# Electronics for Beginners

## A Practical Introduction to Schematics, Circuits, and Microcontrollers

Jonathan Bartlett

Apress®

*Electronics for Beginners: A Practical Introduction to Schematics, Circuits, and Microcontrollers*

Jonathan Bartlett
Tulsa, OK, USA

ISBN-13 (pbk): 978-1-4842-5978-8        ISBN-13 (electronic): 978-1-4842-5979-5
https://doi.org/10.1007/978-1-4842-5979-5

Managing Director, Apress Media LLC: Welmoed Spahr
Acquisitions Editor: Natalie Pao
Development Editor: James Markham
Coordinating Editor: Jessica Vakili

Distributed to the book trade worldwide by Springer Science+Business Media New York, 233 Spring Street, 6th Floor, New York, NY 10013. Phone 1-800-SPRINGER, fax (201) 348-4505, e-mail orders-ny@springer-sbm.com, or visit www.springeronline.com. Apress Media, LLC is a California LLC and the sole member (owner) is Springer Science + Business Media Finance Inc (SSBM Finance Inc). SSBM Finance Inc is a **Delaware** corporation.

For information on translations, please e-mail booktranslations@springernature.com; for reprint, paperback, or audio rights, please e-mail bookpermissions@springernature.com.

Apress titles may be purchased in bulk for academic, corporate, or promotional use. eBook versions and licenses are also available for most titles. For more information, reference our Print and eBook Bulk Sales web page at http://www.apress.com/bulk-sales.

Any source code or other supplementary material referenced by the author in this book is available to readers on GitHub via the book's product page, located at www.apress.com/978-1-4842-5978-8. For more detailed information, please visit http://www.apress.com/source-code.

Printed on acid-free paper

*This book is dedicated to Forrest M. Mims III, whose Engineer's Mini-Notebook series of books I read endlessly as a youth and whose work as a citizen scientist has been an inspiration to me and to many others.*

# Table of Contents

# About the Author

**Jonathan Bartlett** is a senior software R&D specialist at Specialized Bicycle Components, focusing on creating initial prototypes for a variety of IoT (Internet of Things) projects. Jonathan has been educating the tech community for well over a decade. His first book, *Programming from the Ground Up*, is an Internet classic and was endorsed by Joel Spolsky, co-founder of Stack Exchange. It was one of the first open source books and has been used by a generation of programmers to learn how computers work from the inside out, using assembly language as a starting point. He recently released *Building Scalable PHP Web Applications Using the Cloud* as well as the calculus textbook *Calculus from the Ground Up*. Jonathan also writes a mix of technical and popular articles for a number of websites, including the new MindMatters.ai technology blog. His other articles can be found on IBM's DeveloperWorks website, Linux.com, and Medium.com. He is also the head of Tulsa Open Source Hardware, a local group focusing on do-it-yourself electronics projects.

Jonathan also participates in a variety of academic work. He is an associate fellow of the Walter Bradley Center for Natural and Artificial Intelligence. There, he does research into fundamental mathematics and the mathematics of artificial intelligence. He also serves on the editorial board for the journal *BIO-Complexity*, focusing on reviewing information-theoretic papers for the journal and assisting with LaTeX typesetting.

Additionally, Jonathan has written several books on the interplay of philosophy, math, and science, including *Engineering and the Ultimate* and *Naturalism and Its Alternatives in Scientific Methodologies*. Jonathan served as editor for the book *Controllability of Dynamic Systems: The Green's Function Approach*, which received the RA Presidential Award of the Republic of Armenia in the area of "Technical Sciences and Information Technologies."

Jonathan serves on the board of Homeschool Oklahoma along with his wife, Christa, of 20 years. They inspire their community in several ways including writing educational material, creating educational videos, tutoring students through Classical Conversations, and sharing their own stories of tragedy and success with others.

# About the Technical Reviewer

**Mike McRoberts** is the author of *Beginning Arduino* by Apress. He is the winner of Pi Wars 2018 and a member of Medway Makers. He is an Arduino and Raspberry Pi enthusiast.

Mike McRoberts has expertise in a variety of languages and environments, including C/C++, Arduino, Python, Processing, JS, Node-RED, NodeJS, Lua.

# Acknowledgments

I would like to thank, first and foremost, my homeschool co-op community. This book originally started from a series of classes that I taught in our local co-op, and my students were the guinea pigs for this content. I received a lot of encouragement from that class, with both the students and the parents enjoying the material. I want to thank my wife who put up with me always typing on my computer to put this together. I also want to thank the Tulsa Open Source Hardware community (as well as the larger Tulsa WebDevs community), who gave me a lot of encouragement while putting together this book and who also sat through many presentations based on this material.

# CHAPTER 1

# Introduction

Welcome to the world of electronics! In the modern world, electronic devices are everywhere, but fewer and fewer people seem to understand how they work or how to put them together. At the same time, it has never been easier to do so as an individual. The availability of training, tools, parts, instructions, videos, and tutorials for the home experimenter has grown enormously, and the costs for equipment have dropped to almost nothing.

However, what has been lacking is a good guide to bring students from *wanting* to know how electronic circuits work to actually understanding them and being able to develop their own. For the hobbyist, there are many guides that show you how to do individual projects, but they often fail to provide enough information for their readers to be able to build projects of their own. There is plenty of information on the physics of electricity in physics books, but they fail to make the information practical. One exception to this is Horowitz and Hill's *The Art of Electronics*. This book is a wonderful reference guide for practical circuit design. However, its target audience is largely electrical engineers or other very advanced circuit designers. Not only that, the book itself is prohibitively expensive.

What has been needed for a long time is a book that takes you from knowing nothing about electronics to being able to build real circuits that you design yourself. This book combines theory, practice, projects, and design patterns in order to enable you to build your own circuits from scratch. Additionally, this book is designed entirely around safe,

© Jonathan Bartlett 2020
J. Bartlett, *Electronics for Beginners*, https://doi.org/10.1007/978-1-4842-5979-5_1

low-current DC (direct current) power. We stay far away from the wall outlet in this book to be sure that you have a fun and largely worry-free experience with electronics.

This book is written with two groups of people in mind. First, this book can be used as a guide for hobbyists (or wannabe hobbyists) to learn on their own. It has lots of projects to work on and experiment with. Second, this book can also be used in electronics classes for high school and college students. It has problems to be worked, activities to do, and reviews at the end of each chapter.

The needs of these groups are not so different from each other. In fact, even if you are a hobbyist and plan on using this book to learn on your own, I suggest that not only do you read the main parts of the chapter but that you also do the activities and homework as well. The goal of the homework is to train your mind to think like a circuit designer. If you work through the example problems, it will make analyzing and designing circuits simply a matter of habit.

# 1.1  Working the Examples

In this book, all examples should be worked out using decimals, not fractions. This is an engineering course, not a math course, so feel free to use a calculator. However, you will often wind up with very long strings of decimals on some of the answers. Feel free to round your answers, but always include at least a single decimal point. So, for instance, if I divide 5 by 3 on my calculator, it tells me 1.66666667. However, I can just give the final answer as 1.7. This only applies to the final answer. You need to maintain your decimals while you do your computations.

Also, if your answer is a decimal number that *begins* with a zero, then you should round your answer to include the first two to four nonzero digits. So, if I have an answer of 0.0000033333333, I can round that to 0.00000333. If you want to be precise about the proper way to round results, see the section on significant figures in the next chapter.

For beginners and hobbyists, this is less of a concern, and we will generally be in a hobbyist mindset for the book.

In short, as engineers, we wind up being, at minimum, as precise as we *need* to be or, at maximum, as precise as we *can* be. The amount of precision we need will vary from project to project, and the amount of precision that we can be will depend on our tools, our components, and other things we interact with. Therefore, there is not a lot of focus on this book on how many decimals exactly to use. You can get more detailed descriptions in other science books for dealing with significant figures. In the problems in the chapters, if you are off by a single digit due to rounding errors, don't worry about it.

## 1.2 Initial Tools and Supplies

You can get started in electronics with a minimum set of tools, but you can also be as fancy as you have money to afford. This book will focus on the more modest tools that are within the reach of pretty much every budget.

While the book will walk you through a wide variety of parts for different types of circuits, every electronics hobbyist should start out with the following components:

1. Multimeter: Multimeters will measure voltage, current, resistance, and other important values. For these projects, the cheapest digital multimeter you can find will work just fine. You only need one of these.

2. Solderless Breadboards: Solderless breadboards will hold your projects in place and connect your components together. Breadboards are sold based on the number of holes, known as "tie points," the breadboard contains. If you want to keep your projects around, you should have a separate breadboard for each project. However, the beauty of solderless breadboards is that they are in fact reusable if you want.

3. Jumper Wires: Jumper wires are just like normal insulated wires, except that their ends are solid and strong enough to be pushed into your breadboard. The wires themselves may be flexible or rigid. Jumper wires with female ends (a hole instead of a wire) also exist for plugging into circuits which have metal pins sticking out of them (known as headers) to connect to. Every hobbyist I know has a huge mass of jumper wires. They usually come in bundles of 65 wires, which is plenty to get started.

4. Resistors: Resistors do a lot of the grunt work of the circuit. They resist current flow, which, among other things, prevents damaging other parts of the circuit. Resistors are measured in ohms ($\Omega$). Most hobbyists have a wide variety of resistors. You should have a range of resistors from 200 $\Omega$ to 1, 000, 000 $\Omega$. However, if you had to pick one value for your resistors, 1, 000 $\Omega$ resistors work in a wide variety of situations. Resistors for this book should be rated for 1/4 watt of power.

5. LEDs: LEDs (light-emitting diodes) are low-power lights often used in electronic devices. I recommend getting a variety of colors of LEDs just because it makes life more fun. Most standard single-color LEDs have about the same specifications, so the main difference is the color.

6. Buttons and Switches: Buttons and switches will be the primary method of input and output in these circuits. You should buy buttons and switches *which are specifically made to go on breadboards.*

7.  Power Regulator: While most of these projects can be operated directly from a battery, a power regulator board will make sure that, no matter how well charged or drained the battery is, you get a predictable voltage from your battery. The YwRobot breadboard power supply is extremely cheap (cheaper than most batteries) and also provides your project with an on/off switch. You should buy one of these for each breadboard you have. Other breadboard power supplies are available as well (make sure they output 5 volts), but our drawings will assume the YwRobot one.

8.  9 V Battery and Connector: The easiest way to supply power to the power regulator is with a 9 V battery with a standard barrel plug (2.1 mm × 5.5 mm), which will fit into the YwRobot power supply.

Later projects will require specialized components, but these are the components that are needed for nearly every project you will encounter or design yourself. If you would like to order a kit with all of the components you need for this book, you can find them at `www.bplearning.net`.

# 1.3  Safety Guidelines

This book deals almost entirely with direct current from small battery sources. This current is inherently fairly safe, as small batteries are not capable of delivering the amount of current needed to injure or harm. For these projects, you can freely touch wires and work with active circuits without any protection, because the current is incapable of harming you. The main issue that sometimes arises is that, in poorly made circuits, components can overheat and occasionally (but rarely) catch fire.

Additionally, the battery itself may become overheated/compromised, and batteries are often made from potentially toxic chemicals.

Please follow the following safety guidelines when working on projects (both projects from this book and projects you build yourself). They will help keep you safe and help prevent you from accidentally damaging your own equipment:

1. If you have any cuts or other open areas on your skin, please cover them. Your skin is where most of your electric protection exists in your body.

2. Before applying power to your circuit, check to be sure you have not accidentally wired in a short circuit between your positive and negative poles of your battery.

3. If your circuit does not behave as you expect it to when you plug in the battery, unplug it immediately and check for problems.

4. If your battery or any component becomes warm, disconnect power immediately.

5. If you smell any burning or smoky smells, disconnect power immediately.

6. Dispose of all batteries in accordance with local regulations.

7. For rechargeable batteries, follow the instructions on the battery for proper charging procedures.

Please note that if you ever deal with alternating current (AC) or large batteries (such as a car battery), you must exercise many more precautions than described in this book, because those devices generate sufficient power in themselves and within the circuits to harm or kill you if mishandled (sometimes even after the power has been disconnected).

# 1.4 Electrostatic Discharge

If you have ever touched a doorknob and received a small shock, you have experienced electrostatic discharge (ESD). ESD is not dangerous to you, but it can be dangerous to your equipment. Even shocks that you can't feel may damage your equipment. With modern components, ESD is rarely a problem, but nonetheless it is important to know how to avoid it. You can skip these precautions if you wish, just know that occasionally you might wind up shorting out a chip or transistor because you weren't careful. ESD is also more problematic if you have carpet floors, as those tend to build up static electricity.

Here are some simple rules you can follow to prevent ESD problems:

1.  When storing IC components (i.e., electronics chips), store them with the leads enmeshed in conductive foam. This will prevent any voltage differentials from building up in storage.

2.  Wear natural 100% cotton fabrics.

3.  Use a specialized ESD floor mat and/or wrist strap to keep you and your workspace at ground potential.

4.  If you don't use an ESD strap or mat, touch a large metal object before starting work. Do so again any time after moving around.

# 1.5 Using Your Multimeter Correctly

Even though we haven't covered the details we need to use our multimeter yet, since we are covering proper handling of devices, I am including this section here with the others. Feel free to skip over this until we start using multimeters in the book.

In order to keep your multimeter functioning, it is important to take some basic precautions. Multimeters, especially cheap ones, can be easily broken through mishandling. Use the following steps to keep you from damaging your multimeter or damaging your circuit with your multimeter:

1.  Do not try to measure resistance on an active circuit. Take the resistor all the way out of the circuit before trying to measure it.

2.  Choose the appropriate setting on your multimeter *before* you hook it up.

3.  Always err on the side of choosing high values first, especially for current and voltage. Use the high value settings for current and voltage to give your multimeter the maximum protection. If you set the value too large, it is easy enough to set it lower. If you had it set too low, you might have to buy a new multimeter!

# CHAPTER 2

# Dealing with Units

Before we begin our exploration of electronics, we need to talk about **units of measurement**. A unit of measurement is basically a standard against which we are measuring something. For instance, when measuring the length of something, the units of measurement we usually use are feet and meters. You can also measure length in inches, yards, centimeters, kilometers, miles, and so on. Additionally, there are some obscure units of length like furlongs, cubits, leagues, and paces.

Every type of quantity has its own types of units. For instance, we measure time in seconds, minutes, hours, days, weeks, and years. We measure speed in miles per hour, kilometers per hour, meters per second, and so on. We measure mass in pounds, ounces, grams, kilograms, grains, and so on. We measure temperature in Fahrenheit, Celsius, Kelvin, and Rankine.

Units for the same type of quantity can all be converted into each other using the proper formula.

## 2.1 SI Units

The scientific community has largely agreed upon a single standard of units known as the **International System of Units**, abbreviated as **SI Units**. This is the modern form of the metric system. Because of the large number of unit systems available, the goal of creating the SI standard was to create a single set of units that had a basis in physics and had a standard way of expressing larger and smaller quantities.

The imperial system of volumes illustrates the problem they were trying to solve. In the imperial system, there were gallons. If you divided a gallon into four parts, you would get quarts. If you divided quarts in half, you'd get pints. If you divided a pint into twentieths, you'd get ounces.

The imperial system was very confusing. Not only were there an enormous number of units but they all were divisible by differing amounts. The case was similar for length—12 inches in a foot, but 3 feet in a yard and 1,760 yards in a mile. This was a lot to memorize, and doing the calculations was not easy.

| Unit Type | Unit | Abbreviation |
|---|---|---|
| Length | Meter | m |
| Time | Second | s |
| Mass | Gram[a] | g |
| Temperature | Kelvin | K |
| Luminous intensity | Candela | cd |
| Current | Ampere | A |
| Quantity[b] | Mole | mol |

[a]Technically, for historical reasons, the base unit of mass is actually the *kilogram*, but it makes more sense when thinking about it to view the gram it self as the base unit. The kilogram is a base unit in the sense that the standardized weight is based off of the kilogram. However, the gram is a base unit in the sense that all of the prefixes are based off of the weight of a gram.

[b]This is primarily used in chemistry for counting small things like atoms and molecules.

***Figure 2-1.*** *SI Base Units*

The imperial system does have some benefits (the quantities used in the imperial system match the sizes normally used in human activities—few people order drinks in milliliters), but for doing work which requires a lot of calculations and units, the SI system has largely won out. Scientific quantities are almost always expressed in SI units. In engineering it is more of a mix, just as engineering itself is a mix between scientific inquiry and human usefulness. However, the more technical fields have generally moved to SI units and stayed with them.

There are only seven base units in the SI system. Other units are available as well, but they all can be measured in terms of these base units. The base units for the SI system are shown in Figure 2-1.

Many other units are derived from these and are known as SI derived units. For instance, for measuring volume, liters are often used.[1] A liter, however, is not defined on its own, but in terms of meters. A liter is a thousandth of a cubic meter. Thus, we can take the unit of length and use it to describe a unit of volume.

A more complicated example is the newton, which is a unit of force. In the SI system, the newton is defined as being a "kilogram-meter per second squared." This is another way of saying that a newton is the amount of force which accelerates 1 kilogram 1 meter per second, per second.

All of the things of interest to us in this book are ultimately defined in terms of SI base units. For the purposes of this book, it is not important to know which units are base units or derived units, and it is especially unnecessary to know how they are derived. The important thing to keep in mind is that you will be using a well-thought-out, standardized system of units. If the units seem to fit together well, it's because they were designed to do so.

---

[1]Technically, the liter is not defined by the SI, but it is listed here because it is the simplest illustration of the point.

| Conversion Factor | Prefix | Abbreviation | Examples |
|---|---|---|---|
| 1,000,000,000,000 | Tera | T | Terameter, terasecond, teragram |
| 1,000,000,000 | Giga | G | Gigameter, gigasecond, gigagram |
| 1,000,000 | Mega | M | Megameter, megasecond, megagram |
| 1,000 | Kilo | K | Kilometer, kilosecond, kilogram |
| 1 | | | Meter, second, gram |
| 0.001 | Milli | m | Millimeter, millisecond, milligram |
| 0.000001 | Micro | μ or u | Micrometer, microsecond, microgram |
| 0.000000001 | Nano | n | Nanometer, nanosecond, nanogram |
| 0.000000000001 | Pico | p | Picometer, picosecond, picogram |

***Figure 2-2.*** *Common SI Prefixes*

# 2.2 Scaling Units

Now, sometimes you are measuring really big quantities, and sometimes you are measuring very small quantities. In the imperial system, there are different units altogether to reach a different scale of a quantity. For instance, there are inches for small distances, yards for medium-sized distances, and miles for large distances. There are ounces for small volumes and gallons for larger volumes.

In the SI system, however, there is a uniform standard way of expressing larger and smaller quantities. There are a set of modifiers, known as **unit prefixes**, which can be added to *any unit* to work at a different scale. For example, the prefix *kilo-* means thousand. So, while a meter is a unit of length, a kilometer is a unit of length that is 1,000 times as large as a meter. While a gram is a unit of mass, a kilogram is a unit of mass that is 1,000 times the mass of a gram.

It works the other way as well. The prefix *milli-* means thousandth, as in $\frac{1}{1000}$. So, while a meter is a unit of length, a millimeter is a unit of length that is $\dfrac{1}{1000}$ of a meter. While a gram is a unit of mass, a milligram is a unit of mass that is $\dfrac{1}{1000}$ the mass of a gram.

Therefore, by memorizing one single set of prefixes, you can know how to modify all of the units in the SI system. The common prefixes occur at every power of 1,000, as you can see in Figure 2-2.

To convert between a prefixed unit (i.e., kilometer) and a base unit (i.e., meter), we just apply the conversion factor. So, if something weighs 24.32 kilograms, then I could convert that into grams by multiplying by 1,000. $24.32 * 1000 = 24{,}320$. In other words, 24.32 kilograms is the same as 24,320 grams.

To move from the base unit to a prefixed unit, you *divide* by the conversion factor. So, if something weighs 35.2 grams, then I could convert that into kilograms by dividing it by 1,000. $35.2/1000 = 0.0352$. In other words, 35.2 grams is the same as 0.0352 kilogram.

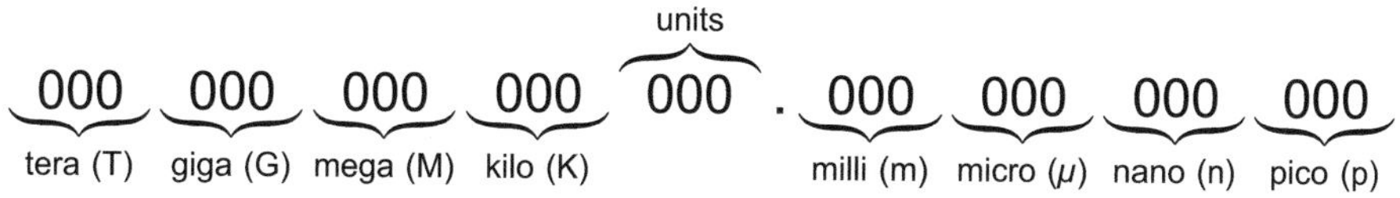

units

$$\underbrace{000}_{\text{tera (T)}}\ \underbrace{000}_{\text{giga (G)}}\ \underbrace{000}_{\text{mega (M)}}\ \underbrace{000}_{\text{kilo (K)}}\ \overbrace{000}^{}\ .\ \underbrace{000}_{\text{milli (m)}}\ \underbrace{000}_{\text{micro ($\mu$)}}\ \underbrace{000}_{\text{nano (n)}}\ \underbrace{000}_{\text{pico (p)}}$$

***Figure 2-3.*** *Visualizing Common Unit Prefixes*

You can also convert between two prefixed units. You simply multiply by the starting prefix and divide by the target prefix. So, if something weighs 220 kilograms and I want to know how many micrograms that is, then I will multiply using the kilo- prefix (1,000) and divide by the micro- prefix (0.000001):

$$\frac{220 \cdot 1000}{0.000001} = 220000000000$$

In other words, 220 kilograms is the same as 220,000,000,000 micrograms.

You can do all of the unit scaling that you need just by knowing the multipliers. However, what usually helps me deal with these multipliers intuitively is to simply visualize where each one lands in a single number. Figure 2-3 shows all of the prefixes laid out in a single number.

So let's say that I was dealing with fractions of a meter and I had something that was 0.000000030 meter. If you line this number up with the chart in Figure 2-3, there are only zeros in the unit, the milli-, and the micro- areas. The first nonzero digits appear in the "nano-" group. When lined up with the chart, the number in the nano- area is 030. Therefore, the number under consideration is 30 nanometers.

# 2.3 Using Abbreviations

Typing or writing words like kilogram, microsecond, and micrometer isn't terribly difficult, but, when it occurs a lot (as what can happen in equations), it can get overwhelming. Therefore, every prefix and every unit has an abbreviation. Since the abbreviation for gram is g, and the abbreviation for kilo- is k, we can abbreviate kilogram as kg. Occasionally the abbreviation for the unit and the scaling prefix are identical, as in the case of meter (m) and milli- (also m). That's fine, as, when you put them together, you get millimeter, which is abbreviated as mm.

The hardest one to write is the one for micro-, $\mu$. This is the Greek letter mu (pronounced "mew"). It's essentially the Greek way of writing the letter m, and it is used because we already have a lowercase m (milli-) and an uppercase M (mega-) in use. Since micro- begins with an m, lacking any additional English/Latin way of writing an m, it is written with the Greek $\mu$. However, this is sometimes hard to type. Therefore, since the squashed way that it is written makes it look kind of like a u, sometimes people will write u instead of $\mu$ if they don't know how to type out $\mu$ with their computer/keyboard. In this book, we never use u for this purpose, but, if you are reading elsewhere something like 100 us, that means 100 microseconds.

# 2.4 Significant Figures

Significant figures are the bane of many science books. Nearly everything in science has to be rounded, and significant figures are basically the rounding rules for science. We need to talk about them simply so that you are aware of how I achieve the rounding that I do in my exercises.

These rules aren't hard, but they can cause some newer students to stumble. If you just are wanting to play with electronics, you can skip this section; just be aware that I may have rounded the answers to problems differently than you do.

The goal of significant figures is to prevent us from thinking that we are being more precise than we really are. Let's say that I measured a piece of wood to be 1 meter long, but I wanted to cut that wood into thirds. How should I report the distance, in decimal, of the length of each desired piece? Well, 1 divided by 3 is 0.33333333333... I can keep writing three's until the cows come home. But do I really need the length to be that precise? Is my measurement of the initial length of the wood precise enough to warrant that sort of precise request? Significant figures allow us to answer that question and report numbers with a justifiable precision.

So, for any measured quantity, we need to count the number of significant figures. For the most part, the number of significant figures in a number is the same as the number of digits, with a few exceptions. First, significant figures ignore all leading zeros. So, if I measured something as being 102 feet, it has three signficant figures, even if I add leading zeros. So 102 feet and 0000000000102 feet both have three significant figures. Additionally, these leading zeros are still ignored even if they are after the decimal point. So the number 0.00042 has two significant figures.

The second rule in counting is that trailing zeros aren't counted as significant if the measuring device isn't capable of measuring that accurately (or the quantity isn't reported that accurately). For instance, the value 1 meter and the value 1.000 meter refer numerically to the same number. However, the second one is usually used to indicate that we can actually measure that precisely. We wouldn't report 1.000 meter unless our scale can actually report accurately to a thousandth of a meter.

The situation is a little more complicated with zeros on the left side of the decimal. If I say, "1,000 people attended the event," how precise is that number? Did you count individuals and get exactly 1,000? Is it possibly estimated to the tens or hundreds place? This gets murky. To simplify the issue for this book, you can assume that all digits on the right count as significant figures. So, if we say "1,000 people" attended the event, that is a number with four significant digits. However, if we say "1 kilopeople" attended the event, that is a number with one significant digit. If we say " 1.03 kilopeople" attended the event, that is a number with three significant digits. We will use this convention when writing down problems, but results may just be a rounded number with trailing zeros (i.e., instead of writing "1.03 kilopeople," we might write the result as 1,030 people).

One other small rule: If a number is exact, then it is essentially considered to have infinite significant digits. So, for instance, it takes two people to have a baby. This is an exact number. It isn't 2.01 or 2.00003 people, it is exactly two. So, for the purposes of significant figures, this value has an infinite number of digits. Conversion factors are generally considered to be exact values.

So that is how to count significant digits. This is important because the significant digits affect how caclulations are rounded. There are two rules—one for multiplying and dividing and another for adding and subtracting.

For multiplying and dividing, you should find the input value with the fewest significant figures. The result should then be rounded to that many significant figures. For instance, if we had $103 * 55$, then the result should be rounded to two significant figures. So, even though the result is 5,665, we should report it as 5,700. Let's say we have 55.0 ÷ 3.00. Since both of the input values have three significant figures, then the result should have three significant figures. Therefore, the result is 18.3.

For addition and subtraction, instead of using significant figures, the decimal points for the numbers are lined up, the operation is performed, and the result is rounded to the number of decimal places available in the input value that has the least precision (fewest numbers to the right of the decimal). So, for instance, if I have 1.054 + 0.06, the result is 1.104. However, this would be rounded to 1.10 because that is how many digits to the right the decimal 0.06 had.

If there are a series of operations, significant figures are usually applied at the end of the whole calculation, or when necessary to limit the complication of intermediate results. Calculators will round for you at some point anyway, so there is no getting around some amount of intermediate rounding. Therefore, you should recognize that if your answer differs from the book's answer by the least significant digit, it is likely that you are correct, but that you rounded in different stages in your calculation.

In professional science and engineering data reporting, significant figures are important. In playing around with electronics, they are much less so. Additionally, even the rules for significant figures aren't perfect—there are places where their usage leads to problematic results. Entire books have been written on the subject.[2] Significant figures are there not because they are perfect, but so that we all have a common, straightforward way of communicating the precision of our results. The most important thing to keep in mind is that the degree to which you are precise in your measurements affects the degree to which you can be precise in your calculations.

---

[2]For instance, see Nicholas Higham's *Accuracy and Stability of Numerical Algorithms*.

# Apply What You Have Learned

1. How many nanometers is 23 meters?

2. How many seconds is 23.7 microseconds?

3. How many grams is 89.43 megagrams?

4. How many meters is 15 nanometers?

5. How many kilograms is 0.3 microgram?

6. How many milliseconds is 45 kiloseconds?

7. What is the abbreviation for picosecond? What is the abbreviation for microgram?

8. What is the abbreviation for a terameter?

9. How many significant figures does the number 476 have?

10. How many significant figures does the number 5 have?

11. How many significant figures does the number 000352 have?

12. How many significant figures does the number 0.00043 have?

13. How many significant figures does the number 1.0004 have?

14. How many significant figures does the number 2.34000 have?

Calculate the following problems taking into account significant figures.

15.  What is $23 * 5$?

16.  What is $23 + 0.6$?

17.  What is $0.005 * 209$?

18.  What is $0.0023 * 45$?

19.  What is $0.5 + 0.5$?

20.  Why are significant figures important?

# PART I

# Basic Concepts

# CHAPTER 3

# What Is Electricity?

The first thing to tackle in the road to understanding electronics is to wrap our minds around what electricity is and how it works. The way that electricity works is very peculiar and unintuitive. We are used to dealing with the world in terms of physical objects—desks, chairs, baseballs, and so on. Even if we never took a class in physics, we know the basic properties of such objects from everyday experience. If I drop a rock on my foot, it will hurt. If I drop a heavier rock, it will hurt more. If I remove an important wall from a house, it will fall down.

However, for electricity, the only real experience we have is that we have been told to stay away from it. Sure, we have experience with computers and phones and all sorts of devices, but they give us the result of processing electricity a million times over. But how does electricity itself work?

## 3.1 Charge

To answer this question, we need to answer another question first: What *is* electricity? Electricity is the flow of **charge**. So what is charge?

Charge is a fundamental quantity in physics—it is not a combination (that we know of) of any other quantity. A particle can be charged in one of three ways—it can be positively charged (represented by a + sign), negatively charged (represented by a – sign), or neutrally charged (i.e., has no charge). Figure 3-1 shows what an atom looks like. In the center of the atom are larger, heavier particles called **protons** and **neutrons**. Protons are positively charged particles, and neutrons are neutrally charged particles.

© Jonathan Bartlett 2020
J. Bartlett, *Electronics for Beginners*, https://doi.org/10.1007/978-1-4842-5979-5_3

Together, these form the **nucleus** of the atom and determine *which* atom we are talking about. If you look on a periodic table, the large printed number associated with an element is known as its **atomic number**. This number refers to how many protons it has in its nucleus. Sometimes, there is a number in smaller print as well. This is the total number of protons and neutrons combined.[1] Note that the number of neutrons in an element can vary, so this number is often a decimal representing the average number of combined protons and neutrons in any particular element.

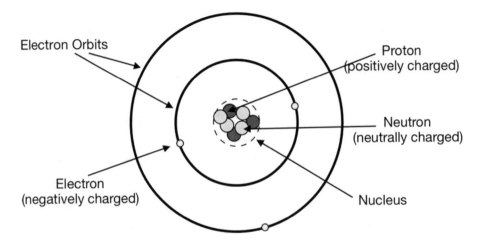

*Figure 3-1.  Charged Particles in an Atom*

Circling around the nucleus are **electrons**. Electrons are negatively charged particles. Even though electrons are much smaller and lighter than protons, the amount of negative charge of one electron is equal to the amount of positive charge of one proton. Positive and negative charges attract each other, which is what keeps electrons contained within the atom.

---

[1]This is technically the *atomic mass* of the element, given in special units called atomic mass units (AMUs). However, the weights of protons and neutrons are each extremely close to 1 AMU, and the weight of electrons is extremely close to zero, so the atomic mass and the combined number of protons and neutrons are nearly identical.

Electrons are arranged in shells surrounding the nucleus. The outermost shell, however, is the most important one when thinking about how atoms work.

When we think about individual atoms, we think about them when they are isolated and alone. In these situations, the number of electrons and the number of protons are equal, making the atom as a whole electrically neutral. However, especially when atoms interact with other atoms, the configuration of their electrons can change. If the atoms gain electrons, then they are negatively charged. If the atoms lose electrons, then they are positively charged. Free electrons are all negatively charged.

If there are both positively and negatively charged particles moving around, their opposite charges attract one another. If there is a great imbalance of positive and negative charges, usually you will have a *movement* of some of the charged particles toward the particles of the opposite charge. This is a *flow* of charge, and this flow is what is referred to when we speak of electricity.

The movement of charge can be either positively charged particles moving toward negatively charged ones, negatively charged particles moving toward positively charged ones, or both. Usually, in electronics, it is the electrons which are moving through a wire, but just know that this is not the only way in which charge can move.

Electricity can be generated by a variety of means. The way that electricity is generated in a battery is that a chemical reaction takes place, but the reactants (the substances that react together) are separated from each other by some sort of medium. The positive charges for the reaction move easiest through the medium, but the negative charges for the reaction move easiest through the wire. Therefore, when the wire is connected, electricity moves through the wire to help the chemical reaction complete on the other side of the battery.

This flow of electric charge through the wire is what we normally think of as electricity.

---

## MAKING YOUR OWN BATTERY

You can make a simple battery of your own out of three materials: thick copper wire or tubing, a galvanized nail (it *must* be galvanized), and a potato or a lemon. This battery operates from a reaction between the copper on the wire and the zinc on the outside of the galvanized nail. The electrons will flow from the zinc to the copper through the wire, while the positive charge will flow within the lemon or potato.

To build the battery, you must insert the thick copper and the nail into the potato. They should be near each other, but *not touching*. This battery will not produce very much current—less than a milliamp of current at less than 1 volt (we will discuss milliamps later in this chapter and volts in Chapter 4). This is not quite enough to light up an LED, but it should register on a multimeter. See Chapter 6 for how to measure voltage with a multimeter.

Note that the lemon/potato is not actually supplying the current. What the lemon/potato is doing is creating a barrier so that only the positive charges can flow freely in the potato, and the negative charges have to use the wire.

---

# 3.2  Measuring Charge and Current

Atoms are very, very tiny. Only in the last few years have scientists even developed microscopes that can see atoms directly. Electrons are even tinier. Additionally, it takes a *lot* of electrons moving to have a worthwhile flow of charge. Individual electrons do not do much on their own—it is only when there are a very large number of them moving that they can power our electronics projects.

Therefore, scientists and engineers usually measure charge on a much larger scale. The **coulomb** is the standard measure of electric charge. One coulomb is equivalent to the electric charge of about

6,242,000,000,000,000,000 protons. If you have that many electrons, you would have a charge of −1 coulomb. That's a lot of particles, and it takes particles on that scale to do very much electrical work. Thankfully, protons and electrons are very, very small. A typical 9-volt battery can provide about 2,000 coulombs of charge, which is over 10,000,000,000,000,000,000,000 charged particles (ten thousand billion billion particles).

However, electricity and electronics are not about electric charge sitting around doing nothing. Electricity deals with the *flow* of charge. Therefore, when dealing with electricity, we rarely deal with coulombs. Instead, we talk about how fast the electric charge is flowing. For that, we use **amperes**, often called amps and abbreviated as A. One ampere is equal to the movement of 1 coulomb of charge out of the battery each second.

For the type of electronics we will be doing, an ampere is actually a lot of current. In fact, a full ampere of current can do a lot of physical harm to you, but we don't usually deal with full amperes when creating electronic devices. Power-hungry devices like lamps, washers, dryers, printers, stereos, and battery chargers need a lot of current—that's why we plug them into the wall. Small electronic devices don't usually need so much current. Therefore, for electronic devices, we usually measure current in **milliamperes**, usually called just milliamps and abbreviated as mA. Remember that the prefix *milli-* means one-thousandth of (i.e., $\frac{1}{1000}$ or 0.001). Therefore, a milliamp is one-thousandth of an amp. If someone says that there is 20 milliamps of current, that means that there is 0.020 amp of current. This is important, because the equations that we use for electricity are based on amps, but since we are dealing with low-current devices, most of our measurements will be in milliamps.

So, to go from amps to milliamps, multiply the value by 1,000. To go from milliamps to amps, divide the value by 1,000 (or multiply by 0.001) and give the answer in decimal (electronics always uses decimals instead of fractions).

**Example 3.1** If I were to have 2.3 amps of electricity, how many milliamps is that? To go from amps to milliamps, we multiply by 1,000. 2.3 * 1,000 = 2,300. Therefore, 2.3 amps is the same as 2,300 milliamps.

**Example 3.2** If I were to have 5.7 milliamps of electricity, how many amps is that? To go from milliamps to amps, we divide by 1,000. 5.7/1,000 = 0.0057. Therefore, 5.7 milliamps is the same as 0.0057 amp.

**Example 3.3** Now, let's try something harder— if I say that I am using 37 milliamps of current, how many coulombs of charge has moved after 1 minute? Well, first, let's convert from milliamps to amps. To convert from milliamps to amps, we divide by 1,000. 37/1000 = 0.037. Therefore, we have 0.037 amp. What is an amp? An amp is 1 coulomb of charge moving per second. Therefore, we can restate our answer as being 0.037 coulomb of charge moving each second.

However, our question asked about how much has moved after 1 *minute*. Since there are 60 seconds in each minute, we can multiply 0.037 by 60 for our answer. 0.037 * 60 = 2.22. So, after 1 minute, 37 milliamps of current moves 2.22 coulombs of charge.

# 3.3  AC vs. DC

You may have heard the terms AC and DC when people talk about electricity. What do those terms mean? In short, DC stands for **direct current**, and AC stands for **alternating current**. So far, our descriptions of electricity have dealt mostly with DC. With DC, electricity makes a route from the positive terminal to the negative. It is the way most people envision electricity. It is "direct."

However, DC, while great for electronics projects, very quickly loses power over long distances. If we were to transmit current that simply flows from the positive to the negative throughout the city, we would have to have power stations every mile or so.

So, instead of sending current in through one terminal and out through another, your home is powered with **alternating current**. In alternating current, the positive and negative sides continually reverse, switching back and forth 50–60 times per second. So the current direction (and thus the direction the electrons are moving) continually switches back and forth, over and over again. Instead of moving in a continuous flow, it is more like someone is pushing and pulling the current back and forth. In fact, at the generator station, that is almost exactly what is going on! This may seem strange, but this push and pull action allows for much easier power generation and also allows much more power to be delivered over much longer distances.

AC, such as the current that comes out of a wall socket, is much more powerful than we require for our projects here. In fact, converting high-power AC to low-power DC voltage used in electronic devices is an art in itself. This is why companies charge so much money for battery chargers—it takes a lot of work to get one right!

Now, not all AC is like this. We call this current AC "mains," because it comes from the power mains from the power stations. It is supposed to operate at about 120 volts, and the circuits are usually rated for about 15–30 amps (that's 15,000–30,000 milliamps). That's a lot of electricity!

In addition to AC mains, there are also ACs which we will call AC "signal." These currents come from devices like microphones. They are AC because the direction of current does in fact alternate. When you speak, your voice vibrates the air back and forth. A microphone converts these air vibrations into small vibrations of electricity—pushing and pulling a small electric current back and forth. However, these ACs are so low powered as to be almost undetectable. They are so small we have to actually amplify these currents (see Chapter 25) just to work with them using our DC power!

So, in short, while we will do some work with AC signal voltages later in the book, all of our projects will be safe, low-power projects. We will often touch wires with our projects active or use multimeters to measure currents and voltages in active circuits. This is perfectly safe for battery-operated projects. But *do not* attempt these same maneuvers for anything connected to your wall outlet unless you are properly trained.

# 3.4 Which Way Does Current Flow?

One issue that really bungles people up when they start working with electronics is figuring out which way electric current flows. You hear first that electric current is the movement of electrons, and then you hear that electrons move from negative to positive. So one would naturally assume that current flows from negative to positive, right?

Good guess, but no—or, at least, not quite.

Current is not the flow of physical stuff like electrons, but the flow of *charge*. So, when the chemical reaction happens in the battery, the positive side gets positively charged, and the influence of that charge moves down the wires. The electrons are a negative charge that moves toward that positive charge. The positive charge is just as real as the negative charge, even though physical stuff isn't moving with the positive charge.

Think about it this way. Have you ever used a vacuum cleaner? Let's say we are tracing the action of a vacuum cleaner. Where do you start? Usually, you start at the inside where the suction happens and then trace the flow of suction through the tube. Then, at the end of the tube, the dust comes into the tube.

Engineers don't trace their systems from the dust to the inside, they trace their systems from the suction on the inside out to the dust particles on the outside. Even though it is the dust that moves, it is the suction that is interesting.

Likewise, for electricity, we usually trace current from positive to negative even though the electrons are moving the other way. The positive charge is like the suction of a vacuum, pulling the electrons in. Therefore, we want to trace the flow of the vacuum from positive to negative, even though the dust is moving the other way.

The idea that we trace current from positive to negative is often called **conventional current flow**. It is called that way because we conventionally think about circuits as going from the positive to the negative, and it is the common convention to draw them that way (any arrow in an electronics diagram is pointing toward the movement of *positive* charge).

If you are tracing charge the other way, that is called **electron current flow**, but it is rarely used.

# Review

In this chapter, we learned the following:

1. Electric current is the flow of charge.

2. Charge is measured in coulombs.

3. Electric current flow is measured in coulombs per second, called amperes or amps.

4. A milliampere is one-thousandth of an ampere.

5. In an atom, protons are positively charged, electrons are negatively charged, and neutrons are neutrally charged.

6.  Batteries work by having a chemical reaction which causes electricity to flow through wires.

7.  In DC, electricity flows continuously from positive to negative.

8.  In AC, electricity flows back and forth, changing flow direction many times every second.

9.  Even though electrons flow from negative to positive, in electronics, we usually think about circuits and draw circuit charges as flowing from positive to negative.

10. AC mains (the kind in your wall outlet) is dangerous, but battery current is relatively safe.

11. Small signal AC (like that generated by a microphone) is not dangerous.

# Apply What You Have Learned

1.  If I have 56 milliamps of current flowing, how many amps of current do I have flowing?

2.  If I have 1,450 milliamps of current flowing, how many amps of current do I have flowing?

3.  If I have 12 amps of current flowing, how many milliamps of current do I have flowing?

4.  If I have 0.013 amp of current flowing, how many milliamps of current do I have flowing?

5.  If I have 125 milliamps of current flowing for 1 hour, how many coulombs of charge have I used up?

6.  What is the difference between AC and DC?

7.  In AC mains, how often does the direction of current go back and forth?

8.  Why is AC used instead of DC to deliver electricity within a city?

9.  In working with electronic devices, do we normally work in amps or milliamps?

# CHAPTER 4

# Voltage and Resistance

In Chapter 3, we learned about current, which is the rate of flow of charge. In this chapter, we are going to learn about two other fundamental electrical quantities—**voltage** and **resistance**. These two quantities are the ones that are usually the most critical to building effective circuits.

Current is important because limiting current allows us to preserve battery life and protect precision components. Voltage, however, is usually the quantity that has to be present to do any work within a circuit.

## 4.1  Picturing Voltage

What is voltage? Voltage is the amount of power each coulomb of electricity can deliver. If person A has 1 coulomb of charge at 5 volts and person B has 1 coulomb of charge at 10 volts, that means that person B's coulomb can deliver twice as much power as person A's.

A good analogy to electronics is the flow of water. When comparing water to electricity, *coulombs* are a similar unit to *liters*—coulombs measure the amount of electric charge present just like a liter is the amount of water volume present. Both charge and water move as a flow. In water, we can measure the flow of a current of a stream in liters per second. Likewise, in electronics, we measure the flow of charge through a wire in coulombs per second, which are also called amperes.

Now, I want you to image the end of a hose through which water is flowing. Normally, the water just falls out of the hose, especially if the hose is just sitting on the ground. That hose just sitting on the ground is like a current with 0 volt—each unit of water or charge is just not doing that much.

Let's pretend we added a spray nozzle to the hose. What happens now? Water shoots out of the nozzle forcefully. We haven't added any more water—it is actually the same amount of water (i.e., current) flowing. Instead, we increased the pressure of the water, which is just like increasing the voltage on an electric charge. By increasing the pressure, we changed the amount of work that each liter of water is available to perform.

Likewise, when we increase voltage, we change the amount of work that each coulomb of electricity can do.

One way we might measure the pressure of water coming out of a hose is to measure how far up it can shoot out of the hose. By doubling the pressure of the water, we can double how far out of the hose it can shoot. Similarly, with voltages, large enough voltages can actually jump air gaps across circuits. However, to do this, it takes a lot of voltage—about 30,000 volts per inch of gap. If you have been shocked by static electricity, though, this is what is happening! The power of the charge is extreme (thousands of volts), but the amount of charge in those shocks is so small that it doesn't harm you (about 0.00000001 coulomb).

# 4.2 Volts Are Relative

While charge and current are fairly concrete ideas, voltage is a much more relative idea. You can actually never measure voltage absolutely. All voltage measurements are actually relative to other voltages. That is, I can't actually say that my electric charge has exactly 1, 2, 3, or whatever volts. Instead, what I have to do is say that one charge is however many volts more or less than another charge. So let's take a 9-volt battery. What that means is not that the battery is 9 volts in any absolute sense, but rather that there is a 9 -volt *difference* between the charge at the positive terminal and the charge at the negative terminal. That is, the pressure with which charge is trying to move from the positive terminal to the negative terminal is 9 volts.

# 4.3 Relative Voltages and Ground Potential

When we get to actually measuring voltages on a circuit, we will only be measuring voltage *differences* on the circuit. So, to measure voltage, I can't just put a probe on one place on the circuit. Instead, I have to put my probe on two *different* places on the circuit and measure the voltage difference (also called the **voltage drop**) between those two points.

However, to simplify calculations and discussions, we usually choose some point on the circuit to represent "0 volt." This gives us a way to standardize voltage measurements on a circuit, since they are all given relative to the same point. In theory, this could be any point on the circuit, but, usually, we choose the negative terminal on the battery to represent 0 volt.

This "zero point" goes by several names, the most popular of which is **ground** (often abbreviated as **GND**). It is called the ground because, historically, the physical ground has often been used as a reference voltage for circuits. Using the physical ground as the zero point allows you to also compare voltages between circuits with different power supplies. However, in our circuits, when we refer to the ground, we are referring to the negative terminal on the battery, which we are designating as 0 volt.

Another, lesser-used term for this designated 0-volt reference is the **common** point. Many multimeters label one of their electrodes as **COM**, for the common electrode. When analyzing a circuit's voltage, this electrode would be connected to whatever your 0-volt point is.

This "ground" analogy also makes sense with our water hose analogy. Remember that a voltage is the potential for a charge to do work. What happens to water after it lands on the ground? By the time the water from my hose lands on the ground, it has lost all its energy. It is just sitting there. Sure, it may seep or flow around a bit, but nothing of consequence. All of its ability to do work—to move quickly or to knock something over—has been drained. It is just on the ground. Likewise, when our electric charge is all puttered out, we say that it has reached "ground potential."

So, even though we could designate any point as being zero, we usually designate the negative terminal of the battery as the zero point, indicating that by the time electricity reaches that point, it has used up all of its potential energy—it now has 0 volt compared to the end destination (i.e., the other battery terminal).

# 4.4 Resistance

**Resistance** is how much a circuit or device resists the flow of current. Resistance is measured in **ohms** and is usually represented by the symbol $\Omega$. Going back to our water hose analogy, **resistance** is how small the hose is, because a smaller hose will resist the flow of water more than a larger hose will. Think about a 2-liter bottle of pop. The bottle has a wide base, but the opening is small. If I turn the bottle upside down, the small opening limits the amount of liquid that flows out at one time. That small opening is giving *resistance* to the flow of liquid, making it flow more slowly. If you cut off the small opening, leaving a large opening, the liquid will come out much faster because there is less resistance.

Ohm's law, which we will use throughout this book, tells us about the relationship between resistance, voltage, and current flow. The equation is very simple. It says

$$V = I * R \tag{4.1}$$

In this equation, V stands for voltage, I stands for current (in *amperes*, not milliamperes), and R stands for resistance (in ohms). To understand what this equation means, let's think again about water hoses. The water that comes out of the faucet of your house has essentially a constant current. Therefore, according to the equation, if we add resistance, it will increase our voltage.

We know this to be true from experience. If we have a hose and just point it forward, water usually comes out about a foot or two. Remember, voltage is how much push the water has, which determines how far the water will go when it leaves the hose. However, if my children are on the other side of the yard and I want to hit them with a water spray, what do I do? I put my thumb over the opening. This increases the resistance, and, since the current is relatively constant, the voltage (the force the water will have when it leaves the hose) will increase, and this force will cause the water to spray further.

However, in circuits, we usually don't have a constant current source. Instead, batteries provide a constant voltage source. A 9-volt battery will provide 9 volts in nearly every condition. Therefore, for electronics work, we usually rearrange the equation a little bit. Using a little bit of algebra, we can solve our equation for either current or resistance, like this:

$$I = \frac{V}{R} \tag{4.2}$$

$$R = \frac{V}{I} \tag{4.3}$$

Equation 4.2 is the one that is usually most useful. To understand this equation, think back to the example of the bottle turned upside down. There, the liquid had a constant amount of push/voltage (from gravity), but we had different resistances. With the small opening, we had a large resistance, so the liquid came out slower. With the large opening, we had almost no resistance, so the liquid came out all at once.

**Example 4.4** Let's put Ohm's law to use. If I have a 5-volt voltage source with 10 ohms of resistance in the circuit, how much current will flow? Since we are solving for current, we should use Equation 4.2. This says $I = \dfrac{V}{R}$. Therefore, plugging in our voltage and resistance, we have $I = \dfrac{5}{10}$, which is $I = 0.5$ ampere (remember, Ohm's law always uses amperes for current).

**Example 4.5** Now let's say that we have a 10-volt source and we want to have 2 amps worth of current flowing. How much resistance do we need in order to make this happen? Since we are now solving for resistance, we will use Equation 4.3, which says $R = \dfrac{V}{I}$. Plugging in our values, we see that $R = \dfrac{10}{2} = 5\,\Omega$. Therefore, we would need 5 $\Omega$ of resistance.

**Example 4.6** Now let's say that I have a 9-volt source and I want to limit my current to 10 *milliamps*. This uses the same equation, but the problem I have is that my units are in milliamps, but my equation uses amps. Therefore, before using the equation, I have to convert my current from milliamps to amps. Remember, to convert milliamps to amps, we just divide by 1,000. Therefore, we take 10 milliamps and divide by 1,000, and we get 0.010 amp. Now we can use Equation 4.3 to find the resistance we need.

$$R = \frac{V}{I} = \frac{9}{0.010} = 900\Omega$$ . Therefore, with 900 $\Omega$ of

resistance, we will limit our current to 10 milliamps.

# Review

In this chapter, we learned the following:

1.  Voltage is the amount of power that each coulomb of charge delivers.

2.  The volt is the electrical unit that we use to measure voltage.

3.  Voltage is always given relative to other voltages—it is not an absolute value.

4.  The ground of a circuit is a location on the circuit where we have chosen to use as a universal reference point—we define that point as having zero voltage for our circuit to make measuring other points on our circuit easier.

5.  In DC electronics, the chosen ground is usually the negative terminal of the battery.

6.  Other terms and abbreviations for the ground include common, GND, and COM.

7.  Resistance is how much a circuit resists the flow of current and is measured in ohms ($\Omega$).

8.  Ohm's law tells us the relationship between voltage, current, and resistance: $V = I * R$.

9.  Using basic algebra, we can rearrange Ohm's law in two other ways, depending on what we want to know. It can be solved for current, $I = \dfrac{V}{R}$, or it can be solved for resistance, $R = \dfrac{V}{I}$.

# Apply What You Have Learned

1.  If I have a 4-volt battery, how many volts are between the positive and negative terminals of this battery?

2.  If I choose the *negative* terminal of this battery as my ground, how many volts are at the *negative* terminal?

3.  If I choose the *negative* terminal of this battery as my ground, how many volts are at the *positive* terminal?

4.  If I choose the *positive* terminal of this battery as my ground, how many volts are at the *negative* terminal?

5.  If I have a Point A on my circuit that is 7 volts above ground and I have a Point B on my circuit that is 2 volts above ground, what is the voltage difference between Point A and Point B?

6.  Given a constant voltage, what effect does increasing the resistance have on current?

7.  Given a constant current, what effect does increasing the resistance have on voltage?

8.  If I have a 10 V battery, how much resistance would I need to have a current flow of 10 amps?

9.  If I have a 3-volt battery, how much resistance would I need to have a current flow of 15 amps?

10. Given 4 amps of current flow across 200 ohms of resistance, how much voltage is there in my circuit?

11. If I am wanting to limit current flow to 2 amps, how much resistance would I need to add to a 40-volt source?

12. If I am wanting to limit current flow to 2 milliamps, how much resistance would I need to add to a 9-volt source?

13. If I am wanting to limit current flow to 20 milliamps, how much resistance would I need to add to a 5-volt source?

# CHAPTER 5

# Your First Circuit

In the last two chapters, we have learned about the fundamental units of electricity—charge, current, voltage, and resistance. In this chapter, we are going to put this information to use in a real circuit.

## 5.1  Circuit Requirements

For a circuit to function properly, you usually need several things:

1.  A source of power which provides electricity for your circuit (this is usually a combination of both a source *and destination* for the electricity)

2.  A network of wires and components that ultimately lead from the source to the destination

3.  Some amount of resistance in your circuit

We need the source because, without a source of power, the charge won't move! If we have a circuit, but no electrical power, it will just sit there. In our circuits, batteries will usually provide the power we need. They will do this by providing a (relatively) constant voltage to our circuits.

We need the wires because unless we provide a *complete pathway* from a higher voltage (the source) to a lower voltage (the destination), the electricity won't be able to move. If we want the charge to move, we have to

J. Bartlett, *Electronics for Beginners*, https://doi.org/10.1007/978-1-4842-5979-5_5

make a *pathway* from the higher voltage to the lower voltage. Without this pathway, we have what is known as an **open circuit**. No electricity flows in an open circuit.

The components in the pathway from the source to the destination do the "electrical stuff" that we want to accomplish, whether that is turning on a light, running a motor, running a computer, or whatever else it is we want to do. In order for them to take advantage of the electrical power, they have to be in the pathway in which the current is moving. Think of this like a watermill—those structures that sit near a river and use the power of the water moving through the river to turn a wheel and therefore operate whatever is inside the house. In order for that to work, the water must flow through the watermill-connected structure. If the watermill is not built next to the river or if the river runs dry, the watermill doesn't work. Similarly, if the components are not in the flow of moving electric charge, they will not operate.

However, in addition to the wires and components, we must also have resistance (though sometimes this is added by the components themselves). Without resistance, the current would be too high. If you had zero resistance, the current would be so high that it would immediately drain your battery and likely destroy all of your components that you have connected. You can actually see this using Ohm's law. If we have a 10-volt source with no resistance, the current is given by the equation $I = V/R = 10/0 \approx \infty$. Dividing by zero gives you, essentially, infinite current. Now, wires and batteries *themselves* have some amount of resistance, so the current wouldn't be infinite, but it would be very, very large and would quickly drain your battery and destroy any sensitive components you had connected. Therefore, every pathway from the positive side of the battery to the negative *must* have some measurable amount of resistance. When a pathway from positive to negative occurs without resistance, this is known as a **short circuit**.

In other words, to accomplish real tasks with electricity, we must control its flow. If it doesn't flow (as in an open circuit), it can't do anything. If it flows without resistance (as in a short circuit), it does damage rather than work. Therefore, the goal of electronics is to provide a controlled route for electric charge to follow so that the power of electricity does the things we want it to do on its way from the source to the destination.

---

### SHORTING OUT

If you've ever heard the phrase "shorting out," that refers to the fact that if you have a short circuit, it will often run too much current through a component and break the component. Sometimes this causes sufficient damage to actually damage the connections within the circuit. So, although the *original problem* was that there was a short circuit (i.e., something that created a pathway which bypassed resistance in the circuit), the *resulting problem* is that the damage leaves you with a permanent open circuit.

Interestingly, shorting out is actually usually a better result than having a permanently short circuit, which would leave you open to your project heating up and potentially catching on fire. This is why many projects which have larger power sources often use fuses. The goal of the fuse is to break either before other parts of the circuit break or before something catches fire.

---

## 5.2  Basic Components

The first circuits that we will build will only use four basic types of components:

- Batteries (9-volt)

- Battery regulator

- Resistors

- LEDs

As we have discussed, batteries provide a relatively constant amount of voltage between the positive and negative terminals. A 9-volt battery, therefore, is supposed to have a 9-volt difference between the positive and negative terminals. However, there is an actual range that 9-volt batteries have. A 9-volt battery, depending on the battery chemistry, will deliver between 7 and 10 volts. Additionally, when the battery is worn out, its voltage will decrease as well.

Therefore, in order to make the projects operate more uniformly across different power sources, our projects will often include a regulator, which will take the battery's voltage (which can vary from 7 to 10 volts) and return a constant 5-volt output. So keep in mind that if the project does not have a regulator attached, the actual voltages in the circuit may vary depending on the battery. If the project does have a regulator attached, it should be reliably yielding a 5-volt difference from the positive to the negative. We will treat the regulator just like a battery, but one that is more stable and reliable than a battery.

A resistor is a device that, as its name implies, adds resistance to a circuit. Resistors have colors that indicate how much resistance they add to the circuit. You don't need to know the color codes yet, but if you are curious, you can see the resistor datasheet in Appendix E. So, if we want to add 100 $\Omega$ to our circuit, we just find a resistor with a value of 100 $\Omega$. Resistors are not the only devices that add resistance to a circuit, but they are usually what are used when you want to add a fixed amount of resistance. Resistors have two terminals (connecting points), but they both function identically—unlike other components, there is no backward or forward for a resistor. You can put them in your circuit either way, and they will function just fine.

Of the components in this section, the LED is probably the strangest. LED stands for "light-emitting diode." A diode is a component that only allows current to flow in one direction. It blocks the flow of electricity in the other direction. However, more importantly, LEDs emit light when current passes through them. However, LEDs do not resist current, so they must be used with a resistor to limit the amount of current flowing through them (most of them will break at 20–30 milliamps). Also, since LEDs only allow current to flow one way, they have to be wired in the correct direction. To find out which way to wire an LED, look at the legs of the LED—one is longer than the other. To allow current flow, the longer leg of the LED should be on the more positive side of the circuit.

Most of your components (especially your resistors) come with very long legs. You can feel free to bend or cut these legs however you please to better fit in your circuit. However, on LEDs (and any other component where leg length matters), be sure to keep the longer legs longer so you don't get confused about which way it should be inserted in your circuit.

## 5.3  Creating Your First Circuit

Now we will put together a simple first circuit. What you will need is

- One 9-volt battery

- One red LED (other colors will work too)

- One 1,000 Ω resistor (anything from 400 ohms to 2,000 ohms should work)

If you already have resistors, you can use a multimeter to determine the resistance, or you can use the color chart in Appendix E. Most electronics enthusiasts I know don't actually use the color codes, because they are too small. If you have better vision than we do, then the color chart may work great. Otherwise, use a multimeter to check the resistance, or, better yet, keep your resistors organized so it is easy to find the value you want. If you don't have resistors, it is even easier—just buy a resistor with the resistance you are looking for!

| READING A RESISTOR'S VALUE FROM A MULTIMETER |
| --- |

Multimeters are incredibly flexible tools, and they are pretty cheap too. For the purposes of this book, you don't need anything fancy—the cheapest one will do just fine! Be sure that the resistor is not connected to anything else before testing.

To find the value of the resistor, look for values on the multimeter marked with the ohm sign ($\Omega$). Set the dial to the lowest resistance value it has (remember to think about the metric suffixes from Chapter 2—for instance, 10 M means 10,000,000). Then, test the resistor by putting the two multimeter probes on the two legs of the resistor. It is okay to hold the probes on the resistor legs with your fingers. Many multimeters require you to only use the pointed tips of the probes in order to measure values accurately.

If the screen shows a 0 or 1, that means that the resistor's value is actually too large for it to register at that setting. In that case, move the dial on the multimeter to the next setting higher and try again. If the screen shows a more precise value, then use that value plus whatever metric suffix the multimeter is set to. For instance, if the multimeter is set to 10 M, then you would add the M suffix to whatever value is shown on the screen. That is the value of the resistor.

If you did buy a fancy, expensive multimeter, it may only have one spot for measuring resistance, marked as ohm without listing any number by it. In this case, it will automatically do that same process internally and report the results to you like magic.

More information about multimeter use is found in Chapter 6.

To make this circuit, take one leg of the resistor and twist it together with the *short* leg of the LED. It should look like Figure 5-1.

Now, take the long leg of the LED and touch it to the positive terminal of the battery. Nothing happens—why not? Nothing happens because, even though we have connected the wires to the positive side of the battery, the electricity has nowhere to go to, so the current won't move. We have an open circuit because there is not a complete path from positive to negative.

Now, touch the long leg of the LED to the battery and, at the same time, touch the unattached end of the resistor to the battery. The LED should give a nice glow of its color. Congratulations! You have built your first circuit!

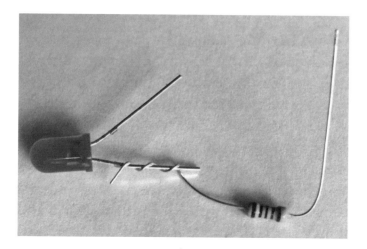

**Figure 5-1.** *Wrapping the Resistor Around the LED's Short Leg*

Even though we can't see the electricity moving, I hope you understand how it will flow through the circuit. We can trace the current flow from the positive terminal of the battery through the LED. The resistor limits the amount of current flowing through the circuit and therefore through our LED (the resistor can actually go on either side of the LED; it will limit the flow no matter which side it is on). Without the resistor, the battery would easily go over the 30-milliamp rating of our LED, and it would short out and no longer work. If you connected it without a resistor, you might see it turn on for a moment and then very quickly turn off, and then it would never work again. If you have an extra LED, you can try this out if you want. It is not dangerous—it will just cost you the price of an LED.

If your LED is backward, no current will flow at all. It won't hurt the LED, but it won't turn on unless it is oriented in the right direction.

# 5.4 Adding Wires

We are not going to physically add wires to our circuit at this time, but I did want to make a note on wires. Changing the lengths of wires will not affect our circuits in any way. On advanced projects (usually projects with extremely high precision or extremely long wires), the length of a wire will sometimes have an effect on such circuits. We are not doing any high-precision circuits, and our wire lengths are all less than a meter. Therefore, for the electronics we are doing, we can totally ignore wire length.

Therefore, if we connected our components using wires rather than directly wrapping their legs around each other directly, it would have no effect on the circuit at all. What is important is not the wires but the connections—what components are connected together and how are they connected. The length of the wire used to connect them is not important. You can connect them with a really long wire or directly touch the legs of each component together with no wires. It doesn't matter because the result is the same—the components are connected.

| Symbol | Component | Description |
|---|---|---|
| ⏚ | Battery | A battery is represented by a long line and a short line stacked on top of each other. Sometimes, there are two sets of long and short lines. The long line is the positive terminal and the short line is the negative terminal (which is usually used as the ground). |
| ⌁ | Resistor | A resistor is represented by a sharp, wavy line with wires coming out of each side. This represents that the resistor is not an easy way for current to flow. |
| ⧨ | LED | An LED is represented by an arrow with a line across it, indicating that current can flow from positive to negative in the direction of the arrow, but it is blocked going the other way. The LED symbol also has two short lines coming out of it, representing the fact that it emits light. |

*Figure 5-2.* *Basic Component Diagram Symbols*

# 5.5  Drawing Circuits

So far, we have only described circuits in words or by showing you pictures. This, however, is a lousy way of describing circuits. In complicated circuits, trying to trace the wires in a photograph is difficult. If you wanted to draw a circuit that you wanted built, you would have to be an artist to render it correctly. Likewise, reading through text describing a circuit takes a long time, and it is easy to get lost when discussing large circuits.

Therefore, in order to communicate information about how a circuit is put together in a way that is easy to read and write, engineers have developed a way of drawing circuits called **circuit diagrams** or **electronic schematics** (often just called *diagrams* or *schematics*). In a circuit diagram, each component is represented by an easy-to-draw symbol that helps you remember what the component does. Figure 5-2 shows the symbols for the components we have used so far. Note that everybody draws the symbols slightly differently and some components have more than one symbol. However, these are the symbols we will use in this book. For more symbols, see Appendix B.

Then, the components are connected together using lines to represent the wires and connections between the components.

53

Therefore, we can redraw our original circuit using these symbols as you see in Figure 5-3.

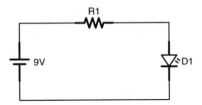

***Figure 5-3.*** *Basic LED Circuit Drawn as a Diagram*

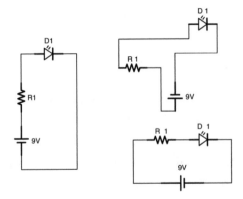

***Figure 5-4.*** *Alternative Ways of Drawing the Basic LED Circuit*

Notice that our components are laid out on the diagram with wires connecting them. Remember that it doesn't matter if we have very long wires or very short wires or if the components are directly placed end to end—the resulting circuits will operate identically. Also notice that each component is labeled (R1 and D1) because, as we make more complicated circuits, it is important to be able to refer back to them.

It does not matter in a diagram which way you have your components turned, how long or short your wires are, or what the general spacing looks like. When you actually wire it, all of those things will change. The important part of a circuit diagram is to convey to the reader what the parts are, how they are connected, and what the circuit does in the way that is easiest to read.

For instance, all of the circuits in Figure 5-4 are equivalent to the circuit in Figure 5-3, they are just drawn differently. All of them have the positive terminal of a battery connected to a resistor, with the other leg of the resistor connected to the positive end of an LED, with the other leg of the LED connected to the negative side of the battery. Since the connections are identical, the circuits are identical. Schematics don't care how long the lines are that you draw or how the components are oriented or even where the components are drawn on the page. The only thing important in the schematic is how the components are connected.

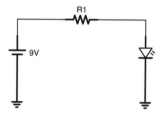

**Figure 5-5.**  *Basic LED Circuit Drawing Using the Ground Symbol*

For consistency, I like to draw all of my batteries to the left of the drawing with the positive side on top. By keeping the battery positive-side-up, components with higher voltage are usually closer to the top, and components with lower voltages are usually closer to the bottom, with the ground (i.e., 0 volt) coming back into the negative terminal. I also try to make my wire lines as simple as possible in order to make following them easier.

By keeping some amount of consistency, it is easier to look at a drawing and see what is happening.

# 5.6  Drawing the Ground

Remember that for electricity to move, every circuit must be fully connected from the positive side to the negative side. That means that in larger circuits, there are numerous connections that come from the positive or go back to the ground/negative. Because of this, a special symbol has been adopted to refer to the ground point in a circuit. This symbol, the ground symbol, has three lines, each shorter than the next. Points on a circuit that have this symbol connected to them are connected to each other (usually they are all connected to the negative side of the battery).

Therefore, the circuit in Figure 5-5 is the same circuit as before, just drawn using the ground symbol. Since points with the ground symbol are all connected together, using this symbol on both the negative terminal and the negative side of the LED means that they are wired together.

This doesn't help us a lot for this circuit (and, in fact, it makes it a little less easy to read). However, in complex circuits, it is much easier to write the ground symbol than trying to have 20 lines drawn back to the negative terminal.

Additionally, the same is true with the positive side of the battery. Many components require a direct connection to a specific voltage to work correctly. These are usually marked with just a disconnected wire with the end of the wire marking what voltage it requires. We make less use of that symbol in this book than the ground symbol, but it does come in handy sometimes.

So, using both the voltage source and ground symbols, we could rewrite the same circuit again in the manner shown in Figure 5-6. This circuit, again, is not *wired* any differently than before. We are just *drawing* it differently. For this circuit, it doesn't matter, but in more complex circuits, if we need a specific voltage at a specific location, this symbol tells us to put it there.

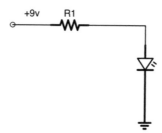

***Figure 5-6.*** *Simple LED Circuit Using Positive and Ground Symbols*

# Review

In this chapter, we learned the following:

1. Every circuit requires a source of power (usually a battery), wires and components, some amount of resistance, and a complete path back to the negative side of the power source.

2. An open circuit is one that does not connect back to the negative side (and thus does not provide any electricity), and a short circuit is one that connects back to the negative side without any resistance (and thus overwhelms the circuit with current).

3. A battery supplies a fixed voltage between its two terminals.

4. A resistor provides a fixed resistance (measured in ohms) within your circuit.

5. An LED allows current to flow in only one direction, gives off light when current is flowing, but is destroyed when the current goes above 20–30 milliamps.

6.  The longer leg of the LED should be on the positive side of the circuit.

7.  Wires on simple circuits can be almost any length (from zero to a few meters) without changing the functionality of the circuit.

8.  A circuit diagram is a way of drawing a circuit so that it is easy to read and understand what the circuit is doing.

9.  Each component has its own symbol in a circuit diagram.

10. Components labeled with the ground symbol are connected together, usually at the negative side of the battery.

11. Voltage sources can be similarly labeled by a wire connected on one side labeled with the voltage that it is supposed to be carrying.

## Apply What You Have Learned

**Special Note**: In the following problems, since we have not yet studied LED operation in depth, we are ignoring the electrical characteristics of the LED and just focusing on the resistor. If you know how to calculate the circuit characteristics using the LED, please ignore it anyway for the purpose of these exercises.

1.  Calculate the amount of current running in the circuit you built in this chapter using Ohm's law. Since Ohm's law gives the results in amps, convert the value to milliamps.

2.  Let's say that the minimum amount of current needed for the LED to be visibly on is 1 milliamp. What value of the resistor would produce this current?

3.  Let's say that the maximum amount of current the LED can handle is 30 milliamps. What value of the resistor would produce this current?

4.  Draw a circuit diagram of a short circuit.

5.  Take the circuit drawing in this chapter, and modify it so that it is an open circuit.

6.  Draw a circuit with just a battery and a resistor. Make up values for both the battery and the resistor and calculate the amount of current flowing through.

# CHAPTER 6

# Constructing and Testing Circuits

In Chapter 5, we learned how a circuit works. However, the method of putting together a circuit in the chapter doesn't translate to the real world well. In this chapter, we will learn how to use solderless breadboards to construct circuits in a more robust manner. Additionally, we will put our understanding of Ohm's law to the test as we learn how to measure voltages in circuits using our multimeter.

## 6.1 The Solderless Breadboard

The most important piece of equipment to use for making circuits is the **solderless breadboard**. Before solderless breadboards, if you wanted to put together a circuit, you had to attach them to a physical piece of wood to hold them down and then **solder** the pieces together. Soldering is a process where two wires are physically joined using heat and a type of metal called solder, which melts at much lower temperatures than other types of metal. So what you would have to do is attach the electrical components to the board, wrap the components' legs around each other, and then heat them up with a soldering iron and add solder to join them permanantly.

This was an involved process, and, though it was sometimes possible to get your components back by reheating the soldered joints, you were generally stuck with your results. The solderless breadboard is an amazing invention that allows us to quickly and easily create and modify circuits without any trouble at all. Figure 6-1 shows what a solderless breadboard looks like, and Figure 6-2 has the different parts of the breadboard labeled.

The solderless breadboard has a number of spring clips (usually about 400 or 800 of them) called **connection points** which will allow you to insert wires or component leads and will hold them in place. Not only that, the breadboard itself will connect the components for you!

The way that this works is that the breadboard is broken up into little half-rows called **terminal strips**. Each terminal strip has multiple connection points—usually five. Each connection point on a given terminal strip is connected by wire *inside* the breadboard. Therefore, to connect two wires or leads together, all you need to do is connect them to the same terminal strip. Any two wires or leads connected to the same terminal strip are themselves connected.

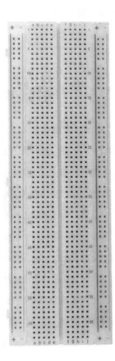

*Figure 6-1. A Solderless Breadboard*

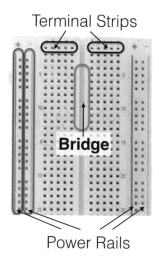

**Figure 6-2.** *Parts of a Solderless Breadboard*

In most breadboards, the two sides of the breadboard are separated by a gulf known as the **bridge**. The bridge is a visual indication that the two sets of terminal strips are not connected, but it also serves a practical purpose. If you have an integrated circuit (a small chip), the bridge is the right width so that you can place your integrated circuit right over the bridge, and each leg of the chip will receive its own terminal strip for you to easily connect them to what you need. We will cover this in more depth in later chapters.

In addition to the terminal strips, most breadboards have two strips running down each side, one with a red line and one with a blue line. These are known as **power rails** (some people call them **power buses**).

Power rails are very similar to terminal strips, with a few exceptions. The main difference is that, in terminal strips, only the five connection points grouped together are connected. On power rails, many more of the connection points are connected together, even when there are short gaps. Some boards will split the power rails at the halfway point, but others go all the way down the board. A split in the power rails is usually visually indicated by a break in the red and blue lines that indicate the power rails.

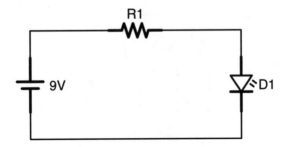

***Figure 6-3.*** *Basic LED Circuit*

Note that the positive and negative are *not* connected to each other (that would create a short circuit) and they are *not* connected to the power rails on the other side of the breadboard (unless you connect them manually). On some breadboards, even a single side isn't connected all the way down, but may be broken into sections at the halfway point.

In many projects, many components need direct access to the positive or negative power supply. Power rails make this easy by providing a connection point with positive and negative power a very short distance away from wherever you need it on the breadboard. If you plug your power source's positive and negative terminals into the positive and negative rails on the breadboard, then any time you need a connection to the positive or negative terminal, you can just bring a wire to the closest connection point on the appropriate power rail.

# 6.2 Putting a Circuit onto a Breadboard

To see how a simple circuit works on a breadboard, let's go back to the circuit we first looked at in Chapter 5. Figure 6-3 has the drawing again for ease of reference.

So how do we translate what we see in the drawing to what we need to put in the breadboard? Well, let's take a look at what is in the circuit—a 9-volt battery, an LED (we will go with a red LED), and a 1,000 Ω resistor.

Let us not concern ourselves with the battery at the moment. So, without the battery, we have a resistor connected to an LED.

Let us start out by simply placing our components onto the breadboard. What you will want is to place them on the breadboard so that each of their legs is on a *different* terminal strip. It doesn't matter *which* terminal strips you use—just make sure the legs all get plugged into different ones. Figure 6-4 shows how your breadboard should look so far. Note that the longer leg of the LED is closer to the resistor. The longer leg is depicted in the diagram as having an extra bend in the leg.

Figure 6-5 shows the *wrong* way to do it. In that figure, the legs of both the components are on the same row, which is the same thing as placing a wire between the legs, creating a short circuit. Don't do that! Make sure each leg goes into its own row.

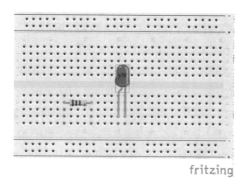

fritzing

***Figure 6-4.*** *Putting the Components onto the Breadboard*

Now, to connect the resistor to the LED, we need to add a wire. So all we need to do is connect a wire to any empty connection point that is on the same terminal strip of the right leg of the resistor and connect the other side of that wire to the left leg of the LED as shown in Figure 6-6.

Note that wires used on breadboards are often called "jumper wires." The difference between these and other kinds of wires is that jumper wires usually have solid, hard ends, making them easier to push into the breadboard. If you use regular wire or speaker wire, the ends are flexible, and it is almost impossible to get them into the breadboard properly to connect.

A common mistake that people will make is to connect the wire to the row right before or after the component. Take some time and be extra certain that the wire is connected to the *very same* row as the leg of your components.

Now, we need to connect our project to the power rails. So take a red wire from the left leg of the resistor to the positive power rail (remember, as long as it is in the same terminal strip as the resistor, they will be connected). Likewise, take a black wire from the right leg of the LED to the negative power rail. I always use red wires for connecting to the positive power rail and black wires for connecting to the negative/ground rail, as it makes it more clear when I am looking at my project what wire carries what. Your project should look like Figure 6-7.

Now your project is almost done. All you need to do now is to connect your power rails to a power supply. Connect a T-connector to a 9-volt battery, and then connect the red (positive) wire to the positive power rail on the breadboard.[1] You can plug it in anywhere on the rail, but I usually connect the power to the edge of the rail to leave more room for components. Then, connect the black (negative) wire to the negative power rail on the breadboard. As soon as you do this, the LED should light up! Figure 6-8 shows the final circuit.

---

[1]A T-connector is just a cap on the battery that has wires coming out of it. If you don't have a T-connector, you can manually plug a jumper wire into the breadboard and hold the other end on the battery terminal. T-connectors have their own drawbacks, as most of them have flexible ends, making them difficult to plug into breadboards. Shortly, we will move to an easier way of handling power with power regulators.

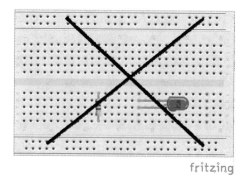

***Figure 6-5.*** *The Wrong Way to Put Components onto the Breadboard*

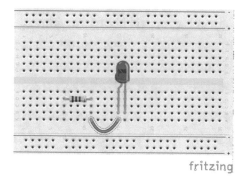

***Figure 6-6.*** *Adding a Wire to Connect the Components*

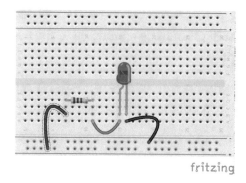

***Figure 6-7.*** *Adding Wires to the Power Rails*

Note that many T-connectors for 9-volt batteries have very flimsy wires that are difficult to insert into a breadboard. Usually, as long as you can get both terminals in far enough to touch the metal within the connection point, it will work. We will move to using power regulators shortly, which makes the process a bit easier.

If your circuit doesn't work, here is a list of things to check:

1.  Make sure your battery is properly connected to the breadboard—the red should go to positive and the black to negative.

2.  Make sure there are *no* wires directly connecting positive to negative on the board. Any direct pathway from positive to negative without going through a component will cause a short circuit and can destroy your components and battery.

3.  Make sure that your wires are connected to the same terminal strip as the component lead that they are supposed to be connected to. If they are on a different row, *they are not connected*!

4.  Make sure the LED is inserted in the right way. The longer leg should be connected to the resistor, and the shorter leg should be connected to the negative power supply.

5.  Make sure your components are good. Try replacing your LED with another LED to see if it works.

6.  If all of those things fail, take a picture of your project and post it to an online forum. Someone will likely be able to spot your problem and/or lead you in the right direction. Many forums are also available on the Web for this.

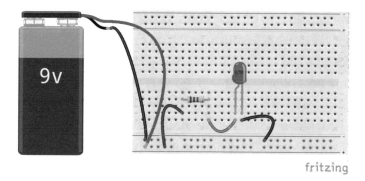

**Figure 6-8.** *Final LED Circuit with Power Connected*

# 6.3 Using Fewer Wires

In the previous section, we used three wires to connect our components, plus two more wires from the battery. We can improve our project by reworking it so that most of the wires are not necessary.

Remember that any two leads or wires plugged in next to each other on the same terminal strip are connected. Therefore, we can remove the wire that goes from the LED to the resistor simply by moving the LED and resistor so that the right leg of the resistor is on the same terminal strip. Figure 6-9 shows what this looks like.

However, that middle wire is not the only redundant wire. If you think about it, we could also save a wire by actually using the LED's own lead to go back to the negative rail. Figure 6-10 shows how this is set up. Now, in order to make the LED fit better, it is now on the *other* side of the resistor in the terminal strip. Remember that this does not matter at all! No matter where a component is connected on the terminal strip, it is joined with a wire to every other component on the same terminal strip.

Now, there is one last wire that we can get rid of. Can you think of which one it is? If you said the wire going from the positive rail to the resistor, you were right.

What we can do is to directly connect the resistor to the positive rail. Doing this gives us what is shown in Figure 6-11.

Therefore, as you can see, there are any number of ways that you can arrange parts on a breadboard to match a given schematic. All of these arrangements we have seen match the schematic given in Figure 6-3. As long as your circuit matches the configuration in the schematic, the specifics of where you put the wires and components is up to you. Some people like to place the components on their breadboard first, spaced out, and then add wires to connect them as needed. This works, though it does make for a messier board, with lots of wires going every which way. Other people like to use as few wires as possible and have their layouts as clean as possible (i.e., they don't like a tangled mess).

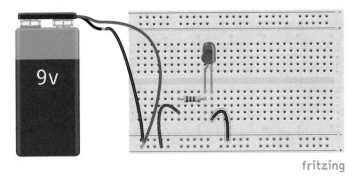

***Figure 6-9.*** *Joining Components by Putting Their Leads on the Same Terminal Strip*

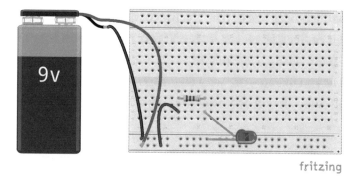

**Figure 6-10.** *Directly Connecting the LED to the Negative Rail*

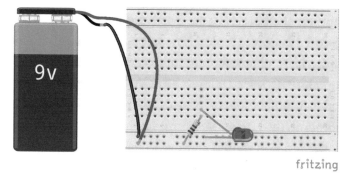

**Figure 6-11.** *Connecting the Resistor Directly to the Positive Rail*

Some people like to use flexible jumper wires that go up and over the board. Other people like to use rigid jumper wires that lie down close to the board and are the exact length needed. The flexible wire allows more flexibility in building your circuits (they are easier to move around and reconfigure), while the solid, rigid wire makes the final result a lot cleaner and easier to follow.

You can also trim the legs of your components to make them fit better, if you want. Some people like to leave their components as intact as possible, while others like to trim the legs of their leads to be the exact right size for their project. However, if you do trim the leads on your LEDs, be sure to keep the positive leg longer!

However you like to work with electronics is up to you. There are lots of options, and they all end up with the same circuit.

# 6.4  Testing Circuits with a Multimeter

Now that we know how to put circuits together, we need to know how to *test* our circuits. The main tool used to test simple circuits is the **multimeter**. It is called a multimeter because it measures *multi*ple different things about a circuit. Figure 6-12 shows a typical low-cost multimeter.

There are a lot of different multimeters around which have a lot of different functions. However, almost all of them will measure voltage, current, and resistance. Each of these values is measured by testing two different points on the circuit. Most multimeters have a red lead and a black lead. The red lead should connect to the more positive side of the circuit, and the black lead should connect to the more negative side of the circuit. However, if you get it reversed, it is usually fine—the multimeter may just report negative values if you are measuring for voltage or current.

To illustrate how to use a multimeter, we will start out measuring the voltage in a 9-volt battery. Remember from Chapter 4 that there is no absolute zero voltage—voltages are merely measured with reference to each other. Therefore, a multimeter doesn't tell you the exact voltage of something—there is no exact voltage. Instead, a multimeter allows you to choose two points on your circuit and measure the voltage difference (also known as the **voltage drop**) between them.

***Figure 6-12.*** *A Low-Cost Multimeter*

Now, remember that a 9-volt battery means that the battery should have 9 volts between its positive and negative terminals. Don't try it yet, but when we measure voltage, we will expect that the multimeter will tell us that the voltage difference is near 9 volts.

When using your multimeter, you must set *what* you are going to test *before* you test it. Otherwise, you can easily damage your multimeter or your circuit. Therefore, since we are going to measure voltage, select the DC Voltage setting on your multimeter (*do not* select the DC Current or DC Resistance setting!). If you are using a high-quality **auto-ranging** multimeter, that is all you need to do. However, when starting out, most people buy the bottom-of-the-line multimeter. That's not a problem, but just know that you will probably accidentally break it at some point.

If you are using a lower-quality multimeter, you will need to select not only *what* you want to measure but the *estimated range* of values that you want to measure. On my multimeter, the DC Voltage has five different settings—1000, 200, 20, 2000 m, and 200 m. These are the upper boundaries (in volts) that these settings can read.

So, for a 9-volt battery, using the 1,000-volt setting is probably unwise. It may give a reading, but it probably won't be accurate. However, if I try it on too low of a setting (say, 2000 m), it either won't read, or it will blow out my multimeter. So the safe thing to do is to start with the highest reasonable setting (or just the highest setting if you don't know what's reasonable) and test it and then reduce the setting until it gives you a good reading.

So, for instance, for my 9-volt battery, let's say I didn't know the voltage. Therefore, I'm going to measure the battery using the 1,000-volt setting. After setting the multimeter to 1,000 volts, I will put the red lead on the positive terminal of the battery and the black lead on the negative terminal. Be sure that you *firmly* press the *tip* of your leads against the positive and negative terminals. If it is not firm or if you use the sides of your terminals, you will not get a good reading.

When I do this, my multimeter reads 9.

Now, notice that this reading is significantly less than our 1,000-volt setting. Therefore, it may not be entirely accurate. So I will reduce the setting to the 200-volt setting and measure again. This time, my multimeter reads 9.6. This is definitely a more accurate reading—it is giving me an extra digit of accuracy! However, this reading is still significantly below the setting.

Therefore, I will reduce the setting again to the 20-volt setting and remeasure. This time, the measurement is 9.66. Again, it is more accurate. Now, can I reduce the setting even more? Well, the next setting is 2000 m, which is basically 2 volts. Our reading is 9.66 volts, so it is above the cutoff point for the next setting. Therefore, I should not try it on a lower setting, both for the sake of accuracy and for the sake of my multimeter's lifespan.

However, I should note that if I did use a lower setting, since the setting is listed as being in millivolts (i.e., 2000 m), then the reading would also be in millivolts. That is, if we were to read the value of the battery on that setting, it would say 9660, because that is how many millivolts the battery has.

Now, you could be wondering, why is a 9-volt battery anything other than exactly 9 volts? Well, it turns out that in electronics, no value is exact, and no formula works perfectly. When we talk about a 9-volt battery, we are actually talking about a battery that runs anywhere from 7 volts to

9.7 volts. In fact, my battery that started out at 9.66 volts will slowly lose voltage as it discharges. This is one of the reasons why measurement is so important.

Also, this means that in our circuits, we will have to find ways to compensate for varying values. Our circuits should work across a wide range of possible values for our components. We will discuss strategies for this as we go forward.

The next thing we will measure is resistance. Pull out a resistor—any resistor. The resistor datasheet in Appendix E shows you how to find the resistor values based on the color bands on the resistor. I don't know about you, but my eyes are not that good at looking at those tiny lines on the resistor and figuring out which color is which. Many times, it is easier just to test it with the multimeter.

The process is the same as with measuring the voltage, except that you start at the lowest setting and work up. First, find the resistance settings on your multimeter (perhaps just marked with the symbol for ohms—$\Omega$). Start with the smallest value (200 in my case). On this setting, the multimeter read 1, which means that it didn't pick up a signal. So I turned it up to the next setting, 2000. This time, it read 1002. Remember that if the value that the meter is set to includes a metric suffix (i.e., m, k, or M), that suffix gets applied to the value that is displayed on the screen.

Note that you should *never test for resistance in a live circuit*. The multimeter uses power to measure resistance, and if there is already power in the circuit, it can damage the multimeter and/or the circuit. However, to test for current and voltage the circuit must be powered.

## 6.5  Using a Multimeter with a Breadboard

We can use our multimeter with our breadboard too. Let's say that we wanted to measure the voltage between the positive and negative rails of the breadboard.

There are two ways to do this. The first, if the size of your multimeter probes and the size of your breadboard connection points allow it, is to simply shove the probes of your multimeter into connection points on the positive and negative rails. Since these will be connected to the power by a wire, these will be at the same voltage levels as the battery itself.

Second, if your breadboard/multimeter combination does not support this, you can do the same thing by simply connecting two jumper wires into the positive and negative rails and then testing the voltage on the other end of the wires.

Also, if you are testing components for voltage, you can also use your multimeter on the exposed legs of the component. This is often easier than either trying to push your probes into the breadboard or running extra wires to your multimeter.

To try out using your multimeter with your breadboard, configure your breadboard similar to Figure 6-8. Use this layout, and *not* one of the ones with fewer wires (you will see why in a minute). With the battery connected to the breadboard, set your multimeter to the highest voltage setting, and put the red lead in any empty hole in the positive rail. While that lead is there, put the black lead in any empty hole in the negative rail.

This should give you the same reading that you received for the battery terminals. Remember that the power rails are connected all the way across—that is why putting your probes in any hole on the line works! If you work your way down the ranges on your multimeter, you should find that you get the same value that you did when you measured directly on the battery's terminals. Again, if your probes do not fit inside the connection points, you can also use wires to connect out from your breadboard to your multimeter probes.

You can now do the same to any component on your board. Let's find the voltage difference between one side of the resistor and the other. To do this, find an empty hole on the same terminal strip as the left-hand side of the resistor, and put the red lead from your multimeter in that hole. Then, find an empty hole on the same terminal strip as the right-hand side of the resistor, and put the black lead from your multimeter in that hole. Now you can measure the voltage difference. Note that to measure voltage differences, the circuit *must* be active. If the power is gone, the voltage difference will likely drop to zero. Use the same ranging procedure to find the voltage drop between the left-hand and right-hand sides of the resistor.

Even though we have not discussed diodes, this doesn't prevent you from measuring the voltage difference between the legs of the diode in your circuit. Use the same procedure as before to measure the voltage drop.

# 6.6  Measuring Current with a Multimeter

Now we will learn to measure current using the same circuit layout from Figure 6-8. Like voltage, measuring current requires that the power to your circuit be on. To measure current, use the DC Amperage (sometimes called DC Current) settings on your multimeter.

Measuring current is a little different than measuring voltage in a circuit. Instead of just placing your probes in the breadboard as it is, you are going to use your probes to *replace a wire*. You will remove a wire and then place your probes in the holes (connection points) where the wire used to be. Alternatively, if your multimeter probes do not fit into the connection points, you can again run two wires, one from each hole, from the breadboard to your multimeter probes.

Using either of these approaches, the circuit will then use your multimeter *as the wire* that was removed, and the multimeter will then measure how much current is running through it and report it to you on the screen. You will need to use the same ranging technique as you used before with voltages to get an accurate report.

Let's say that you wanted to measure the current going through the wire that connects the resistor to the LED. To do this, we will start by *removing* that wire, and connecting the red lead to where the wire used to be on the left (since it is more positive) and the black lead to where the wire used to be on the right (since it is more negative). The multimeter should now report back how much current the circuit is using. This will vary for a number of reasons, but should be about 17 mA.

Now, put the wire back, and remove another wire and measure current there. No matter which wire you choose, they should all measure the same current. The reason is that, since all of these components are in series (one right after the other), they must all have the same amount of electricity flowing through them (otherwise, where would the electricity be going?).

# 6.7 Using a Power Regulator

So far, we have discussed several problems of using batteries in electronics projects. First, with batteries, we don't know exactly how much voltage they will deliver. A 9 V battery will deliver between 7 V and 10 V, and the actual amount will vary across its life. Additionally, the connectors available from batteries usually don't have the solid jumper wire ends, so it is hard to connect them to breadboards.

Both of these problems can be solved with a power regulator module. A power regulator module will take power from other sources (such as a battery) and reduce the voltage to a value which, while lower, will be constant. The power regulator we will use is the YwRobot breadboard power supply.

This low-cost device will take an input between 6.5 and 12 volts and deliver a constant voltage at the output of either 3.3 or 5 volts (we will use the 5 V setting). This device can be connected to a battery with an appropriate battery clip.[2] Figure 6-13 shows what this looks like.

---

[2]This can also be connected to a wall outlet using an appropriate adapter or connected to your laptop for a USB power supply. For the purposes of this book, we recommend against both of these options as it adds additional risk if something is wired incorrectly.

As you can see, the power module clips onto the power rails of the breadboard. The most important thing is to make sure that the power module is oriented correctly so that the positive and negative markings on the power module line up with the positive and negative power rails. Additionally, this power module has a shunt which, depending on where it is placed, sets whether it outputs 3.3 V or 5 V or is switched off. You need to be sure that the shunts on both sides are set to the 5 V position.

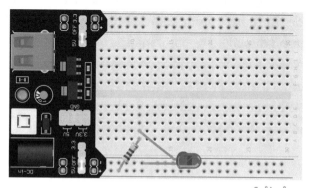

***Figure 6-13.*** *Breadboard with a Power Module*

***Figure 6-14.*** *9 V Battery Clip*

Finally, you need to plug the battery in. A 9 V battery can be plugged into the power module using a battery clip designed for CCTV cameras. They have a 9 V clip on one side and a barrel plug on the other side, which plugs nicely into the power module. You can see one in Figure 6-14.

After that is set up, don't forget to turn it on! The power module has an LED that lights up when the power module is turned on. This is really convenient because you don't have to include an on/off switch or an on light on your project, because the power module has one for you.

So how does the power module show up in the schematic? Well, actually, it doesn't directly. The combination of battery and power module basically just yields a 5 V battery in the schematic. So we will just represent it with the normal battery symbol, but set to 5 volts.

There are other power modules available as well, and they all basically work the same way. Just be sure that the voltage is set to 5 volts.

# Review

In this chapter, we learned the following:

1.  Solderless breadboards can be used to quickly create circuits.

2.  Solderless breadboards allow circuits to be easily constructed and destructed in such a way that the components are reusable from one project to the next.

3.  Both wires and the legs of a component are attached to connection points on the breadboard.

4.  Connection points in the same terminal strip are connected by a wire behind the breadboard.

5.   To connect two components together, all you have
     to do is put their legs on the same terminal strip of
     the breadboard.

6.   The power rails on a breadboard extend either all
     the way down the board or sometimes split at the
     halfway point.

7.   The bridge of a breadboard divides and separates
     different groups of terminal strips. This allows a chip
     to be placed over the bridge, allowing each of its
     pins a separate terminal strip.

8.   The schematic drawing of a circuit can be
     assembled onto a breadboard, giving a definite
     implementation of the drawing.

9.   There are multiple different ways to place a given
     circuit drawing onto a breadboard.

10.  Components on a breadboard can be connected by
     wires, or they can be connected by placing their legs
     in the same terminal strip.

11.  There are many different styles of placing
     components onto breadboards, which have
     tradeoffs between how easy it is to reconfigure and
     how clean the result is.

12.  A multimeter allows you to measure several
     important values on a circuit, including resistance,
     voltage, and current.

13. If your multimeter is not auto-ranging, you must test your value several times, starting with the highest range setting for the value you are looking for and decreasing it through the settings until you find a precise value. For resistance values, this is reversed—we start with the lowest range setting and move upward.

14. Always be sure your multimeter is set to the right setting *before* measuring.

15. Always turn your circuit off before measuring resistance.

16. Your circuit must be on to measure voltage or current.

17. Voltage is measured by connecting your multimeter to empty connection points in the terminal strips that you want to measure. This can be done either by putting your multimeter leads directly into the relevant connection points or by running wires from those connection points to your multimeter leads.

18. Current is measured by using your multimeter to replace a wire that you want to measure current running through.

19. Many circuit values vary much more than what you might think, so it is good to design circuits in a way that will handle these variances.

20. Power modules can deliver consistent voltages even when the components feeding into them (such as batteries) may have a significant amount of variance.

# Apply What You Have Learned

All measured values should be measured using the ranging technique discussed in this chapter:

1.  Start with the circuit you built in Figure 6-8. Measure the voltage drop across the resistor, and then measure the voltage drop across the LED. Now, measure the voltage drop across both of them (put the red multimeter lead on the left side of the resistor and the black multimeter lead on the right side of the LED). Write down your values.

2.  Using the same circuit, change the LED from red to blue. Measure the values again and write them down. Measure the current going through the circuit using any wire. Is it the same or different than before?

3.  Add another LED in series with the one you have already. Measure the voltage drops on each side of each component in the circuit. Measure the current going through any given wire. Write down each value.

4.  Take the new circuit you built in the previous problem and draw the schematic for the circuit.

# CHAPTER 7

# Analyzing Series and Parallel Circuits

In Chapter 5, we looked at our very first circuit and how to draw it using a circuit diagram. In this chapter, we are going to look at different ways components can be hooked together and what they mean for your circuit.

## 7.1  Series Circuits

The circuit built in Chapter 5 is considered a **series circuit** because all of the components are connected end to end, one after another. In a series circuit, there is only one pathway for the current to flow, making analyzing the circuit fairly simple.

It does not matter how *many* components are connected together—as long as all of the components are connected one after another, the circuit is considered a series circuit. Figure 7-1 shows a series circuit with several components included.

© Jonathan Bartlett 2020
J. Bartlett, *Electronics for Beginners*, https://doi.org/10.1007/978-1-4842-5979-5_7

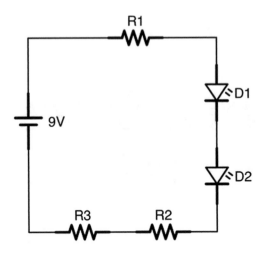

**Figure 7-1.** *A Series Circuit with Several Components*

If all of the components are in a series, then, even if there are multiple resistors scattered throughout the circuit, you can figure out the total resistance of the circuit just by adding together all of the resistances. This is known as the **equivalent resistance** of the series.

In this example (Figure 7-1), if R1 is 100 Ω, R2 is 350 Ω, and R3 is 225 Ω, then the total series resistance of the circuit will be 100 + 350 + 225 = 675 Ω.

That means that the current is easy to figure out as well. If we ignore the LEDs (since we have not yet learned to calculate using them), then we can use the total series resistance to calculate current the same way we did with the single resistor.

Since the voltage is 9 volts, then we can use Ohm's law to find out the current going through the system.

$$I = V / R = 9 / 675 = 0.013\text{A}$$

Note that A stands for ampere, and we will be using this in our calculations from here on out. However, we usually measure in milliamps (abbreviated as mA), so let us convert:

$$0.013 * 1000 = 13\text{mA}$$

So our circuit will draw about 13 milliamps of current. This amount of current is the same amount running through all of the components in the series.

## 7.2  Parallel Circuits

Circuits are wired into a **parallel circuit** if one or more of their components are arranged into multiple branches.

Figure 7-2 shows a simple circuit with two resistors in parallel. In this figure, the circuit has *two* branches. R1 is in the first branch, and R2 is in the second branch. The place where the branch occurs is called a **junction**, and is usually marked with a dot to show that all the wires there are connected.

In a parallel circuit, electricity will flow through both branches simultaneously. Some of the current will go through R1 and some of it will go through R2. This makes determining the total amount of current more difficult, as we have to take into account more than one branch.

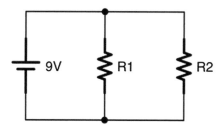

***Figure 7-2.*** *Two Resistors Wired in Parallel*

However, there are two additional laws we can use to help us out, known as **Kirchhoff's circuit laws**. The guy's name is hard to spell, but his rules are actually fairly easy to understand.

# 7.2.1 Kirchhoff's Current Law

The first law is known as **Kirchhoff's current law**. Kirchhoff's current law states that, at any junction, the total amount of current going *into* a junction is exactly the same as the total amount of current going *out* of a junction. This should make sense to us. Think about traffic at a four-way intersection. The same number of cars that enter that intersection must be the same number of cars that leave the intersection. We can't create cars out of thin air; therefore, each car leaving must have come in. Cars don't magically disappear; therefore, each car entering must leave at some point. Therefore, Kirchhoff's circuit law says that if you add up all of the traffic going in, it will equal the amount going out.

---

## ADVANCED: ANOTHER WAY OF LOOKING AT IT

Another way to say this is that the total amount of all of the currents at a junction is zero. That is, if we consider currents coming in to the junction to be positive and currents going out of the junction to be negative, then their total will be zero since the size of the currents coming in must equal the size of the currents going out.

---

So let's look at a junction. Figure 7-3 shows a junction where one wire is bringing current in and it branches with two wires bringing current out. The first wire going out has 0.75 A of current, and the second wire going out has 0.34 A of current. How much current is going into the junction from the left?

Since the total coming in must equal the total coming out, then that means the total coming in must be

$$0.75 \text{ A} + 0.34 \text{ A} = 1.09 \text{ A}$$

Therefore, the total amount of current coming into the circuit is 1.09 A.

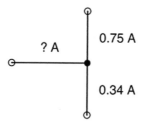

**Figure 7-3.** *A Simple Junction*

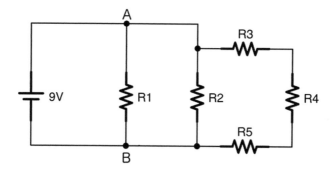

**Figure 7-4.** *A Circuit with Many Parallel Paths*

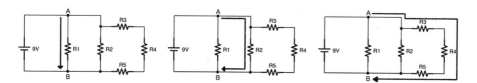

**Figure 7-5.** *All Paths Between Two Points Have the Same Voltage Drop*

Now, let's say we had a junction of four wires. On the first wire, we have 0.23 A of current coming in. On the second wire, we have 0.15 A of current going out. On the third wire, we have 0.20 A of current going out. What must be happening on the fourth wire? Is current coming in or going out on that wire?

To figure that out, we have to look at the totals so far. Coming in, we have the one wire at 0.23 A. Going out, we have the two wires for a total of 0.15 A + 0.20 A = 0.35 A. Since we only have 0.23 A coming in, but there is 0.35 A going out, that means that the fourth wire must be bringing current in. Therefore, the amount that this fourth wire must be bringing in is 0.35 A − 0.23 A = 0.12 A.

## 7.2.2  Kirchhoff's Voltage Law

Kirchhoff's current law makes a lot of sense, because the amount of "stuff" coming in is the same as the amount of "stuff" going out. This is similar to our everyday experience. Kirchhoff's voltage law, however, is a bit more tricky. **Kirchhoff's voltage law** states that, given any two specific points on a circuit at a particular time, the difference in voltage between the two points (known as the **voltage drop**) is the same *no matter what pathway you take to get there.*

Figures 7-4 and 7-5 illustrate this point. If we wanted to measure the voltage drop between the two points indicated (A and B), then that voltage drop, at least at a particular point in time, would be the same no matter what pathway electricity travels. The direct route between the two points has the same voltage drop as the more winding pathways, no matter what the values of the resistors are.

So how does that square with Ohm's law?

The way it works is that Ohm's law will cause all of the *currents* through each part of the circuit to adjust in order to make sure that the *voltage* stays the same.

As you can see, the voltage drop between A and B *must* be 9 volts because the battery is a 9-volt battery, and there are no components (only wires) between the battery terminals and A and B. Since batteries always have a constant voltage between their terminals, that means that A and B will have the same voltage—9 volts.

Therefore, that means that the voltage drop across R1 is 9 volts, because it is one of the pathways between A and B, and all pathways get the same voltage. Let's put in some real values for these resistors and see if we can figure out how much voltage and current is happening in each part of the circuit. Let's set R1 = 1,000 $\Omega$, R2 = 500 $\Omega$, R3 = 300 $\Omega$, R4 = 400 $\Omega$, and R5 = 800 $\Omega$. Now, let's find out what our circuit looks like.

As we have noted, *every* path must have the same voltage drop—9 volts. So let's start with the easiest one, the current going across R1. Since we have a 9-volt drop and 1,000 $\Omega$, we can just use Ohm's law for current:

$$I = V / R = 9\text{V} / 1,000\Omega = 0.009\,\text{A}$$

So we have 0.009 A running across R1.

Now, what about R2? R2 is connected to point A simply by a wire. As we mentioned in Chapter 5, wires can be considered to be zero length. Therefore, R2 is just as much directly connected to point A as R1 is. Therefore, the voltage drop across R2 is also going to be 9 volts. Again, using Ohm's law, we can see that

$$I = V / R = 9\text{V} / 500\Omega = 0.018\,\text{A}$$

So the current going across R2 is 0.018 A.

What about the current going across R3, R4, and R5? Well, if you notice, those resistors are all in series, so we can add them all up and just use the total resistance.

So the total resistance for this section of the circuit will be

$$R3 + R4 + R5 = 300\Omega + 400\Omega + 800\Omega = 1,500\Omega$$

So, using Ohm's law, the current running through this part of the circuit will be

$$I = V / R = 9\text{V} / 1,500\Omega = 0.006\,\text{A}$$

Now, remember that the total current flowing into any junction has to be equal to the current flowing out of it. So let's look at the junction between R2 and R3. We calculated that the current flowing to R2 is 0.018 A and the current flowing to the series starting with R3 is 0.006 A. Therefore, there has to be 0.018 + 0.006 = 0.024 A flowing into that junction.

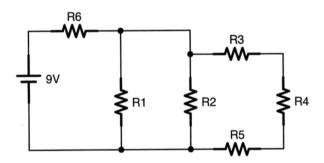

***Figure 7-6.*** *Kirchhoff's Voltage Law with Series and Parallel Components*

Now, how much current is flowing out of junction A? Well, earlier, we noted that the amount of current flowing across R1 was 0.009 A, and we just calculated that there is 0.024 A flowing out the junction between R2 and R3. That means that there must be 0.033 A total flowing into junction A.

While there were a lot of steps to determine this, each individual step was fairly straightforward. We simply combined Ohm's law, Kirchhoff's voltage law, and Kirchhoff's current law to figure out each step.

Now, one important thing to notice is that there is *less* current running through the pieces of the circuit with more resistance than there is with the pieces of the circuit with less resistance. The electric current is more likely to go down the path of least resistance. This is a very important point and should not be overlooked, as it will come in handy in later chapters.

# 7.3 Equivalent Parallel Resistance

The sort of calculation that we have done in the previous section gets trickier if there is a series resistance before or after the parallel resistance. Figure 7-6 gives an example of this. The setup is just like the previous circuit, except there is a single resistor (R6) in series with the battery *before* the parallel branches. This will prevent our simple calculations from working because the current flowing in each of the branches of the circuit will all add together to tell us the amount of current flowing through R6. However, the voltage drop across R6 will depend on the current flowing through it. If this voltage changes, then it will change our starting voltage for our calculations to figure out the parallel branches.

Thus, we have ourselves in a loop—in order to find out the current flowing through the parallel branches, we have to know their starting voltage. In order to find out their starting voltage, we have to know how much the voltage dropped across R6. In order to know how much the voltage dropped across R6, we have to know how much current was flowing through it!

This may seem like an impossible problem, but basic algebra allows us to work it out, though the details are kind of ugly. Instead, there is an equation that we can use for parallel resistors which will give us an **equivalent resistance** for a group of parallel resistors. That is, we can take a group of parallel resistors, and we can calculate the total resistance of those resistors, as if they were acting together as one resistor. In other words, we can find out what value we would need for a single resistor to replace all of the other resistances.

If you have resistors in parallel to each other (let's call them $R_1$, $R_2$, and $R_3$) and you want to know the resistance of their *combined* action (which we will call total $RT$), then you would use the following equation:

$$R_T = \frac{1}{\dfrac{1}{R_1} + \dfrac{1}{R_2} + \dfrac{1}{R_3}} \qquad (7.1)$$

This equation works for any number of resistances that we have in parallel. We can just keep on adding them to the end of the list:

$$R_T = \frac{1}{\dfrac{1}{R_1} + \dfrac{1}{R_2} + \ldots + \dfrac{1}{R_N}} \tag{7.2}$$

So let's look at our circuit and see how we can find out the current flowing through each resistor. For this example, we will again say that $R1 = 1{,}000\ \Omega$, $R2 = 500\ \Omega$, $R3 = 300\ \Omega$, $R4 = 400\ \Omega$, and $R5 = 800\ \Omega$. Additionally, $R6 = 250\ \Omega$.

In order to compute this, we first have to figure out *what* is in series and what is in parallel. Notice the loop made by R3, R4, and R5. Those are all connected end to end, so they are in series. Because they are in series, we can get their equivalent resistance just by adding them together—300 + 400 + 800 = 1,500 Ω. Therefore, we can actually *replace* these resistors with a single, 1, 500 Ω resistor. We will call this "combined" resistor R7. Now, if you look at the new picture, with R7 standing in for the loop, you will see that R1, R2, and R7 are in parallel with each other.

Therefore, we can find out their combined resistance by using Equation 7.2:

$$R_T = \frac{1}{\dfrac{1}{R1} + \dfrac{1}{R2} + \dfrac{1}{R7}}$$

$$R_T = \frac{1}{\dfrac{1}{1{,}000} + \dfrac{1}{500} + \dfrac{1}{1500}}$$

$$R_T = \frac{1}{0.001 + 0.002 + 0.00067}$$

$$R_T = \frac{1}{0.00367}$$

$$R_T = 272.5\,\Omega$$

Therefore, the equivalent resistance of all of the parallel resistances is about 272.5 Ω, which means that we could in theory replace *all* of these resistors (R1, R2, R3, R4, and R5) with a single resistor that is 272.5 Ω. Also notice that this resistance is actually *less* than each of the individual resistances.

Now, to get the total resistance of the circuit, we notice that this parallel resistance (272.5 Ω) is in series with R6, which is 250 Ω. Since they are in series with each other, we can simply add them together. The total resistance of this circuit is 250 + 272.5 = 522.5 Ω. We can now use Ohm's law to find the total amount of current running through this circuit:

$$I = \frac{V}{R}$$
$$I = \frac{9}{522.5}$$
$$I = 0.0172\text{A}$$

Thus, the whole circuit has 0.0172 ampere of current running through it. Using this, we can now go back through and identify how much current and voltage is flowing through each individual piece.

Because the entirety of the 0.0172 ampere is going through the first resistor (R6), that means that the voltage drop of the R6 resistor will be, using Ohm's law

$$V = I \cdot R$$
$$V = 0.0172 \cdot 250$$
$$V = 4.3\text{V}$$

That means that this resistor will chew up 4.3 V. This leaves us with 9 − 4.3 = 4.7 V after the series resistor.

We now know the starting and ending voltages of each branch of the parallel resistors—4.7 V at the beginning (what we just calculated the voltage to be after the series resistor) and 0 V at the end (because it connects to the negative terminal of the battery, which we have designated as the 0-volt reference).

Therefore, we can use Ohm's law to find the amount of current flowing through each of them. For R1:

$$I = \frac{V}{R}$$
$$I = \frac{4.7}{1,000}$$
$$I = 0.0047\,\text{A}$$

For R2:

$$I = \frac{V}{R}$$
$$I = \frac{4.7}{500}$$
$$I = 0.0094\,\text{A}$$

And finally, for the series that is in a loop at the right (R3, R4, and R5):

$$I = \frac{V}{R}$$
$$I = \frac{4.7}{1500}$$
$$I = 0.0031\,\text{A}$$

Since the loop is all in series, that means all of the resistors in that series will have 0.0031 A going through them.

If we add all of these currents, we will see that 0.0031 + 0.0094 + 0.0047 = 0.0172 A, which is the amount of current we originally figured out.

What we have learned is that we can replace the entire circuit with a single value for its resistance to figure out how the circuit will behave as a whole. For a simple circuit like this, having all of these parallel branches doesn't do much, so it may seem pointless. However, in a real circuit, each of these branches may be, instead of a resistor, a more complicated component that has some amount of resistance. If you know the resistance, you can calculate how much current is flowing through it the same way.

However, we start with only resistors in order to make the problems simpler.

# 7.4  Wires in a Circuit

In complicated circuits, sometimes we run out of room and must draw wires on top of each other even though the wires aren't connected. In this book, we try to make clear which wires are connected by placing a dot on the junction point. Another way to show this is to show the wires crossing if the wires are joined but showing one of the wires as being broken across the intersection point if the wires are not joined. Figure 7-7 demonstrates the difference. The wires on the left are joined together as indicated by the dot. The wires on the right are not joined in any way; they just had to be drawn across each other because of space reasons in the diagram. In this book, the convention we follow is to use dots to indicate joined wires, but we do not break lines for unjoined wires.

Also, the lengths of wires that we draw are irrelevant. Usually, in simple circuits, we should consider that wires are all zero length. If, after a resistor, the voltage in the circuit has dropped to 5 V, then we can consider that the *whole wire* until the next circuit is at 5 V. If a wire branches into multiple branches, even though each branch will have a different amount of *current* running on it, each branch of the wire will all have the *exact same voltage* until they reach another component.

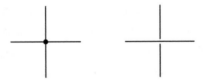

**Figure 7-7.** *Showin Joined Wires (Left) vs. Showing Unjoined Wires (Right)*

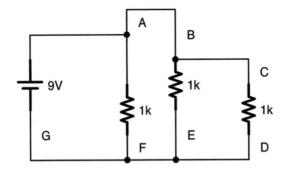

**Figure 7-8.** *Several Points on a Circuit*

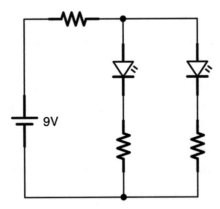

**Figure 7-9.** *A Circuit with Series and Parallel Components*

Therefore, in the circuit in Figure 7-8, you can see several points labeled A, B, C, D, E, F, and G. In this circuit, A, B, and C all have equivalent voltages (though not equivalent currents) since there are only wires (and not components) between them. Likewise, D, E, F, and G all have equivalent voltages since there are only wires between them. Also, since D, E, F, and G are all connected to the battery negative (i.e., ground) with no components between them, that means that they are all at 0 volt. Likewise, since A, B, and C are all directly connected to the battery positive with no intervening components, they are all at 9 volts.

# 7.5  Wiring Parallel Circuits onto a Breadboard

One other issue we need to look at is how to wire parallel circuits onto the breadboard. It is actually very simple to do. In this section, we are going to put the circuit in Figure 7-9 onto a breadboard.

Notice that, in this circuit, there is a series resistor at the beginning and then two parallel circuits that branch off from it. It doesn't matter much what the value of the resistors are, but we will put them at 1,000 $\Omega$ if you need a specific value (anything between 200 and 2,000 $\Omega$ should work fine).

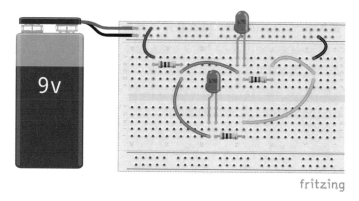

***Figure 7-10.*** *A Circuit with Series and Parallel Components on the Breadboard*

To get the circuit onto the breadboard, remember that anything that is connected in the same terminal strip on a breadboard is connected together. This means that, when we have a parallel subcircuit, we connect all of the branches of the subcircuit into the same terminal strip. Figure 7-10 shows what this looks like.

Let's follow the path of electricity through the breadboard. First, the current flows from the positive terminal to the positive rail on the breadboard. A wire then pulls the positive +9 V power onto the board. This wire is connected to a resistor by putting one leg of the resistor in the same terminal strip as the wire. On the other leg of the resistor, there are *two* wires that are in the same terminal strip. Each of these goes to a different part of the circuit. We have one LED with a resistor on the top and one LED with a resistor on the bottom. These are just normally connected components.

However, after the resistor, the two subcircuits come back together to a terminal strip on the right. Then, a wire on the same terminal strip takes that back to the negative rail on the breadboard (which connects to the negative terminal on the battery).

Note that I could have used a lot fewer wires to accomplish the same circuit. However, I thought that using more wires would make it more clear what is happening at each junction, especially when the circuit gets divided into branches or comes back together.

Take a moment to look at both the schematic drawing and the breadboard picture, and be sure that you can trace the flow of the schematic on the actual breadboard.

# Review

In this chapter, we learned the following:

1.  In a series circuit, electricity flows in a single line through all of the components.

2.  In a parallel circuit, electricity branches and flows in multiple branches.

3.  Most real circuits are combinations of series and parallel circuits.

4.  When you have resistors together in series, the total resistance of all of the resistors combined is simply the sum of their individual resistances. $R_T = R_1 + R_2 + \ldots + R_N$.

5.  In a parallel circuit, Kirchhoff's current law says that the total amount of current entering a branch/junction is the same as the total amount of current leaving the branch.

6.  In a parallel circuit, Kirchhoff's voltage law says that, between any two points on a circuit at a given point in time, the voltage difference between those two points will be identical no matter what pathway the electricity follows to get there.

7.  When resistances are in parallel, the total resistance for the parallel circuit is given by the equation

$$R_T = \frac{1}{\dfrac{1}{R_1} + \dfrac{1}{R_2} + \ldots + \dfrac{1}{R_N}}$$

8.  By using these laws in combination, we can predict how current will flow in each part of our circuit.

9.  Series circuits are placed onto a breadboard by putting the connected legs of two connected components onto the same terminal strip.

10. Parallel circuits are placed onto a breadboard by connecting each subcircuit branch to the same terminal strip.

# Apply What You Have Learned

1.  There is a junction in a circuit that has one wire with current flowing in and two wires with current flowing out. There is 1.25 A of current coming in, and the first wire going out has 0.15 A of current. How much current is leaving through the second wire?

2.  There is a junction in a circuit that has two wires with current flowing in and two wires with current flowing out. The first wire with current flowing in has 0.35 A of current, the first wire with current flowing out has 0.25 A of current, and the second wire with current flowing out has 0.42 A of current. How much current is flowing in on the second incoming wire?

3.  At a junction of four wires, wire 1 has 0.1 A of current flowing in, wire 2 has 0.2 A of current flowing in, and wire 3 has 0.4 A of current flowing out. Is the current in wire 4 going in or out? How much current is flowing on it?

4.  If I have three 100 Ω resistors in series, what is the total resistance of the series?

5.  If I have a 10 Ω resistor, a 30 Ω resistor, and a 65 Ω resistor in series, what is the total resistance of the series?

6.  If I have a 5 Ω resistor and a 7 Ω resistor in series, what is the total resistance of the series?

7. If I have two resistors in parallel, a 30 Ω resistor and a 40 Ω resistor, what is the total resistance of this circuit?

8. If I have three resistors in parallel—25 Ω, 40 Ω, and 75 Ω—what is the total resistance of this circuit?

9. If I have four resistors in parallel—1,000 Ω, 800 Ω, 2,000 Ω, and 5,000 Ω—what is the total resistance of this circuit?

10. If I have three resistors in parallel—100 Ω, 5,000 Ω, and 10,000 Ω—what is the total resistance of this circuit? Which of the resistors is the total resistance most similar to?

11. Take a look at the following circuit diagram. If the voltage drop between B and C is 2 volts and the voltage drop between C and D is 3 volts, what is the voltage drop between A and E? What is the voltage at E? What is the voltage at A?

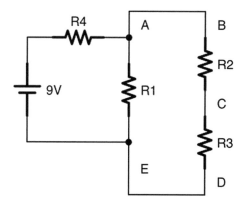

12. If the preceding circuit runs with 2 A total current, what is the value of the resistor R4?

13.  The following circuit is a combination of series and parallel resistances. Each resistor is labeled with its resistance value, given in ohms. Find out how much current is flowing through each resistor and how much each resistor drops the voltage.

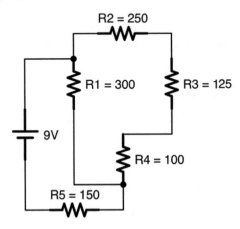

14.  Build the circuit in Figure 7-10 on your own breadboard. Measure the voltage drops across every component, and measure the amount of current flowing into the first series resistor.

# CHAPTER 8

# Diodes and How to Use Them

This chapter introduces the **diode**. We have used light-emitting diodes (LEDs) in previous chapters, but have not really discussed their function except for emitting light. In this chapter, we are going to look at regular diodes, light-emitting diodes, and Zener diodes, to get a feel for what these devices are and how they might be used in circuits for more than just light.

## 8.1  Basic Diode Behavior

Unlike resistors, diodes have both a positive and negative side. For any component with both positive and negative legs, the positive leg of the component is termed the **anode** and the negative leg is termed the **cathode**. On LEDs, the anode is longer than the cathode. However, for other types of diodes, the cathode is marked with a line. You can remember this because in the schematic of a diode, the cathode has the blocking line.

The diode performs two fundamental "actions" with electric current. The first action of a diode is to drop voltage by an essentially fixed amount *without* affecting or limiting current. This amount of voltage is called the **forward voltage drop** and it is usually around 0.6 V for most non-LED diodes. Forward voltage is often abbreviated as $V_F$. For most LEDs, the

© Jonathan Bartlett 2020
J. Bartlett, *Electronics for Beginners*, https://doi.org/10.1007/978-1-4842-5979-5_8

forward voltage drop depends on the color of the LED, with a red LED dropping about 1.8 V and a blue LED dropping about 3.3 V. The forward voltage drop can vary among the other colors as well.

To remind you, when we say "voltage drop," we are referring to the difference in voltage between the positive and negative legs of the diode. Therefore, no matter what the voltage is coming into the diode, the voltage coming out of the diode will be that voltage minus the voltage drop.

The second action of a diode is to limit the direction of current to a single direction. With some exception, the diode only allows current to flow one way in the circuit. The "normal flow" of a current through the diode is to flow from the anode to the cathode. Looking at the schematic symbol, current flows in the direction that the arrow is pointing, and current is blocked from flowing the other way (you can think of the line as a "block" preventing reverse flow).

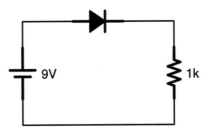

***Figure 8-1.*** *A Diode and Single Resistor Circuit*

However, diodes are limited in the amount of reverse flow they can block. At a certain point, diodes reach their **breakdown voltage**. The breakdown voltage is the voltage at which they will stop blocking voltage. In regular diodes, this is a failure mode, and the precise value shouldn't be relied upon (we will see an exception to this with Zener diodes). Usually, though, this value is high enough not to worry about (i.e., around 100 volts).

# 8.2 Circuit Calculations with Diodes in Series

Now let's talk about how to properly calculate the behavior of circuits with diodes. Remember, the key to a diode is that if current is flowing through the diode, the voltage drop across the diode will be essentially constant. For a normal non-LED diode, this voltage drop is almost always 0.6 V. This is so common it is usually assumed, and never listed in the circuit itself.

Therefore, take a look at the circuit in Figure 8-1. Since the voltage source is 9 volts, that means that the total voltage drop between the positive and negative is 9 volts. The diode will eat 0.6 V of the voltage, but will not limit the current in any way. The resistor, then, since it is the only component left, will use up the rest of the voltage—8.4 V. Therefore, we can calculate the current in the circuit using Ohm's law:

$$I = V / R = 8.4 / 1000 = 0.0084\text{A} = 8.4\text{mA}$$

Therefore, our circuit will use 8.4 mA of current. So, as you can see, when doing calculations, the diodes simply provide a drop in voltage, they do not limit (or even affect) current.

This is true no matter how many diodes or resistors I have in my circuit. Figure 8-2 shows a circuit like that. To figure out the behavior of this circuit, remember that *every* diode has a 0.6 V voltage drop. Since the circuit has three diodes, that means that the diodes will drop a total of 0.6 * 3 = 1.8 V.

Therefore, we will have 1.8 V taken up by diodes, which drop voltage without limiting current. Since we have a 9 V source, there will be 9 − 1.8 = 7.2 V that is not eaten by diodes. This voltage will go to our two resistors. These resistors, even though they are separated by diodes, are essentially in series with each other. Therefore, we can treat them as a single resistor in series. So the total resistance on the circuit will be $1k + 2k = 3k\,\Omega$.

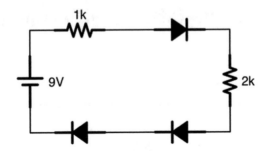

**Figure 8-2.** *A Circuit with Multiple Diodes and Resistors*

We can then find the total current running through the circuit using Ohm's law:

$$I = V / R = 7.2\text{V} / 3,000\Omega = 0.0024\text{A} = 2.4\text{mA}$$

However, it is possible to put too many diodes in your circuit. Since they each eat 0.6 V in their forward voltage drop, that puts a limit on how many you can string together in series from a given battery. For a 9 V battery, if I try to put 20 diodes together in series, I will have used *more* than the total 9 volts that I have available. Therefore, current will not flow. With 20 diodes, the voltage drop will be $20 * 0.6 = 12$ V. Since this is more voltage than the battery can put out, no current will flow.

So we have seen two conditions for which current will not flow through a diode—the first is that the diode will block current from flowing in the wrong direction, and the second is that the diode will not conduct if the voltage source cannot provide enough voltage to bridge the forward voltage drop of the diode.

# 8.3 Circuit Calculations with Diodes in Parallel

The real magic of diodes comes when using them in parallel circuits. Remember the rules that we learned in Chapter 7. Kirchhoff's voltage law says that between any two points, the voltage drop between those two points will be the same *no matter what path the current follows*. Therefore, since the voltage drop across a diode is *fixed*, that means that we can guarantee a maximum voltage drop between two points on a circuit by putting diodes between them.

Figure 8-3 shows what this looks like. The voltage drop from one side of the diode to the other is 0.6 V. Period. End of story (actually, it could be less, which would keep the diode from conducting altogether, but we won't consider that at the moment).

Kirchhoff's voltage law tells us that *no matter what path is traveled*, the voltage difference between those two points will be the same. Since the 2k resistor is attached to the same two points that the diodes are attached to, Kirchhoff's voltage law tells us that the voltage across the resistor *must* be the same as the voltage across the diode. Thus, the voltage across the resistor *must* be 0.6 V.

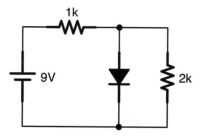

***Figure 8-3.*** *A Single Diode in Parallel with a Resistor*

Using Ohm's law, we can deduce the amount of current flowing through that resistor:

$$I = V / R = 0.6 / 2,000 = 0.0003A = 0.3mA$$

So how much current is flowing through the diode? To find this out, we need to use Kirchhoff's current law. The amount entering the junction where the diode and the 2k resistor split off is the same as the amount leaving it. We know that 0.3 mA leaves the junction to go to the resistor. Therefore, if we could figure out how much current was coming *into* the junction, we could figure out how much is going through the diode.

To discover that value, we need to know how much current is going through the 1k resistor. To figure that out, we need to know the voltage drop across the resistor. However, we can figure this out easily. Since the tail end of the diode is connected to ground (the negative terminal), that means that after the diode, we are at 0 V. Therefore, since the diode voltage drop is 0.6 V, then the voltage before the diode must be 0.6 V. That means that the rest of the voltage must have been consumed by the 1k resistor.

Since the voltage source is 9 V, that means that the voltage for the entire circuit from positive to negative is 9 V, and therefore, the voltage drop across the resistor must have been 9 − 0.6 = 8.4 V. Using this value, we can determine the current going through the resistor using Ohm's law:

$$I = V / R = 8.4 / 1,000 = 0.0084A = 8.4mA$$

In this circuit, there is 8.4 mA going through the first resistor. That means that there is 8.4 mA coming into the junction. We know that 0.3 mA is going out of the junction through the 2k resistor. That means that the rest of the current is going through the diode. Therefore, we can calculate that the current going through the diode is 8.4 − 0.3 = 8.1 mA.

Diodes don't make the math harder, but they do force you to *think* a little harder about how you apply the rules.

Let's take a look at a slightly harder example, using Figure 8-4. In this circuit, we have two diodes in parallel with two resistors in parallel. This parallel circuit is in series with a resistor on the front and another diode at the end.

It is almost always easiest to analyze circuits starting with the diodes because their voltage drops are fixed. If we look at this circuit, the diode at the end gives the circuit a voltage drop of 0.6 V.

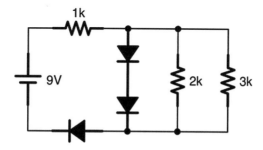

**Figure 8-4.** *A Circuit with Multiple Diodes*

Now let's look at the parallel part of the circuit. Here, we have three pathways—one through two diodes and two other pathways through resistors. However, one of the pathways contains all diodes. We know that diodes give a constant voltage drop, and we know that Kirchhoff's voltage law says that all pathways between two points have the same voltage drop. Since we have two diodes, the voltage drop of this parallel pathway is 0.6 * 2 = 1.2 V.

Now we have the parallel resistors to worry about. However, we can use the formula for parallel resistance (Equation 7.2) to figure out the total resistance of the parallel resistors.

$$R_T = \cfrac{1}{\cfrac{1}{R1} + \cfrac{1}{R2}} = \cfrac{1}{\cfrac{1}{2,000} + \cfrac{1}{3,000}} \approx \cfrac{1}{0.0005 + 0.0003333} = \cfrac{1}{0.0008333} \approx 1200\Omega$$

However, we technically don't even need that number, because, since we already know the voltage drop across each resistor (it *must* be 1.2 V because of Kirchhoff's voltage law), we can just apply Ohm's law to each resistor.

Now, using Ohm's law, we can calculate the current flowing through the resistors. So, for the 2k resistor, we have

$$I = V / R = 1.2\text{V} / 2,000\Omega = 0.0006\text{A} = 0.6\text{mA}$$

For the 3k resistor, we have

$$I = V / R = 1.2\text{V} / 3,000\Omega = 0.0004\text{A} = 0.4\text{mA}$$

The total current going into both resistors is simply the sum of each of the currents, 0.4 + 0.6 = 1.0 mA. So there is 1 mA total flowing through the two resistors. To find out how much current is flowing through the diode, we will need to know how much current is coming into the circuit itself out of the first resistor.

So how much current is flowing through the first resistor? Well, the voltage drops we have calculated so far include a 0.6 V drop at the end and a 1.2 V drop in the middle. That is a total of 1.2 + 0.6 = 1.8 V. Since the battery is 9 V, that means that there is 9 − 1.8 = 7.2 V left to be consumed by the circuit. Therefore, that must be the voltage drop of the first resistor. Using Ohm's law, we find that

$$I = V / R = 7.2\text{V} / 1,000\Omega = 0.0072\text{A} = 7.2\text{mA}$$

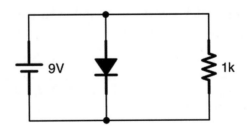

***Figure 8-5.*** *A Bad Diode Circuit*

Therefore, we have 7.2 mA flowing through that first resistor. So, if we have 7.2 mA coming into the parallel circuit in the middle and 1 mA flowing to the resistors, the amount of current flowing through the diodes down the middle is 7.2 − 1 = 6.2 mA. The amount of current going through the final diode is the full 7.2 mA of current in the circuit.

Again, there are a lot of steps, but none of the steps are individually very hard. You simply start with the easiest-to-find values (in this case, the voltage drops from the diodes) and work out from there.

## 8.4  Diode Short Circuits

Next, let's look at a very bad design with a diode. Let's say that someone wanted to use a diode to regulate the amount of voltage across a resistor to 0.6 V. Therefore, they built the circuit shown in Figure 8-5. Can you figure out what the problem is here?

Well, the voltage drop across the diode will be 0.6 V. However, the battery operates at 9 V. This means that there is 8.4 V left in the circuit with *zero* resistance. Using Ohm's law, that gives us

$$I = V / R = 8.4 / 0 = \infty$$

Thus, having a diode going direct from the positive to the negative of your voltage source is essentially the same as a short circuit. That is why the circuit is bad! To use a diode, there must *always* be resistance somewhere in series with the diode in order to dissipate the current from the excess voltage. The resistor can be before the diode or after it, but it must be there to absorb the extra voltage.

Additionally, it is important to make sure the amount of current flowing through your diode is within the specifications of the diode you are using. Most LEDs, for instance, are only rated for small currents up to about 30 mA.

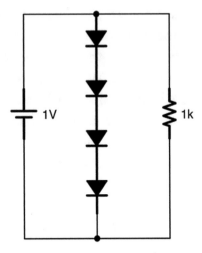

**Figure 8-6.** *Nonconducting Diodes*

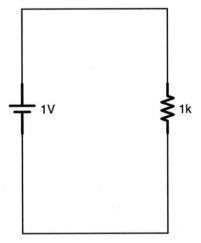

**Figure 8-7.** *A Circuit Equivalent to Figure 8-6 Because of Nonconducting Diodes*

# 8.5 Nonconducting Diodes

There is one case where diodes do not maintain a constant voltage drop, and that is where there is not enough voltage to go across them. Figure 8-6 shows an example of this.

In this figure, the voltage drop across the center diode bridge is $0.6 + 0.6 + 0.6 + 0.6 = 2.4$ V. However, the battery source is only 1 V. Since the voltage drop of the diodes is larger than the available voltage, this part of the circuit is basically turned off. In reality, there is a small but ignorable leakage current (about 0.00000022 mA in this case if you were really curious), but we can think of this circuit as effectively switched off.

So keep that in mind—if you ever wind up with more forward voltage drop from a diode than you have available voltage, you may treat the diode as if it were an open (i.e., unconnected) circuit, as if it were not even there.

Therefore, we would analyze Figure 8-6 as if it were just like Figure 8-7.

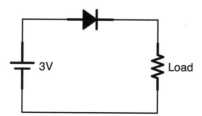

***Figure 8-8.*** *A Simple Diode Protection Circuit*

# 8.6 Usage of Diodes

Diodes can be thought of as circuit traffic cops—they regulate the flow of electricity. They make sure that everything within a circuit is happening in a controlled manner. They regulate the circuit in two different ways—by limiting the direction of current and, in parallel circuits, by establishing fixed voltages between two points.

The simplest usage of a diode is to use it as a device that makes sure that your battery is plugged in the right orientation. If you have a device that will be damaged if someone puts the battery in backward, a simple diode will make sure that the current can only flow in one direction.

The circuit in Figure 8-8 shows what this looks like. Note that we have a resistor labeled "Load." Many times in circuits, a load resistor is shown to represent whatever else is happening in another part of a circuit. Thus, this circuit shows that the diode is protecting the rest of the circuit (whatever it is) from the user putting the battery in backward. However, this has a cost—the diode will eat 0.6 V in order to provide this protection.

Another problem often solved by diodes is voltage regulation. Because diodes provide a fixed voltage drop between two points, you can use diodes to ensure a fixed voltage for devices that require it.

For instance, when we looked at batteries in Chapter 6, we noted that their voltage actually varied quite a bit. A 9 V battery might give you anywhere from 7 V to 9.7 V. This is true of any battery, not just the 9 V variety. In that chapter, we showed how we could use a voltage regulator to accomplish this, but a similar effect can be accomplished with diodes. If you need a fixed amount of voltage, you can use diodes to provide that at the cost of some extra current.

This isn't recommended for a whole project (the excess current can generate a lot of heat), but sometimes makes sense in limited circumstances. However, for demonstrating the concept, let's look at what it would take to provide voltage regulation using diodes.

Figure 8-9 shows a simple voltage regulator using diodes. Given a 5 V battery (actually, a battery of any size significantly over 3 V will work), this circuit will provide a regulated 3 V of electricity to whatever is connected to it as a load (remember a "load" resistor is just a stand-in for whatever we want to attach to this).

Because the diodes provide a fixed voltage drop of 0.6 V each, then that pathway has a total voltage drop for five diodes of $5 * 0.6 = 3.0$ V. Kirchhoff's voltage law says that between two points, *every* pathway between them will have the same voltage drop. This means that the load, since it is connected to those two points, will have the same voltage drop, thus regulating the amount of voltage used by the load.

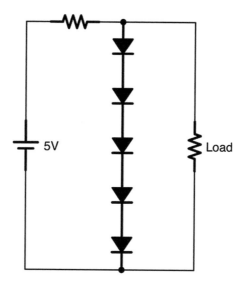

**Figure 8-9.**  *A Simple 3 V Voltage Regulator*

But what about that first resistor at the beginning of the circuit? Remember, if we provide a pathway through diodes only, we create a short circuit in the system. There has to be some element (usually a resistor) that eats up whatever voltage is left over. Therefore, putting a small resistor before our diode pathway will give the circuit a place to use the excess voltage and limit the amount of current that flows.

The size of the resistor will depend on how much current the load requires and how much current you are willing to waste. A small resistor wastes more current, but allows for a higher maximum current used by the load. A larger resistor wastes less current, but if the load needs a lot of current, it could interfere with the voltage regulation.

To see how this could happen, let's say that our load is equivalent to 1,000 Ω. This means that the amount of current that the load will draw can be calculated using Ohm's law:

$$I = V / R = 3V / 1,000\Omega = 0.003A = 3mA$$

So the load will use up 3 mA of current. That means that, however much current goes through our first resistor, however much that is over 3 mA will be drained off through the diodes. So let's calculate what that looks like on a tiny, 20 Ω resistor. The voltage will be $5 - 3 = 2$ V.

$$I = V / R = 2V / 20\Omega = 0.1A = 100mA$$

So, if we just used a 20 Ω resistor, that means that even though the load only used 3 mA, the whole circuit will be using 100 mA to operate! Therefore, we need a bigger resistor to limit the amount of current we use. Let's try a 500 Ω resistor:

$$I = V / R = 2V / 500\Omega = 0.004A = 4mA$$

This is much better—we are only using 4 mA in this circuit, so we are only wasting 1 mA. There has to be *some* amount of waste to do the voltage regulation.

Let's say that, after a while, our battery sags down to only providing 4 V of power. What happens now? Well, using the 500 Ω initial resistor, that means that there is only 1 V extra to drain off, so the current will be

$$I = V / R = 1V / 500\Omega = 0.002A = 2mA$$

Here, the current is only 2 mA, but we need 3 mA to power the circuit! Thus, if we use a 500 Ω resistor, we can't handle our power supply dropping down to 4 V.

What about using the 20 Ω resistor? In this case, Ohm's law would give us

$$I = V / R = 1V / 20\Omega = 0.05A = 50mA$$

So, here, the 20 Ω resistor will still provide plenty of excess current to allow our regulator to keep working. However, it is still eating up an extraordinary amount of current compared to our load.

So how do you choose the right resistor? The way to work situations like this is to think about what are the maximum cases you are designing for and then calculate appropriately. So, if I want this circuit to work when the battery sags down to 4 V, I need to decide how much excess current I'm willing to have at that level. Let's say I decide that I always want at least half a milliamp to run through the diode (somewhat of an arbitrary number, but if the diode has no power, it is not providing any regulation—this is a low number that is still "noticeable" on the circuit). That means that, since my load will be using 3 mA, the total amount of current running through the initial resistor will be 3.5 mA, or 0.0035 A. Therefore, I calculate what the resistor will need to be at 4 V using Ohm's law:

$$R = V / I = 1V / 0.0035A \approx 286\Omega$$

Therefore, for this situation, the initial resistor should be 286 Ω. Now, let's figure out how much current this wastes when the battery is at full charge—5 V (which means that there will be a 2 V drop across this resistor).

$$I = V / R = 2V / 286\Omega \approx 0.007A = 7mA$$

So, at full charge, there is 7 mA going through this resistor, which means we will waste 4 mA. Whether or not that is acceptable to your circuit depends on what you are going to do with it!

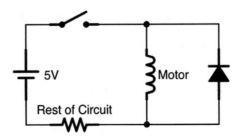

***Figure 8-10.*** *A Diode Protection Circuit*

Note that there are better means of regulating battery voltage for a whole circuit than using diodes. However, many times you need a regulated voltage somewhere *within* a more complex circuit. Diodes are great for that, and the same calculations and considerations apply.

One final note: As mentioned earlier, although we think of diodes as providing a fixed voltage, they actually do vary a little bit with the amount of current flowing through them. In any circuit, you should allow for ±10% variance in the voltage drop of a diode.

# 8.7 Other Types of Diode Protection

Diodes can provide other types of protection for circuits as well. As single-direction control valves, they can be used to prevent a variety of overvoltage conditions. Oftentimes they are wired in such a way that they will not normally conduct, but will conduct under certain conditions to redirect extra voltage in a safe manner.

Figure 8-10 shows an example circuit. In this circuit, a DC motor is connected to a switch. Notice the diode that is wired backward. Normally, this diode does absolutely nothing because the current is flowing in the other direction, so it just goes through the motor. DC motors, however, tend to generate very large voltages for a short time when switched off (see Chapters 20 and 23 for more information about DC motors and inductive loads). Therefore, when the motor is switched off, the motor can produce a very large voltage—up to 50 V in this circuit!

To protect the rest of the circuit from this sudden influx of voltage, the diode provides an alternative path back through the motor. Thus, when the voltage starts to build up after the switch closes, the diode provides a safe pathway back through the motor for it to flow, allowing the voltage buildup to slowly dissipate through the motor, rather than overloading a circuit expecting 5 V with 50 V.

Oftentimes when looking at circuit diagrams, you may find diodes in funny places and oriented in funny ways. These are oftentimes providing some sort of protection to the circuit from potential failure conditions or exceptional circumstances. Many microchips, for instance, use diodes to shunt off excess voltage from static electricity shocks.

**Figure 8-11.** *The Zener Diode Schematic Symbol*

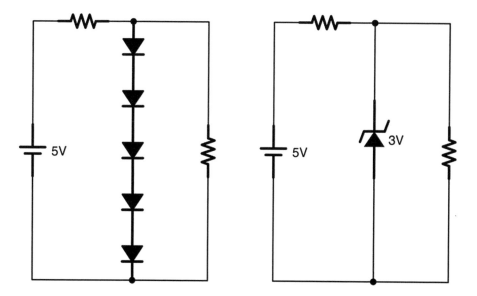

**Figure 8-12.** *A Circuit Regulated by Regular Diodes and a Zener Diode*

# 8.8  Zener Diodes

One problem with using diodes for voltage regulation is that their forward voltage drop is pretty small, so you have to have quite a few of them to regulate larger voltages. Zener diodes can help out in these situations. Figure 8-11 shows the symbol for a Zener diode.

Remember that most diodes have a breakdown voltage if you try to pass voltage the wrong way. However, in most diodes, this is a failure mode—doing this can, at best, be unpredictable, and, at worst, damage your diode. A Zener diode, however, is built so that it has a very predictable operation at its breakdown voltage. In fact, at its breakdown voltage, it acts like a normal diode with a larger voltage drop.

However, since you are using the breakdown voltage rather than the forward voltage, Zener diodes are wired into your circuit *backward*. Figure 8-12 shows what this looks like. In this figure, on the left you have the same 3 V regulated circuit as Figure 8-9. On the right, you have an equivalent circuit regulated by a Zener diode instead. Since we are using the Zener diode's breakdown voltage rather than its forward voltage, it has to be wired backward for it to work.

Not only that, the breakdown voltage drop for a Zener diode is much more constant over a larger range of current than the forward voltage drop of most regular diodes. Because of this, Zener diodes are used much more often for voltage regulation than a series of regular diodes.

Zener diodes come in a variety of breakdown voltages. In any exercise in this book which involves drawing a circuit with a Zener diode, you may presume that the Zener diode with the voltage drop you are looking for exists. When drawing a circuit, be sure to label the Zener diode with the breakdown voltage you are needing.

# 8.9  Schottky Diode

A Schottky diode is very similar to a normal diode, but it is made using a different process, meaning that its voltage drop is significantly reduced. While a "normal" diode's forward voltage drop is about 0.6 V, a Schottky diode's voltage drop can be as low as 0.15 V. This can be very useful in cases where a diode is needed to regulate the direction of electrical flow, but the voltage requirements are sensitive enough that you can't afford the 0.6 V of a regular diode.

# 8.10  Diode-Like Behavior in Other Components

Another important reason for being familiar with diode operation is that other types of components have parts which contain diodes or behave in diode-like ways. When we discuss bipolar junction transistors (BJTs) (see Chapter 24), we will see that these components partially consist of diode-like behavior.

# Review

In this chapter, we learned the following:

1.  Diodes only allow current to flow in one direction.

2.  Diodes have a fixed forward voltage drop across the diode—0.6 V for normal diodes and a range of about 1.8 to −3.3 V for LEDs.

3.  Different color LEDs have different voltage drops.

4. Diodes also have a breakdown voltage—the amount of voltage for which, if applied in the reverse direction, the diode will no longer block current.

5. When analyzing circuits with diodes, it is often easier to analyze the diodes first, since the voltage drop is fixed.

6. Because of Kirchhoff's voltage law, anything wired in parallel with diodes will have the same voltage drop as the diodes (or possibly less).

7. If the forward voltage drop on a diode is greater than the available voltage in the circuit, the diode will not conduct, and it can be treated as an open circuit.

8. If diodes are connected to the positive and negative terminals of a voltage source (such as a battery) with no resistance in series, this will create a short circuit, causing extremely large amounts of current to flow through the diodes.

9. Diodes are often used as control valves to regulate the direction of current flow on a circuit.

10. Diodes are often used to regulate the amount of voltage between two points on a circuit.

11. The series resistor used with voltage-regulating diodes determines both how much current is wasted and how much current the load can draw—lower-value resistors waste more current but allow the load to draw more current, and higher-value resistors waste less current but don't allow as much potential current to your load.

12. When designing circuits, it is often useful to account for the most extreme variations possible. This will allow your circuit to be more flexible.

13. Diodes can also provide protection to circuits against strange failure conditions, such as voltage spikes and static electricity. Diodes in strange places in circuit diagrams are often there to protect the circuit against certain types of failures or events.

14. Zener diodes are built so that they have very reliable operation on their breakdown voltage.

15. Wiring a Zener diode backward gives you the equivalent of several forward diodes in series and can be used for simple voltage regulation.

16. The breakdown voltage of a Zener diode is much more constant than the forward voltage of a regular diode and therefore works even better for voltage regulation.

17. Zener diodes come in a wide variety of breakdown voltages and are usually labeled on the circuit with the necessary breakdown voltage.

18. Schottky diodes are like ordinary diodes except they have a much smaller forward voltage.

19. Understanding diode behavior is important because a number of components contain diodes or exhibit diode-like behavior.

# Apply What You Have Learned

1.  If you have a 9 V voltage source, a blue LED, and a 500 Ω resistor all in series, how much current is running through the LED?

2.  If you have a 3 V voltage source and a red LED, what size resistor do you need to put in series with the LED to have it use 3 mA of current?

3.  If you have a 10 V voltage source, a blue LED, a red LED, and a 200 Ω resistor all in series, how much current is running through the LEDs?

4.  If I have a 12 V voltage source, a blue LED, and a red LED and the LEDs have a maximum current of 30 mA before they break and a minimum current of 1 mA before they turn on, what range of resistors can I put in series with the LEDs to get them to light up without breaking?

5.  In the following circuit, calculate how much current is flowing through each component and each component's voltage drop if R1 is 500 Ω (note that the diode is just a regular diode, not an LED).

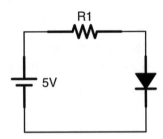

6. Let's say instead of an ordinary diode, the diode is a blue LED. Recalculate the current going through each component and the voltage drops for each component.

7. In the following circuit, calculate how much current is flowing through each component and each component's voltage drop if R1 is 300 Ω, R2 is 400 Ω, and R3 is 500 Ω.

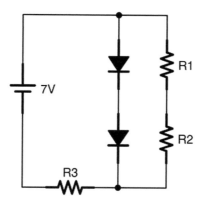

8. Draw a circuit that provides a 6-volt regulated power supply to the circuit load from a 9-volt battery using regular diodes. Choose a resistor that works efficiently for a circuit load of 500 Ω and operates with a battery voltage from 7 V to 9.6 V. What is the current at the lowest and highest ranges of the battery? How much is used by the circuit load, and how much is wasted through the diodes in each configuration?

9. Draw an equivalent circuit to the previous question using a Zener diode instead of normal diodes.

# CHAPTER 9

# Basic Resistor Circuit Patterns

When most people look at a schematic drawing, all they see is a sea of interconnected components with no rhyme or reason combining them. However, most circuits are actually a collection of **circuit patterns**. A circuit pattern is a common way of arranging components to accomplish an electronic task. Experienced circuit designers can look at a circuit and see the patterns that are being used. Instead of a mass of unrelated components, a circuit designer will look at a schematic and perceive a few basic patterns being implemented in a coherent way.

In this chapter, we are going to learn three basic resistor patterns and learn to work with switches as well.

## 9.1 Switches and Buttons

Switches and buttons are very simple devices, but nonetheless we probably need to take a moment to explain them. A switch works by connecting or disconnecting a circuit. A switch in the "off" position basically disconnects the wires so that the circuit can't complete. A switch in the "on" position connects the wires.

There are different types of switches depending on their operation. The ones we are concerned with are called "single pole single throw" (SPST) switches, which means that they control only one circuit (single pole) and the only thing they do is turn it on or off (single throw).

© Jonathan Bartlett 2020
J. Bartlett, *Electronics for Beginners*, https://doi.org/10.1007/978-1-4842-5979-5_9

**Figure 9-1.** *Schematic Symbols for an SPST Switch (Left) and an SPST Button (Right)*

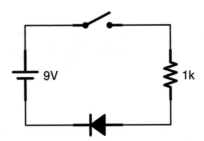

**Figure 9-2.** *A Simple Switch Circuit*

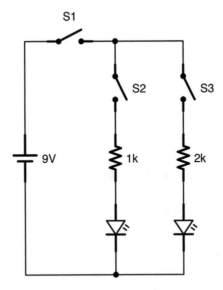

**Figure 9-3.** *A Circuit with Multiple Switches*

Figure 9-1 shows what the schematic symbols for an SPST switch and an SPST momentary switch (i.e., a button) look like. As the drawing indicates, when the switch is open, the circuit disconnects. When the switch closes, it connects the circuit. While the switch holds its position stable (someone has to manually switch it back and forth), the button only connects the circuit *while it is being pushed*. While the button is being pushed, the circuit is connected, but as soon as someone stops pushing the button, the circuit opens back up.

Figure 9-2 shows what a simple circuit with a switch looks like. It is just like a normal LED circuit, but with a switch controlling whether or not electricity can flow. Note that the switch is just as effective on the other side of the circuit. If the switch was the last part of the circuit, it would be equally as effective. Remember, in order for current to flow, there must be a full circuit from positive back to negative.

Switches can also be used to turn on or off individual parts of a circuit—basically reconfiguring the circuit while it is running. In the circuit given in Figure 9-3, a master switch (S1) turns the whole circuit on or off, and two individual switches (S2 and S3) turn parallel branches of the circuit on and off.

To analyze a circuit with switches, you need to analyze the way the circuit behaves with each configuration of switches. In this case, obviously when S1 is open, no current at all flows. However, this circuit will use different amounts of current when S2 is closed, S3 is closed, and both S2 and S3 are both closed. Therefore, to truly know the behavior of the circuit, you need to calculate the current usage in each of these situations.

# 9.2  Current-Limiting Resistor Pattern

The first resistor pattern we are going to learn is one that we already know—the current-limiting resistor pattern. The idea behind this pattern is that a resistor is added to limit the amount of current that can flow through a device. The size of the resistor needed depends on the size of the voltage source, the action of the device itself, and the maximum amount of current to allow. Then, the resistor size needed can be calculated using Ohm's law.

Many resistors are added to circuits to limit current flow. At the beginning, we used resistors to make sure we didn't destroy our LEDs. In Chapter 8, we used a resistor to limit the amount of current flowing through our voltage regulation circuit.

In many different circuits, we will need resistors to limit current for two different reasons—to avoid breaking equipment and to save battery life. Oftentimes, we are actually choosing resistor values to accomplish both of these tasks.

If an LED breaks with 20 mA, then we need a resistor big enough to keep the current that low. However, if the LED light is sufficiently visible with 1 mA, then, to save battery life, we might want a bigger resistor. Battery capacity is often measured in milliamp-hours (mAh), with a typical 9 V battery holding 400 mAh. So, with such a battery, an LED circuit at 10 mA will drain the battery in 40 hours (400 mAh/10 mA = 40 h), but the same LED circuit with a bigger resistor, limiting the current to 1 mA, will take a full 400 hours (400 mAh/1 mA = 400 h) to drain the same battery! That will save you a lot of money in the long run.

# 9.3  Voltage Divider Pattern

A **voltage divider** occurs anytime there are two resistors together with a subcircuit coming out from in between them. They usually are connected to a fixed positive voltage on one side of the first resistor and the ground on the other side of the second resistor, but this isn't strictly necessary. A simple schematic of a voltage divider is shown in Figure 9-4. Notice that there are two resistors between the voltage source and the ground (a 1k on top and a 2k on the bottom) and a subcircuit (indicated by the load resistance) branching off from between them. Under certain circumstances (which will be covered in a moment), we can basically ignore the parallel resistance of the subcircuit and just look at the voltages at each point in the main voltage divider circuit.

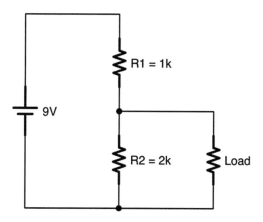

**Figure 9-4.** *A Simple Voltage Divider Circuit*

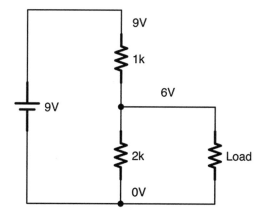

**Figure 9-5.** *Voltage Divider with Voltages Labeled*

# 9.3.1  Calculating the Voltages

We can see that the voltage at the top of the voltage divider is 9 V (because it connects to the positive terminal) and at the bottom of the voltage divider it is 0 V (because it connects to the negative terminal). Therefore, the total voltage drop across both resistors must be 9 V. Since the resistors are in series (remember, we are ignoring the load for now), we can find the total resistance in the circuit by just adding their resistances. So 1,000 Ω + 2,000 Ω = 3,000 Ω. Since the current in a series is the same for the whole series, we can now use Ohm's law to calculate the current flow:

$$I = \frac{V}{R} = \frac{9\text{V}}{3,000\Omega} = 0.003\text{A} = 3\text{mA}$$

So there is 0.003 A (3 mA) in this circuit. That means that *each* resistor in the series will have this amount of current flowing through them. Therefore, we can calculate the voltage drop across each resistor. Let's look at the 1k resistor:

$$V = I * R = 0.003\text{A} * 1,000\Omega = 3\text{V}$$

So the voltage drop across the first resistor is 3 V. That means that, since the battery started at 9 V, at the end of the resistor the voltage compared to ground is 6 V. We can calculate the voltage drop across the second resistor either by Ohm's law again or just by noting the fact that since the other end of the resistor is connected to ground, the voltage *must* go from 6 V to 0 V.

Figure 9-5 shows the voltages at each point (relative to ground). As you can see, the wire from the middle of the voltage divider has a new voltage that can be used by the load. This is what voltage dividers are normally for—they have a simple way of providing a scaled-down voltage to a different part of the circuit.

# 9.3.2 Finding Resistor Ratios

But how do we choose the values of the resistors?

One thing to note is that the second resistor consumed exactly twice as much voltage as the first resistor. Additionally, the second resistor was exactly twice as large as the first resistor. Thus, as a general principle, the relative sizes of the resistors will determine the relative amounts of voltage they eat up. So, if we needed a 4.5 V output—that is half of our input voltage—we would need both resistors to be the same.

A more explicit way of stating this is with an equation. Given a starting voltage $V_{IN}$ connected to the first resistor, $R_1$, and the second resistor ($R_2$) connected to ground, the output voltage ($V_{OUT}$) coming out between the resistors will be given by the equation

$$V_{OUT} = V_{IN} * \frac{R_2}{R_1 + R_2} \qquad (9.1)$$

Note that the specific resistance values don't matter yet—it is the *ratio* we are concerned about so far. To get 4.5 V, we can use two 1 kΩ resistors, two 200 Ω resistors, or two 100 kΩ resistors. As long as the values are the same, we will divide the voltage in half.

If we wanted an 8 V output, we would do a similar calculation. Since we start at 9 V, we need to use up $\frac{1}{9}$ of the voltage in the first resistor, and $\frac{8}{9}$ of the voltage in the second resistor. Therefore, our resistors need to be in similar ratio. We could use a 100 Ω resistor for the first resistor and an 800 Ω resistor for the second resistor. Alternatively, we could use a 10 Ω resistor for the first resistor and an 80 Ω resistor for the second resistor. It is the ratio that matters most.

# 9.3.3 Finding Resistor Values

So how do you determine exactly what value to use? Here is where we start thinking about the load again. While we have been treating the voltage divider as a series circuit, in truth we have one resistor in series and then a parallel circuit with the other voltage divider resistor in parallel with the load. Our simplified model (where we ignore the parallel resistance) will work, *as long as the load resistance does not impact the total parallel resistance by a significant amount.* Therefore, let's look at how the load resistance affects the parallel resistance.

So, using Equation 7.2, we can write a formula for the total resistance of these two, with $R_2$ being our second voltage divider resistor and $R_L$ being our load resistance:

$$R_T = \frac{1}{\dfrac{1}{R_2} + \dfrac{1}{R_L}}$$

Now, let's look back at the circuit in Figure 9-5. Let's say that the resistance of the load ($R_L$) is 400 $\Omega$, which is much less than the resistance of the voltage divider resistor ($R_2$, which is 2,000 $\Omega$). So what is the total resistance?

$$R_T = \frac{1}{\dfrac{1}{R_2} + \dfrac{1}{R_L}} = \frac{1}{\dfrac{1}{2,000} + \dfrac{1}{400}} = \frac{1}{0.0005 + 0.0025} = \frac{1}{0.003} \approx 333\Omega$$

This is significantly different from our simplified model which ignored the load resistance, which gave 2,000 $\Omega$. That means that our simplified model won't work with this value.

Now, let's imagine a bigger load resistance so that it is equal to the $R_2$ resistance (2,000 $\Omega$) and recalculate:

$$R_T = \frac{1}{\dfrac{1}{R_2} + \dfrac{1}{R_L}} = \frac{1}{\dfrac{1}{2,000} + \dfrac{1}{2,000}} = \frac{1}{0.0005 + 0.0005} = \frac{1}{0.001} \approx 1,000\Omega$$

This is still significantly off, but it is much closer. So, now, let's look at what happens if the load resistance is double of $R_2$, or 4,000 $\Omega$:

$$R_T = \frac{1}{\dfrac{1}{R_2} + \dfrac{1}{R_L}} = \frac{1}{\dfrac{1}{2,000} + \dfrac{1}{4,000}} = \frac{1}{0.0005 + 0.00025} = \frac{1}{0.00075} \approx 1,333\Omega$$

Here, we are getting much closer to our original value. Now, let's say that the load is ten times the resistance of our $R_2$ resistor, or 20,000 $\Omega$. That gives us this:

$$R_T = \frac{1}{\dfrac{1}{R_2} + \dfrac{1}{R_L}} = \frac{1}{\dfrac{1}{2,000} + \dfrac{1}{20,000}} = \frac{1}{0.0005 + 0.00005} = \frac{1}{0.00055} \approx 1,818\Omega$$

This is very close to the resistance of $R2$ by itself. So what we can say is that our voltage divider circuit can ignore the resistance of the load *if the resistance of the load is significantly more than the resistance of the voltage divider resistor.* A way of writing this down is that $RL \gg R2$. What "significantly" means depends on how sensitive your circuit is to voltage changes, but, generally (and for the purposes of the exercises), I will say that "significantly more" should mean at least ten times as much.

## 9.3.4 General Considerations

So, for low-resistance loads, a voltage divider does not work well, because it puts too little resistance between the voltage source and ground. However, in Chapter 11, we will see that many circuits have loads of approximately infinite resistance, so voltage dividers work really well in those cases.

In general terms, a voltage divider with smaller resistors is "stiffer" because it varies less in response to variations in a load, but it also eats up more current. A voltage divider with larger resistors doesn't work with low-resistance loads, but it also uses up much less current.

If you need to know full equations for figuring out voltage divider resistors, I have them listed in Equations 9.2 and 9.3. In these equations, $V_{IN}$ is the voltage coming into the voltage divider, $V_{OUT}$ is the voltage going out of the divider into your load, and $R_L$ is the load resistance. $R_1$ is the resistor connected to the positive power supply, and $R_2$ is the resistor connected to the ground. If you are good at algebra, you might see if you can deduce these formulas yourself from the information given in this section:

$$R_2 = \frac{R_L}{10} \qquad (9.2)$$

$$R_1 = \frac{R_2 * \left( V_{IN} - V_{OUT} \right)}{V_{OUT}} \qquad (9.3)$$

## 9.4 The Pull-Up Resistor

The pull-up resistor is a strange circuit, but we will find very good applications for it once we start dealing with ICs in Chapter 11. It is probably easiest to describe by simply showing you a circuit and then describing how it works.

Figure 9-6 shows the circuit diagram for a basic pull-up resistor circuit. Normally, we think of lighting up an LED by pushing the button. However, in this case, pushing the button causes the current to bypass the LED, which turns it off.

If you look at the path from where the circuit branches, when the button is not pressed, the current can only go one way—through the LED. However, when the button is pressed, the electricity has two options—either through the LED or directly to ground through the button. The electricity would always rather go directly to ground rather than through an intermediary, so *all* of the current goes through the closed button, and none of it goes through the LED.

Since the branch point is directly connected to ground when the button is pushed, that means that the voltage *at the branch point* is also zero. Kirchhoff's voltage law says that no matter what path is taken, the voltage drop will always be the same. However, an LED induces a voltage drop, but the voltages on both sides of the LED are zero. Therefore, electricity cannot flow through the LED.

So what is the function of the resistor? The resistor connects the switch and the LED to the positive voltage source and provides a limitation on the current that runs through it. The resistor must be *before* the branch point for it to work.

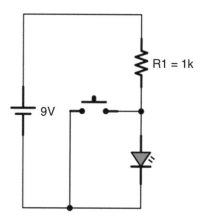

*Figure 9-6.* *Basic Pull-Up Resistor*

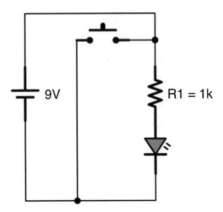

***Figure 9-7.*** *Incorrect Way to Wire the Circuit*

Think about what happens without the resistor or if the resistor is after the branch point. The electricity will have a path directly from the positive voltage source to ground with no resistance—in other words, a short circuit. This will draw an enormous amount of electricity. Figure 9-7 shows what this would look like. Notice that when the button is pushed, you can trace a path from the positive voltage source to ground with no intervening resistance.

The resistor is called a pull-up resistor because it is connected to the positive voltage source and is used to "pull up" the voltage on the circuit to a positive value when the switch is open while still providing safety (by limiting the current) when the switch is closed.

In short, a pull-up resistor is usually used to supply positive voltage to a circuit which might be turned off by redirecting the voltage to ground. The resistor provides both the electrical connection to the positive source and a limit to the amount of current that will flow if the current flow is then routed to ground (usually through some kind of switching mechanism).

# 9.5 Pull-Down Resistors

One more basic resistor circuit that is often used is the pull-down resistor. While the pull-up resistor is connected to the positive power rail, the pull-down resistor is instead connected to ground. So, in a pull-up resistor, if part of the circuit is disconnected, the voltage goes high. In a pull-down resistor, if part of the circuit is disconnected, the voltage goes low. However, we don't yet have enough background really to understand how they are used here. They are covered more fully in Chapter 12. They are merely mentioned here because they are one of the basic resistor circuit patterns that are seen throughout electronics.

# Review

In this chapter, we learned the following:

1. Buttons and switches allow circuits to be altered while they are running by connecting circuits (allowing pathways for electric current) and disconnecting circuits (blocking pathways for electric current).

2. Most circuits are a combination of common, well-understood circuit patterns.

3. The more experienced you are with the basic circuit patterns, the easier it is to see these circuit patterns when you look at a schematic drawing.

4. A current-limiting resistor is a resistor that is used to limit the maximum current flow within a circuit, either to protect other components or to limit overall current usage.

5.   A voltage divider is a pair of two resistors connected in series with one another (usually connected to a positive voltage on one side and the ground on the other), but with another wire coming out in between them to provide voltage to another circuit (called the *load* ).

6.   In a voltage divider, it is assumed that the resistance of the load is significantly more than (i.e., greater than ten times) the resistance of the second half of the voltage divider because then the load can be basically ignored for calculating voltage drops.

7.   For a voltage divider, the ratio of the voltages consumed by each resistor is the same as the ratio of their resistances. The output voltage coming out of the first resistor is the level of the voltage that will be supplied to the load.

8.   Another way of stating the output voltage is $V_{OUT} = V_{IN} * \dfrac{R_2}{R_1 + R_2}$ , where $R_1$ is the resistor connected to the positive voltage and $R_2$ is the resistor connected to ground.

9.   Voltage dividers with smaller resistances are "stiffer"—they are impacted less by the resistance of the load. Voltage dividers with larger resistances are not as stiff but waste much less current.

10.   A pull-up resistor circuit is a circuit in which a positive voltage which may be switched to ground at some point is provided through a resistor.

11.  The pull-up resistor both (a) connects the circuit to the positive voltage to supply a positive current when the circuit is not switched to ground and (b) limits the current going to ground (i.e., prevents a short circuit) when the output is switched to ground.

12.  It is called a pull-up resistor because it pulls the voltage up when the circuit is not switched to ground.

# Apply What You Have Learned

1.  In Figure 9-3, calculate the amount of current used by the whole circuit for each configuration of the switches S2 and S3 when S1 is closed. You can assume that the LEDs are red LEDs.

2.  Build the circuit given in Figure 9-3 (you may swap out resistors with different but similar values— anything from 300 Ω to about 5 kΩ should work).

3.  Given a 15 V voltage supply, what size of a resistor would be needed to make sure that a circuit never went over 18 mA?

4.  Given a 9 V battery source, design a voltage divider that will output 7 V to a load that has a resistance of 10 kΩ.

5.  Given a 3 V battery source, design a voltage divider that will output 1.5 V to a load that has a resistance of 1 kΩ.

6. In Figure 9-6, how much current is going through the circuit when the switch is open? How much when it is closed? You can assume that the LED is a red LED.

7. How would you modify the circuit in Figure 9-6 to keep the maximum current in the circuit under 2 mA? Draw the full circuit out yourself.

8. Build the circuit you designed in the previous question. If you do not have the right resistor values, use the closest ones you have.

# CHAPTER 10

# Understanding Power

So far we have covered the basic ideas of voltage, current, and resistance. This is good for lighting up LEDs, but for doing work in the real world, what is really needed is **power**. This chapter on its own adds very little to your capabilities as a circuit designer, but it is absolutely critical background information for the chapters that follow. Additionally, this chapter contains information critical to the safe usage of electronics. Knowing about power, power conversions, and power dissipation will be critical to taking your electronics abilities into the real world.

## 10.1 Important Terms Related to Power

To understand what power is, we need to go through a few terms from physics (don't worry—they are all easy terms):

1. **Work** happens when you move stuff.

2. Work is measured in **joules**. A joule is the amount of work performed when a 1-kilogram object is moved 1 meter.

3. The capacity to perform work is called **energy**. Energy is also measured in joules.

4. **Power** is the sustained delivery of energy to a process.

© Jonathan Bartlett 2020
J. Bartlett, *Electronics for Beginners*, https://doi.org/10.1007/978-1-4842-5979-5_10

5. Power is measured in **watts** (abbreviated W). Watts are the number of joules consumed or produced per second.

6. Another measurement of power is horsepower (abbreviated hp). One horsepower is equivalent to 746 watts. Horsepower is not important for electronics, but I wanted to mention this because horsepower is a term you have probably heard, and I wanted you to be able to connect its importance to the ideas in this chapter.

One of the interesting things about work, energy, and power is that they can take on a number of forms that are all basically equivalent. For instance, we can have mechanical energy, chemical energy, and electrical energy (as well as others). We can also perform mechanical work, chemical work, and electrical work. All these types of energy and work can be converted to each other. They are all also measured in joules. Therefore, we have a common unit of energy for any sort of task we want to accomplish.

Now, when we actually apply energy to perform work, we do not get a 100% conversion rate. In other words, if we want to do 100 joules of work, we will probably need more than 100 joules of energy to perform the task. That's because the process of converting energy into work (as well as converting between different types of energy and work) is **inefficient**—not all of the energy gets directed to the task we want to perform. There is no perfectly efficient process of converting energy to work. Additionally, there is no way to create energy from nothing—any time you need additional energy, you will need a source for it.

When energy is converted to work, *all* of the energy does something, even if it isn't work on the task you want. Usually, the inefficiencies get converted to **heat**. So, if I have a process that is only 10% efficient and I give that process 80 joules of energy, then that process will do only 8 joules of work, leaving 72 joules of energy that is converted to heat.

Work and energy are usually the quantities we care about for systems that do a fixed task (i.e., require a fixed amount of energy). In electronics, however, we are usually building systems that stay on for sustained periods of time. Therefore, instead of measuring energy, we measure power, which is the continuous delivery of energy (or the continuous usage of energy in doing work).

As we mentioned, power is measured in watts, where a watt is 1 joule per second. So, if you have a 100 W light bulb, that bulb uses 100 joules of energy each second. True, 100 W incandescent light bulbs are very inefficient, which is why they get so hot—the energy that is not converted to light gets converted to heat instead. Today, incandescent bulbs are rarely used for that very reason. For instance, the LED bulbs that are labeled as "100 W" equivalent generally use about 11 W, but they are as bright as the old 100 W incandescents. What this means is that in an incandescent light, less than 11 W of energy was being put toward actually giving off light, and the rest was wasted as heat, which is why they got quite so hot.[1]

# 10.2  Power in Electronics

So we have a basic idea about what power is in general. In electronics, there are a few equivalent ways of calculating power.

The first is to multiply the number of volts being consumed by the number of amps of current going through a device:

$$P = V * I \qquad (10.1)$$

---

[1]It is actually much less than 11 W, since LEDs are not perfectly efficient either. The point is that since they are both emitting the same amount of light (i.e., producing the same light energy), we can see that the difference in watts used is probably lost in heat.

Here, $P$ indicates power measured in watts, $V$ indicates volts, and $I$ indicates current measured in amps. So, if my circuit is on a 9-volt battery and I measure that the battery is delivering 20 mA to the circuit, then that means I can calculate the amount of power that my circuit is using (don't forget to convert milliamps to amps first!):

$$
\begin{aligned}
P &= V * I \\
&= 9\text{V} * 20\text{mA} \\
&= 9\text{V} * 0.02\text{A} \\
&= 0.18\text{W}
\end{aligned}
$$

So our circuit uses 0.18 watt of power.

You can also measure the amount of power that individual components use. For instance, let's say that a resistor has a 3 V voltage drop and has 12 mA of current running through it. Therefore, the resistor uses up 3 * 0.012 = 0.036 watt of power.

The second way of calculating power comes from applying Ohm's law. Ohm's law say

$$V = I * R \tag{10.2}$$

So, if we have the equation $P = V * I$, Ohm's law allows us to *replace V* with $I * R$. Therefore, our new equation becomes

$$P = (I * R) * I \tag{10.3}$$

Or we can simplify it further and say that

$$P = I^2 * R \tag{10.4}$$

We can also substitute $I = V/R$ and wind up with a third equation for power:

$$P = \frac{V^2}{R} \qquad\qquad (10.5)$$

So, if we have 15 mA running through a 200 Ω resistor, then we can calculate the amount of power being used using Equation 10.4:

$$P = I^2 * R$$
$$= (15\text{mA})^2 * 200\Omega$$
$$= (0.015\text{A})^2 * 200\Omega$$
$$= 0.000225 * 200$$
$$= 0.045\text{W}$$

# 10.3  Component Power Limitations

Now, if you think about it, the resistor in the previous example isn't actually *doing* anything. It is just sitting there. Therefore, since we are not accomplishing any *work* by going through the resistor, the energy gets converted to heat. Electronic components are usually rated for how much power they can **dissipate**, or easily get rid of. Most common resistors, for instance, are rated between 1/16 W and 1/2W (most that I've seen for sale are 1/4 W). This means that they will continue to work as long as their power consumption stays under their limit. If the power consumption goes too high, they will not be able to handle the increased heat and will break (and possibly catch fire!).

So far, our projects have dealt with low enough power that this isn't a concern. In fact, using 9 V batteries, it is hard to generate more than 1/4W of power—you would have to have less than 350 Ω of resistance on the *whole* circuit and have the entire voltage drop occur on the resistor.

In any case, whenever you are building circuits, you should keep in mind how much power the component is rated to handle and how much power it is actually consuming. You can use any of the equations given here to calculate power consumption. The component itself should have information on its maximum ability to handle power consumption and dissipation.

# 10.4 Handling Power Dissipation with Heatsinks

As we mentioned earlier, when power dissipates without doing any work, it is converted to heat. Some devices need to dissipate large quantities of heat under regular workloads. One common device that often needs to dissipate heat is the voltage regulator, like the 7805 regulator we will encounter in Chapter 12.

The way that this regulator performs its job is essentially by dissipating power until the voltage is at the right level. When used with any serious amount of current, this can actually get very, very hot. As such, the back side of these contains a metal plate which is used to dissipate heat. Additionally, it has a metal tab with a hole that can be used to attach a **heatsink**.

A heatsink is a metal structure with a large surface area that helps an electronic component dissipate heat. By being made of metal, it quickly moves the heat into itself. By having a large surface area, it can transfer the heat to the air, where it will then disperse into the environment.

*Figure 10-1.* A 7805 voltage regulator and its heatsink

Figure 10-1 shows a 7805 chip next to its heatsink. To attach the heatsink, just screw it into the 7805. On the 7800 series of regulators, the tab is electrically connected to ground, so it should not produce a voltage. However, other types of chips in the same TO-220 package may actually have a voltage on the tab. In such a case, it would be wise to buy an isolation kit to electrically isolate the chip from the heatsink; otherwise, incidental contact with the heatsink could cause a short circuit. The isolation kit will only allow heat, not electricity, flow into the heatsink.

# 10.5  Transforming Power

As we have discussed, energy (and therefore power) can be transformed among a variety of forms—mechanical, electrical, chemical, and so on. In any case, always remember that energy is only reduced or lost, never gained.

The essence of energy transformation is at the heart of what makes batteries work. A battery contains energy stored in a chemical form. Chemical reactions in the battery allow electrons to move. By drawing the electrons through a specific path (drawing them to the positive from the negative), this reaction generates electrical energy. So we have a conversion from chemical energy (the reaction of the chemicals in the battery) into electrical energy (the pull of the electrons through the circuit).

This can also go the other way. Electrical energy can be used to stimulate chemical reactions. A common one is the separation of water into hydrogen and oxygen.

The same conversion can happen with mechanical energy. In an electric motor, electrical energy is converted into mechanical energy in the motor. But the reverse also can occur. A power generator is made by converting mechanical energy into electrical energy.

We won't go into details on how each of these transformations works (you would need to take courses in chemistry, mechanics, etc. to know more), but the essential ideas are that

1.  Energy and power can be transformed between a variety of forms.

2.  These forms of energy can all be measured with the same measuring stick (joules).

3.  Every energy transformation will lose (never gain) some amount of energy through inefficiencies.

Power and energy are known as **conserved quantities**, because, although they are transformed, they are never created or lost. Note that when we talk about power lost through inefficiencies, the power actually isn't lost in total; it is merely converted to heat. You can think of heat as power that is applied in a nonspecific direction. Energy is lost when it is transformed not because it disappears but rather because all processes which channel one form of energy into another are imperfect.

In Section 10.2, "Power in Electronics," we noted that, in electronics, the power (measured in watts) is determined by *both* the voltage and the current—by multiplying them together. Therefore, what will be conserved in electronics will not be the voltage or the current individually, but their product. What this means is that we can, at least in theory, increase the voltage without needing a power gain, but at the cost of current. Likewise, we can, at least in theory, increase the current without needing a power gain, at the cost of voltage. In both of these cases, rather than transforming electrical power to another form of power altogether, we are transforming it into a different configuration of electrical power.

Devices that convert electrical power between different voltage/current configurations are known as **transformers**. A step-up transformer is one that converts a low voltage to a higher voltage (at the cost of current), and a step-down transformer is one that converts a high voltage to a lower voltage (but can supply additional current).

Technically, for DC circuits, these are usually known as **DC-DC power converters** or **boost converters** instead of being called transformers, but the same rules apply—the total number of watts delivered can never increase, but the voltage can be converted up and down at the expense or gain of the current.[2]

So, if I had a source of 12 V and 2 A, then I would have 12 ∗ 2 = 24 W. Therefore, it may be possible to convert that to 24 V, but I would only be able to get 1 A of current (24 ∗ 1 = 24). However, I could drop the voltage to get more current. If I needed 4 A, I could reduce the voltage to 6 V.

Also remember that in doing these transformations, there is always some amount of power loss as well, but these calculations will give you what the maximum possibilities are. The actual mechanisms that these devices employ for doing power conversions are outside the scope of this book.

# 10.6  Amplifying Low-Power Signals

Many devices, especially integrated circuits, are only capable of processing and generating low-power signals. Microcontrollers (like the ATmega328/P) have limits to how much power they can send or receive. The ATmega328/P can only source up to 40 mA per pin and only about 200 mA total across all pins simultaneously. At 5 V, 40 mA would yield a maximum of 0.2 W. Therefore, if you want to turn on a device that requires more power than that, you will need to **amplify** your signal.

Now, as we discussed previously, you can't actually create more power out of nothing. What you can do is, instead of trying to *create* power, you can instead *control* power. We will discuss several specific techniques on how to do this starting in Chapter 24, but the essential idea is that you can amplify a signal by using a small signal to control a larger one.

---

[2]As a sidenote, if you tried to wire a regular AC transformer to a DC power supply, it would not deliver any power at all—DC-DC converters work on very different principles than AC transformers.

Think about your car. The way that you control your car is by taking a low-power signal, such as the gas pedal, and using it to control a high-power signal, such as the engine. My foot is not directly powering the car. My foot is merely using the pedals to tell another power source—the engine—how much of its energy it should move. My foot doesn't actually interact directly with the engine at all, except as a valve to unleash or not unleash the power available in the gas tank and engine.

In the same way, since the output signals from the microcontrollers are low power, instead of using these signals directly, we will use the signals to control larger sources of power. Devices which can do this include relays, optocouplers, transistors, op-amps, and darlington arrays. We will cover more about amplification starting in Chapter 24.

# Review

In this chapter, we learned the following:

1. Work is what happens when you move stuff and is measured in joules.

2. Energy is the capacity to do work and is also measured in joules.

3. Power is the sustained delivery of energy and is measured in joules per second, also called watts.

4. Power can be converted to a number of different forms.

5. Converting power to another form or using it to do work always has inefficiencies, and these inefficiencies result in energy lost to heat.

6. In electronics, power (in watts) is calculated by multiplying the voltage by the current ($P = V * I$). It can also be calculated as $P = I^2 * R$ or $P = V^2/R$.

7. To calculate the power consumption of an individual component, use the voltage drop *of that component* and multiply it by the current flowing through it (measured in amps, not milliamps).

8. Most components have a maximum rating for the amount of power they can safely consume or dissipate. Be sure you design your circuits so that your components stay under that limit.

9. Some components can handle additional power dissipation by adding a heatsink, which will more effectively dissipate the excess heat into the air.

10. Power can be transformed into other types of power (mechanical, chemical, etc.), but can never go beyond the original amount of power.

11. Electrical power can also be transformed into different combinations of voltage and current, as long as the total power remains the same.

12. Components that do this transformation are called transformers for AC power and DC-DC converters for DC power.

13. Because power cannot be created, the way that signals are amplified is by using a small power signal to control a larger power source.

# Apply What You Have Learned

1.  If I have 50 joules of energy, what is the maximum amount of work I could possibly do with that amount of energy?

2.  If I am using up 10 joules of energy each second, how many watts am I using up?

3.  If I convert 30 watts of mechanical power into electrical power with 50% efficiency, how many watts of electrical power are delivered?

4.  If I have a circuit powered by a 9 V battery that uses 0.125 A, how many watts does that circuit use?

5.  If a resistor has a 2 V drop with a 0.03 A current, how much power is the resistor dissipating?

6.  If a resistor has a 3 V drop with a 12 mA current, how much power is the resistor dissipating?

7.  If a 700 Ω resistor has a 5 V drop, how much power is the resistor dissipating?

8.  If a 500 Ω resistor has 20 mA flowing through it, how much power is the resistor dissipating? If the resistor was rated for 1/8 of a watt, are we within the rated usage for the resistor?

9.  In the following circuit, calculate the voltage drop,
    current, and power dissipation of every component
    (except the battery). If the resistors are all rated for
    1/8 of a watt, are any of the resistors out of spec?

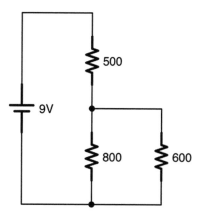

# CHAPTER 11

# Integrated Circuits and Resistive Sensors

So far, the components we have studied are simple, basic components—batteries, resistors, diodes, and so on. In this chapter, we are going to start to look at **integrated circuits**, also called **chips**, **microchips**, or **ICs**. An IC is a miniaturized circuit placed on silicon. It is a whole collection of parts geared around a specific function. These functions may be small, such as comparing voltages or amplifying voltages, or they may be complex, such as processing video or even complete computers. A single chip may hold just a few components, or it may hold billions.

Miniaturized circuits have several advantages—they are cheaper to produce in mass, they use less power, and they take up less space in your overall circuit—all because they have a reduced area and use fewer materials. These miniaturized circuits are what allowed for the computer revolution over the last century.

## 11.1  The Parts of an Integrated Circuit

Integrated circuits, as we have noted, are basically miniaturized circuits placed on a silicon plate, called the die. This die is where all of the action of the integrated circuit takes place.

© Jonathan Bartlett 2020
J. Bartlett, *Electronics for Beginners*, https://doi.org/10.1007/978-1-4842-5979-5_11

The die is then placed into a **package**, which then provides connection points for circuit designers to interface with the IC. These connection points are often called **pins** or **pads**. Each pin on an IC is numbered, starting with pin 1 (we will show you how to find pin 1 shortly). Knowing which pin is which is important, because most of the pins on a chip each have their own purpose, so if you attach a wire to the wrong pin, your circuit won't work or you will destroy the chip. Most packages are marked with the chip's manufacturer and part number. If they weren't, it would be nearly impossible to tell one chip from another.

There are many different types of packaging available, but there are two general types that are often encountered:

Through-Hole: In this packaging type, the connection points are long pins which can be used on a breadboard. This type of packaging is easiest for amateur usage.

***Figure 11-1.*** *Comparison of the Same IC in SMD (Left) and DIP (Right) Packages (Image Credit: Shutterstock/Youra Pechkin)*

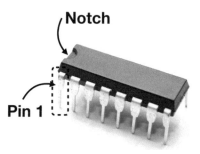

**Figure 11-2.** *Pin 1 is Immediately Counterclockwise of the Notch (Image Credit: Shutterstock/Cristian Storto)*

Surface Mount: In this packaging type, the connection points are small pads which are meant to be soldered to a circuit board. These packages are much smaller (and therefore less expensive) and can be more easily managed by automated systems to build completed circuits. These are also referred to as SMDs (surface mount devices) or SMT (surface mount technology).

Since we are only using breadboards in this book and not doing any soldering, we will only concern ourselves with through-hole packaging. However, through-hole packaging itself comes in a variety of styles. The main one we will concern ourselves with is called a **dual in-line package**, or **DIP**. Figure 11-2 shows the same chip in SMD and DIP configurations.

An integrated circuit in a DIP package has two rows of pins coming out of the package. Most chips either mark the top of the chip with a notch or indentation (where pin 1 is immediately counterclockwise of the notch) or mark pin 1 with an indentation or both. See Figure 11-2 to see how to use the notch to find pin 1. The rest of the pins are numbered counterclockwise around the chip.

*Figure 11-3.* *A DIP IC Inserted Into a Breadboard*

The beauty of a DIP-packaged IC is that it fits perfectly onto most breadboards. Figure 11-3 shows how you can place your IC across the breadboard's bridge and each pin on the chip will have its own terminal strip to connect to.

Be careful, though, when inserting ICs into breadboards. The spacing of the pins on an IC is often slightly wider or shorter than the breadboard's bridge, and pins have to be inserted carefully. If you just jam the IC into the breadboard, you will likely accidentally crush one or more of the pins that aren't exactly aligned on the hole. Instead, compare the spacing of the pins to the bridge spacing on your breadboard. If it doesn't match up, *very gently* bend the pins with your fingers or with pliers to get them to match up. It's usually just a very small amount, but if you don't take care, you can easily damage your IC.

Usually, the ICs that I purchase are just a little wide, and I will squeeze the pins on each side slightly between my thumb and finger until they move close enough together. However you adjust the pins, make sure they line up before pushing them into their connection points on the breadboard. Also, with larger ICs, you may also need to slightly wiggle the IC back and forth as you gently insert it into place on the breadboard.

# 11.2 The LM393 Voltage Comparator

There are thousands and thousands of available chips which do a dizzying array of functions. In this chapter, we are going to focus on a very simple chip—the LM393 voltage comparator. This chip does one simple task. The LM393 compares two input voltages and then outputs either a high-voltage signal or a low-voltage signal depending on which input voltage is greater. The LM393 is actually a *dual* voltage comparator, which means that it will do two separate comparisons on the same chip. Like most chips, the LM393 is an *active* device, which means that it additionally requires a voltage source and a ground connection to provide power to the device.

Figure 11-4 shows the pin configuration (also called the **pinout**) of the LM393. The first thing to note on any pinout is where the voltage and ground connections are. In this case, the voltage is marked as VCC, and the ground is marked as GND. Even though the LM393 has *two* voltage comparators on the chip, they both share the power (VCC) and ground (GND) pins. The left side of the chip diagram shows the inputs and output for the first voltage comparator (1IN+, 1IN-, and 1OUT), and the inputs and output for the second voltage comparator are on the right (2IN+, 2IN-, and 2OUT). In your projects, you can use whichever one is more convenient for you, or even both at the same time if you have more than one voltage comparison task.

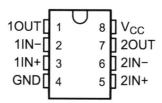

*Figure 11-4.*  *The Pin Configuration of an LM393*

So the 1IN+ pin (pin 3) and the 1IN- pin are where the two voltages are being fed that are being compared by the first comparator. The 1OUT is the pin which will contain the output. If the voltage at 1IN+ is less than the voltage on 1IN-, the output pin will be at a low (i.e., near-zero/ground) voltage. If the voltage at 1IN+ is greater than the voltage on 1IN-, the output pin *will not conduct at all*, but this will be considered a "high" (positive voltage) state. This sounds counterintuitive, but, as we will see, this lets us set our own output voltage to whatever we want without causing too much complexity. This configuration where high-voltage outputs don't conduct is called an **open collector** configuration. Don't worry if this is a little confusing, we will discuss it more in depth later in the chapter.

---

## VOLTAGE SOURCES ON INTEGRATED CIRCUITS

Note that the voltage pins on integrated circuits can be marked in a number of different ways. The positive voltage source is often labeled as $V_{CC}$, $V_{DD}$, or $V+$. The ground connect is often labeled as $GND$, $V_{EE}$, $V_{SS}$, or $V-$. There are additional ways that these are labeled as well. Finding the positive and ground connections for an IC should always be the first thing you do with it.

---

# 11.3  The Importance and Problems of Datasheets

Every IC (and, usually, any other part as well) has a **datasheet** supplied by the manufacturer which tells you important details about how you should use their chip in your circuit. Reading datasheets is one of the worst parts of electronics, in my opinion. For me, datasheets rarely have the information I am actually looking for in a way that is easy to find.

In fact, most datasheets assume that you already know how to use the device, and the datasheets are just there to supply additional details about the limitations of the device. For instance, looking through the LM393 datasheet from Texas Instruments, the actual operation of the device isn't even listed until page 11, and there it is buried within a sub-subsection, almost as a sidenote.

These datasheets are written *by* people who have spent a lot of time being electrical engineers, and they are written *for* people who have spent a lot of time being electrical engineers, so when mere mortals read the datasheets, the important pieces are often shrouded in unintelligible gibberish. For instance, the fact that the "high" output state of the device doesn't conduct isn't mentioned explicitly anywhere at all in the datasheet. Instead, it is implied by the configuration.

The reason for this is that the datasheets are usually read by professionals familiar with the type of device and who just need to know the electrical details so they don't accidentally bend the device beyond the breaking point. Thus, the datasheets oftentimes spend more time just showing and describing the layout of the circuit on the chip and graphs of different chip properties, and then you are left to interpret what that means for your circuit. For advanced circuit designers, this is great. For students and hobbyists, however, this is oftentimes more frustrating than helpful.

However, datasheets do often provide a few basic details that are helpful to everyone. They will often tell you

- What each pin does
- What the power requirements are
- What the outer limits of the chip's operation are
- An example circuit that you can build with the device

For all of these reasons, Appendix E contains simplified datasheets for a number of common devices that are easier to read than the standard ones. For the LM393, the important points are as follows:

1. The input voltage on $V_{CC}$ can be anywhere between 2 V and 36 V.

2. When sensing voltage, the LM393 doesn't really draw any (or at least much) current, so there are no parallel resistances we need to worry about.

3. The output is high when IN+ is greater than IN- and low (i.e., near-ground) when IN+ is less than IN-, with an error range of about 2 millivolts.

4. When the output is low, this means the output pin will conduct current into itself (since it is at ground, positive charge will naturally flow into it), but if it sinks more than 6 mA into it, you will destroy it, so you have to be sure that you know the maximum amount of current that could flow through the pin when it is at ground.

5. When the output is high, this means the output will not conduct any current, but instead act as if it were disconnected. As we will see, this will allow us to supply our own "high" voltage level.

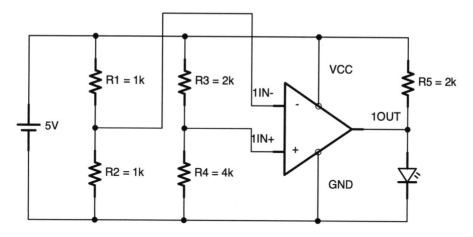

**Figure 11-5.** *A Simple Comparator Circuit*

That isn't to say that the datasheets aren't important, but for a beginner, the datasheets usually aren't what you need to get started.

# 11.4  A Simple Circuit with the LM393

In this section, I am going to show a simple circuit using the LM393 chip. In doing so, we are going to be using several of the resistor circuit patterns that we learned in Chapter 9.

The circuit we are discussing is shown in Figure 11-5. Can you identify the resistor circuit patterns? Take a minute and see if you can find some. Note that the wire coming out of 1IN- crosses two wires that it is *not* joined with.

The first thing to notice is that we have *two* voltage dividers. The first voltage divider is between R1 and R2. Since R1 and R2 are the same resistance and are connected to both 5 V and 0 V, that means that they divide the voltage in half, giving a 2.5 V output. The second voltage divider is between R3 and R4. Since R3 is half of the resistance of R4, that means that it only uses up half as much voltage as R4. Thus, since R3 eats up 1.7 V and R4 eats up 3.3 V, the wire coming out from the middle is at 3.3 V.

Then, to the right of the circuit, you can see that we have a current-limiting resistor in front of the LED. That is not its only function, though. It also functions, as we will see shortly, as a pull-up resistor.

So what is the big triangle? Comparators (and several other circuits commonly placed on ICs) are represented as triangles in the schematic (we could have also placed the chip itself there). Each of the connections is labeled the same as they are labeled in the pinout diagram in Figure 11-4 so they would be easy to locate.

The way that the circuit works is very simple. The voltage coming in to 1IN+ is 3.3 V, and the voltage coming in to 1IN- is 2.5 V. Since 1IN+ is greater than 1IN-, then that will turn 1OUT to high (positive voltage). However, remember that we said that 1OUT *does not conduct* when it is high. It acts like an open switch. Therefore, R5 acts like a pull-up resistor and supplies the positive voltage for us to our LED to turn it on.

Now let's say that the input voltages were reversed. What would happen? If 1IN- is greater than 1IN+, then 1OUT will go low (0 volt) and also conduct. It will act like a closed switch going to ground.

Therefore, current will go the easy route—it will go through 1OUT (directly to ground) instead of through the LED (1.8 V or more), effectively denying power to the LED and switching it off. This works just like the switch in the circuit in Chapter 9, Section 9.4, "The Pull-Up Resistor." When 1OUT is low, it acts like a closed switch to ground and acts as a sink for all current at that point in the circuit. When 1OUT is high, it acts like an open switch, and whatever voltage/current you provided at that point is allowed to continue on.

The resistor R5 does several jobs. The first job is to act as a pull-up resistor, as we just described. Remember that a pull-up resistor prevents the load to ground from going too high when the switch is closed. Without the pull-up resistor, when the switch is closed (1OUT goes low), we would have a short circuit from the voltage source to ground. This would not only waste a large amount of electricity; it would break the LM393, because it can only sink a maximum of 6 mA of current. Having a 2 kΩ resistor, we limit the current for the closed switch to $I = V/R = 5/2{,}000 = 0.0025\,A = 2.5$ mA.

When the switch is open, the current flows through the resistor to the LED, and then the resistor acts as a current-limiting resistor for the LED. The amount of current to the LED will be calculated as $I = V/R = (5 - 1.8)/2{,}000 = 3.2/2{,}000 = 0.0016\,A = 1.6$ mA.

# 11.5  Resistive Sensors and Voltages

One of the more practical uses of the voltage comparator circuit is to measure the values of sensors which act as variable resistors. Many different materials in the world act as resistors. What's really interesting is that many of these materials *change their resistance* depending on external factors. Some of them change their resistance based on temperature, pressure, light, humidity, and any number of other environmental factors.

Now, changing resistance doesn't tell us much by itself. If we put a resistor between a voltage source and ground, it will always eat up that voltage source. However, if you use it in concert with a fixed resistor to make a voltage divider, you can then get the output voltage to vary based on the changes in resistance.

Figure 11-6 illustrates this principle. It is a simple voltage divider, where the top resistor is actually a photoresistor (a resistor that varies based on light) and the bottom resistor has a fixed resistance. Thus, as the light varies, the top resistance will vary. This will change the ratio between the top and bottom resistors, which will affect the output voltage.

To use this circuit, you will need to know the resistances of your photoresistor on the different conditions you are interested in. I usually use the GL5528, which ranges from 10 kΩ in bright light to 1 MΩ in complete darkness. However, depending on your specific photoresistor as well as the light conditions that you think of as "light" and "dark," the resistance values that are relevant for light and dark will be different for you. So, whatever photoresistor you use, it is worthwhile to measure the resistance using your multimeter in the different conditions you think of as light and dark.

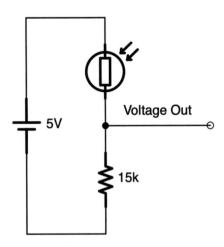

*Figure 11-6. A Simple Resistor Sensor Circuit*

# 11.6 Sensing and Reacting to Darkness

So far in the book, we have focused entirely on example circuits that didn't really do anything. They lit up, they had voltage and current, but there wasn't much interesting that they were doing. However, now, we finally have enough knowledge to start building circuits that *do* something.

We have

1. A way to generate a fixed voltage (using a voltage divider)

2. A way to generate resistances from real-world events (photoresistors and other resistance sensors)

3.  A way to convert changes in resistance to changes in voltage (using a voltage divider with one fixed resistor)

4.  A way to compare our varying voltage to our fixed voltage (using the LM393 comparator)

5.  A way to utilize the output signal from the LM393 to do work (using the pull-up resistor and the LED)

There are a lot of pieces to put together this simple circuit, which is why it has taken so long to do anything worthwhile. However, if you have followed along carefully, now that you are here, you should be able to see how all of this fits together.

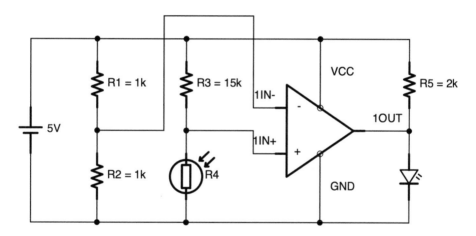

***Figure 11-7.*** *Darkness Sensor Schematic*

What we will do is to take the circuit given in Figure 11-5 and modify R4 to be our photoresistor and R3 to be a fixed resistor. In my own testing, I discovered that the light/dark switchover point for my photoresistor was about 15 kΩ. Therefore, I am going to use a 15 kΩ resistor as the fixed resistor for R3. Yours may need to vary based on your experimentation with your photoresistor.

When there is light in the room, the photoresistor will have a lower resistance than 15 kΩ, which will make the fixed resistor R3 use up more of the voltage. Thus, the voltage at the divider will be less than 2.5 V, which will turn 1OUT to low (which closes the switch and makes a path to ground on the output before it gets to the LED, which turns the LED off).

In low-light conditions, the resistance will jump way up above the resistance of the fixed resistor. If the upper, fixed resistor has less resistance than the bottom resistor, then the voltage at the divider will be larger than 2.5 V, activating the comparator and turning 1OUT to high (i.e., opening the switch and allowing power to flow through the LED).

The final circuit is given in Figure 11-7. You can see a way to lay it out on the breadboard in Figure 11-8.

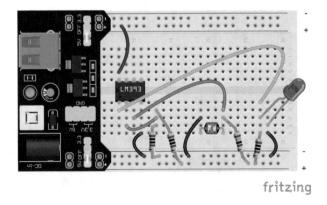

*Figure 11-8. Darkness Sensor Breadboard Layout*

# Sources and Sinks

Two terms that often come up when dealing with circuits are the concepts of a current **source** and a current **sink**. A source is a component whose pins might provide current to other parts of the circuit. A sink is a component whose pins might pull current from other parts of the circuit.

For the LM393, its input pins neither source nor sink current (at least not any significant amount). The input pins more or less just sense the voltage without pulling any measurable current. Therefore, they are neither sources nor sinks of current. Technically, they probably sink a few nanoamps (billionths of an amp), but not nearly enough to affect our circuit analysis.

The output pin, even though it is called an *output*, doesn't source any current. Instead, it acts either as a sink (when low) or as a disconnected circuit (when high). This is known as an **open collector** output.

Anytime an IC sources or sinks current, be sure to read the datasheets on the maximum amount of current it can source or sink. These are usually quantities that *you* have to limit—they are merely telling you at what point their circuit will physically break. Therefore, you must use resistors to limit the currents to make sure that they are within limits.

However, be aware that many (but certainly not all) ICs do not source current, using open collectors for their output operations. This has the disadvantage that you have to supply your own voltage and pull-up resistor to the output pin, but it also has the advantage that the output is set to *whatever voltage level you choose*. In other words, you don't need to pick a new comparator IC to get a different output voltage.

# Review

In this chapter, we learned the following:

1. Integrated circuits (called ICs or chips) are miniaturized circuits packaged up into a single chip that can be added to other circuits.

2. ICs can have a few or several billion components on them, depending on the function.

3.  ICs have different types of packages, including through-hole (optimized for breadboards) and surface mount (optimized for soldering and machine placement).

4.  Dual in-line packages (DIPs) are the most common through-hole packaging type used for students, hobbyists, and prototype builders.

5.  DIP chips should be placed in the breadboard saddling the bridge, so that each IC pin is attached to its own terminal strip.

6.  On most chips, pin 1 is located immediately counterclockwise of the notch in the chip, and remaining pins are numbered counterclockwise.

7.  Most ICs are active devices, meaning that they have a direct connection to a power supply and ground in addition to their normal input and output pins.

8.  An IC datasheet is a document that tells about the electrical characteristics of an IC. However, most of them are difficult to read and assume you are already familiar with the part. However, they are very useful for getting a pinout for the chip as well as telling the maximum ratings for voltages and currents.

9.  The LM393 is a dual voltage comparator IC—it compares two voltages and alters its output based on which is larger.

10. The LM393's inputs do not consume any significant current when sensing the input voltages.

11.   The LM393's outputs are open collectors—which means that they act as a switch to ground. When the output is "low," the pin acts as a closed switch to ground. When the output is "high," the pin acts as a disconnected circuit.

12.   Because the LM393 acts as a disconnected circuit when high, a pull-up resistor circuit is required to get an output voltage.

13.   Many sensors are based on the fact that the resistance of many materials will change with environmental factors. Therefore, the sensor acts as a variable resistor, with the resistance telling you about the environment.

14.   A resistive sensor can be used with a fixed resistor to make a variable voltage divider, essentially converting the resistance to a voltage, which then can be detected.

15.   By putting the sensor-based resistive voltage divider in comparison with a fixed reference, we can use the LM393 comparator to trigger an output when the sensor crosses some threshold of resistance.

# Apply What You Have Learned

1.   Calculate the amount of current flowing through each element of the circuit in Figure 11-5. You can presume that the LM393 uses about 1 mA for its own (internal) operation and that the LED is a red, 1.8 V LED. What is the total amount of current used by the circuit?

2. Take the circuit in Figure 11-5 and swap which voltage divider is attached to 1IN+ and 1IN-. Now calculate the total amount of current used by this circuit.

3. The Spectra flex sensor is a resistive sensor that changes its resistance when bent. When it is straight, it has a resistance of 10 kΩ. When it is bent, it has resistances of 60 kΩ and above. Draw a circuit that turns on an LED when the resistor is bent. Use a resistor symbol for the flex sensor, but label it as FLEX.

4. Build the circuit in Figures 11-7 and 11-8.

5. If you wanted to wait until the room was even darker before the LED went on, how would you change the circuit?

# PART II

# Digital Electronics and Microcontrollers

# CHAPTER 12

# Using Logic ICs

In Chapter 11, we worked with our first integrated circuit, the LM393 voltage comparator. In this chapter, we are going to look at other ICs and talk more about how they are named and used in electronics.

## 12.1 Logic ICs

One of the easiest class of ICs to use are the *logic* ICs. A logic IC is a chip that implements a basic function of **digital logic**. In digital logic, electric voltages are given meanings of either "true" or "false," usually with "false" being a voltage near zero and "true" being a positive voltage (often between 3 and 5 volts). These values are also referred to by a number of other designations—a 1 (for true) and 0 (for false) or HIGH (for true) and LOW (for false).[1] Then, the digital logic ICs implement logic functions that combine different signals (usually designated as A and B) and give an output signal (usually designated as Y or Q).

---

[1]Very rarely, some ICs will reverse the meaning of the positive and zero voltages.

© Jonathan Bartlett 2020
J. Bartlett, *Electronics for Beginners*, https://doi.org/10.1007/978-1-4842-5979-5_12

For instance, the **AND** function will output a "true" (positive voltage) value if both of its inputs are true and will output a "false" (near-zero voltage) value otherwise. In other words, if A *and* B are true, Y is true. As another example, the **OR** function will output a "true" value if either of its inputs is true. In other words, if A *or* B is true, Y is true. Figure 12-1 shows the most common types of logic operations and how they work.

As we have seen, AND yields a true result when both A and B are true, and OR yields a true result when either A or B is true. So what are the others? **XOR** is *exclusive OR*, which means that it is just like OR, but is also false when both inputs are true. **NOR** is *not OR*, which means that it is the exact opposite of OR. Likewise, **NAND** is *not AND*, which means that it is the exact opposite of AND. Finally, **NOT** only has one input and simply reverses its value.

Each digital logic function, when implemented in electronics, is called a **gate**. The nice thing about building circuits with logic gates is that, rather than using math, you can build circuits based on ordinary language.

| Operation | A | B | Y (output) |
|---|---|---|---|
| AND | false | false | false |
| AND | false | true | false |
| AND | true | false | false |
| AND | true | true | true |
| OR | false | false | false |
| OR | false | true | true |
| OR | true | false | true |
| OR | true | true | true |
| XOR | false | false | false |
| XOR | false | true | true |
| XOR | true | false | true |
| XOR | true | true | false |
| NOR | false | false | true |
| NOR | false | true | false |
| NOR | true | false | false |
| NOR | true | true | false |
| NAND | false | false | true |
| NAND | false | true | true |
| NAND | true | false | true |
| NAND | true | true | false |
| NOT | false | N/A | true |
| NOT | true | N/A | false |

*Figure 12-1.* *Common Logic Operations*

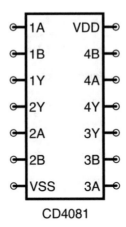

**Figure 12-2.**  *The Pinout of a CD4081 Chip*

If you were to say, "I want my circuit to output a signal if both button 1 *and* button 2 are pressed," then it is obvious that you would use an AND gate to accomplish this.

## INVERTED INPUTS AND OUTPUTS

Sometimes an input or an output on a chip will be labeled with a line on top of the input or output name. This means that the result (or requirement) will be the *opposite* of what you would otherwise expect. For instance, if the output is Y, then $\overline{Y}$ refers to the opposite value of Y. So, if Y is true, then $\overline{Y}$ will be false.

The same can occur on inputs as well. For instance, some chips have a reset on the chip which will reset the chip. However, we would normally consider "signaling" a pin to be sending it a voltage. Sometimes the chips would prefer that you signal the reset by bringing the voltage low instead of high. In these cases, they <u>usually</u> designate this by putting a bar over the name of the input pin, so the reset pin would be labeled $\overline{\text{RESET}}$ in order to indicate this behavior.

These are known as **inverted** inputs and outputs.

Most logic gates are implemented in chips that contain multiple (often four) implementations of the same gate. For instance, the CD4081 chip is a quad–NAND gate chip. The pinout for this chip is shown in Figure 12-2. Note that it has a supply voltage pin (pin 14) as well as a ground pin (pin 7) to supply power to all the gates on the chip. Each logic gate is numbered 1–4, and the inputs are labeled A and B with the output of Y.

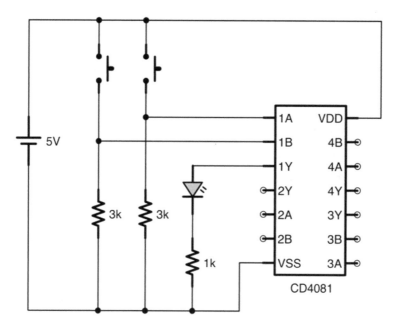

***Figure 12-3.***  *Example Circuit Using an AND Gate*

To use the chip, you pick which one of the four gates you are going to use (it doesn't really matter which). If we want to use Gate 1, then we put our inputs on 1A and 1B, and then our output signal goes to 1Y. Note that, unlike the IC from the last chapter, this logic gate has a powered output—it actually supplies voltage and current to drive a (small) output signal.

Logic gates are wired to expect relatively fixed, predefined voltages on their inputs and output the same voltage levels. They do not need current-limiting resistors for their inputs because the inputs themselves are usually high resistance (i.e., 1,000,000–10,000,000 Ω). Because of the high resistance on the inputs, it also means that even if there is a resistor on the input, it will not affect the input voltage significantly. It also means that the current going into the gate is essentially ignorable:

$$I = \frac{V}{R} = \frac{5}{10,000,000} = 0.0005\text{mA}.$$

For some logic chips, the input voltage is expected to be around 3.3 V or 5 V, while for others, it is based on the supply voltage. However, nearly all ICs are limited in how much current they can put out before they fry. This is usually somewhere in the range of 8–20 mA, depending on the chip. Because of this, if you use a logic gate to directly power a device (such as an LED), you probably will need a current-limiting resistor to keep the output current down below these limits.

There are logic chips that have open collector outputs (like the LM393 from Chapter 11), but they are more rare because they are harder to use.

Let's say that we want to build a circuit which will turn on an LED if *both* of two buttons are pushed at the same time. Figure 12-3 shows a circuit to accomplish this. It has two buttons, one wired to 1A (pin 1) and one wired to 1B (pin 2). The output 1Y (pin 3) then goes to an LED with a current-limiting resistor. You may wonder what the resistors attached to the buttons are doing. Those will be explained in Section 12.3, "Pull-Down Resistors."

For most logic chips, the manufacturers recommend that unused inputs (but not outputs!) be connected to ground. This makes the chip more efficient in power consumption, but for simple projects like these, it isn't really necessary. If you wish to connect the unused inputs to ground, then it is a better circuit design.

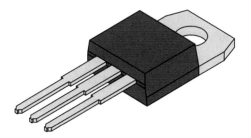

**Figure 12-4.** *A 7805 Voltage Regulator in a To-220 Package*

Note that the circuit shows a 5 V source. While the CD4081 is tolerant of a wide range of input voltages and would operate just fine at 9 V, many digital logic chips are not. Many digital logic chips operate at pre-specified voltages, usually either 5 V or 3.3 V. Therefore, we will take a moment and look at how we can get an input source for a specific voltage.

# 12.2  Getting a 5 V Source

So far in this book, we have used a custom power regulator to regulate the voltage on the board. Thankfully, this voltage is actually selectable— jumpers on the board allow you to select 5 V or 3.3 V, which are precisely the voltages usually required.

However, if we didn't have such fancy regulators, how would we achieve a 5 V source? There are several options for doing this, all depending on your requirements and/or the supplies you have available to you.

One option is to build a simple 5 V power supply using the knowledge you already have. In Chapter 9, we showed how to build a voltage divider to step down the voltage from a higher voltage source to a lower one. Although not ideal, this could work fine for simple test circuits. A better option would be to build the Zener diode voltage regulator that was shown in Chapter 8 if you have a 5 V Zener diode handy (however, you would need to be careful to calculate the output wattage, as these can dissipate a lot of power).

A better option is to use a voltage regulator IC. The LM7805 is a simple voltage regulator circuit you can use to convert a 7–24 V voltage source into a 5 V voltage source with somewhat minimal current loss. It is itself an IC, though with a different kind of packaging than we've seen, known as a **TO-220 package**. You can see what this looks like in Figure 12-4. On these packages, if you are reading the writing on the package, pin 1 (input voltage) is on the left, pin 2 (ground) is in the middle, and pin 3 (output voltage) is on the right. Figure 12-5 shows what this looks like in a circuit diagram.

Figure 12-6 shows how to attach the LM7805 regulator to your breadboard. First, plug the regulator into your breadboard so that each pin is on its own terminal strip. Next, plug the positive wire from the battery into the terminal strip with the voltage regulator's pin 1 and the negative wire from the battery to the negative/ground power rail on the breadboard. Then, connect the voltage regulator's pin 2 (ground) to the negative/ground power rail. Finally, connect the voltage regulator's pin 3 (output voltage) to the positive power rail.

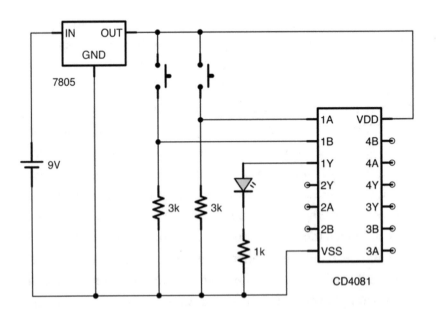

***Figure 12-5.*** *Logic Gate Circuit with a Voltage Regulator*

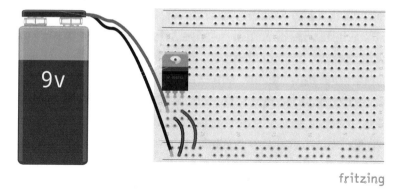

fritzing

**Figure 12-6.** *Simple Way to Attach the LM7805 to Your Breadboard*

This will give you a 5 V supply without all of the circuitry of our previous power regulator. This is especially helpful if you have strange power needs or need to use a minimum of space for your power regulation.

Note that some LM7805s have pins that are too big for breadboards. That's unfortunate, but they are pretty rare. As long as you buy from companies that target hobbyists, you are likely to get a component that will work well with breadboards.

In any case, we will continue to use our power regulators, but I wanted to note that there are other ways to supply the correct amount of power to chips that require fewer components.

# 12.3 Pull-Down Resistors

In Figure 12-3, we looked at the circuit diagram for a simple AND gate. We noted that each button had a resistor connecting it to ground, but we did not mention why. In digital logic circuits, buttons and single-pole switches, when they are open, essentially disconnect the circuit. Because the inputs are high-resistance inputs (i.e., they use very little current), simply disconnecting the input circuits is not always enough to turn them off! Think of it this way—when you connect the circuit by pushing the button, the whole wire becomes positive. When you let go of the button, the state of the wire has not changed. Eventually the positive charge will drain out through the gate, but, since the input uses so little current, it may take a while for that to happen. Therefore, we have to provide another path for the electricity to go when the button is not pressed. These resistors are called pull-down resistors because, when the button circuit is not connected, they pull the voltage level down close to zero.

The resistor is very important because, when the button is connected, it keeps the voltage high and limits the amount of current that leaks out across the resistor. If you directly connected the button to ground without the resistor, then pushing the button would not raise the voltage because it is still directly connected to ground and would therefore remain at 0 volt. Having the resistor there makes sure that the voltage on the inputs remains high while the button is pressed and bleeds off when the button is released.

In short, without a path to ground, when you let go of the button, the input could remain high. Moreover, without the resistor, pushing the button would cause a short circuit. Therefore, a pull-down resistor allows voltage to drain off quickly when the button is not pressed, but also prevents disasters and wasted current when the button is pressed.

Additionally, static electricity in the air can cause the actual voltage on the gate to fluctuate when it is not connected. Physically connecting the gate to the ground through a resistor will make sure there is always *some* complete circuit which provides a deterministic value for the voltage at the gate.

The value of a pull-down resistor is usually somewhere between 1 kΩ and 10 kΩ. Beyond 10 kΩ, the actual function of pulling the voltage down to zero can be slowed down. Additionally, even above 4 kΩ, it is possible to interfere with the actual logic operation of the chip. Having a resistor below 1 kΩ, however, means that you are just wasting current.

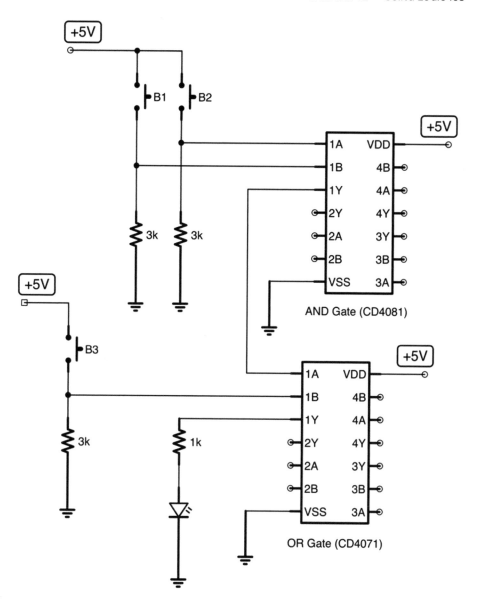

***Figure 12-7.*** *Multiple Logic Gates Combined in a Circuit*

So, for any button-type input to a digital logic circuit (where the circuit is *phyiscally disconnected* when the input is off), a pull-down resistor is needed to make sure that the input *actually* goes low when the button stops being pushed or the switch turns off.

# 12.4 Combining Logic Circuits

Logic chips that operate at the same voltage are very easy to combine together. Let's say that you had three buttons that you wanted to monitor and you wanted the light to come on if someone pushed either buttons 1 *and* 2 together *or* button 3 (or all of them). To do that, you would need an AND gate and an OR gate. Buttons 1 and 2 would be wired with the AND gate, and button 3 would be combined with the output of the AND gate through an OR gate.

Figure 12-7 shows what this looks like. Since there are so many voltage/ground connections, the figure does not have an explicit battery drawn; instead, it simply shows +5 V wherever it should connect to the voltage source and a ground symbol wherever it should connect to the battery negative. As you can see here, there are two logic ICs—the CD4081 having the AND gate and the CD4071 having the OR gate. The output of the first AND gate is wired into one of the inputs of the OR gate.

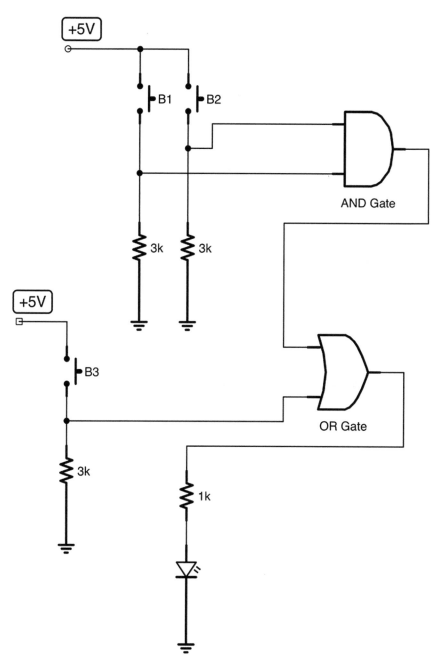

***Figure 12-8.*** *Logic Gates Represented as Shapes Instead of IC Pins*

This works because, unlike the LM393 (discussed in Chapter 11), these logic gates actually supply output voltage and current as well. Because the inputs to the logic gates are high resistance (they act like there is an extremely large resistor connected to the input), there is no need for a current-limiting resistor when combining gates in this way.

Now, it is fine to draw logic circuits the way we have in Figure 12-7. However, as the logic becomes more complex, actually drawing all of the connections to voltage and ground becomes tiring, and trying to get all of the wires to the right spot on the chip can get messy as well. Because of this, engineers have devised a simpler way of describing logic gates and logic circuits in schematics.

Instead of representing the entire chip on a schematic, engineers will represent only the logic gates themselves.

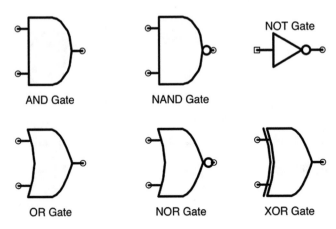

**Figure 12-9.** *Common Gates Used in Schematic Drawings*

Additionally, since the power goes to the whole chip (and not the individual gates), in such a drawing, the power connections for the gates are not shown. The standard that was developed represents each type of gate with a shape. Figure 12-8 shows what this circuit drawing looks like if it is drawn using shaped gates instead of IC pins. The actual physical circuit is the same; this is only to simplify the schematics to make them easier to understand and follow.

Figure 12-9 shows what these gate drawings look like. The AND gate has a flat back panel and a simple, rounded front. The OR gate looks a bit like a space shuttle, with both the back and the front angled. The NOT gate is a triangle with a circle at the tip. This circle can also be added to other gates to show that the gate is the opposite one. For instance, a NAND gate is drawn by first drawing an AND gate and then adding a circle to the front, indicating that the gate behaves like an AND gate with a NOT gate in front of it. Similarly, the NOR gate is an OR gate with a circle in front of it. The XOR gate is similar to the OR gate, but with an extra line going across its inputs.

Many times, the internal schematics of a chip are shown using gate symbols, in order to help you understand the operation of the chip and how the pins work. For instance, Figure 12-10 shows how the CD4081 chip is wired up internally. You can see the inputs going through the logic gate and out toward the output. While this isn't any new information you didn't already know, if may help you understand why the pins are laid out the way that they are.

As an interesting sidenote, every logic function can actually be built from NAND gates, though you have to wire them up in strange ways. You can actually build a computer almost entirely from NAND gates if you wanted to. It is not incredibly important, but Figure 12-11 shows how to build each type of logic gate from NAND gates. As an activity, go through the truth tables in Figure 12-1 and see if you can follow how each set of values becomes the result.

# 12.5  Understanding Chip Names

One of the biggest problems in learning to build electronic devices is the bewildering array of chips, each with some weird name. "Oh, for that you want an NE555P," or "You could use a SN74HC00P or a CD4011BE for that task." What language are such people speaking?

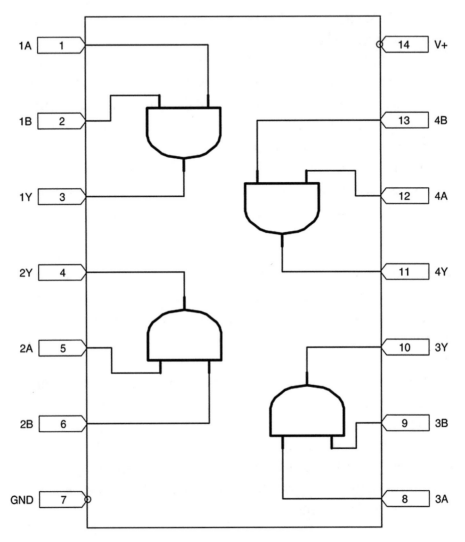

**Figure 12-10.** *The Internal Layout of the CD4081*

There is a huge selection of chips available, and learning their names is a daunting task. Appendix C attempts to offer some method to the madness, but, at the end of the day, chip names are like people's names—you get to know them by using them. Nobody knows everybody's name, but, for the types of projects you like to work on (whatever that happens to be), there will be standard chips whose names you will eventually come to know.

Once you make it through this book, you should have a solid enough background to search for the chips you need, have some understanding of the part names, and be able to find the chips you need for your projects. If you buy the chips from a seller geared toward amateurs and hobbyists, they will likely also include tutorials and additional information available in an easier-to-understand format than just datasheets.

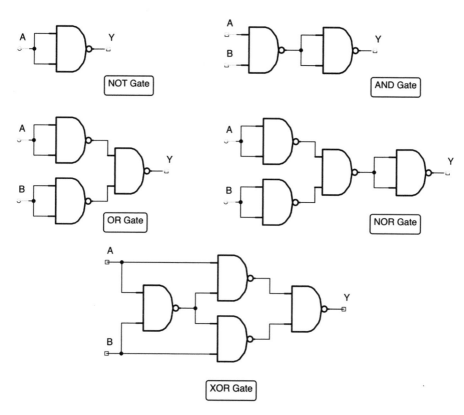

**Figure 12-11.** *How Each Gate Can Be Built from NAND Gates*

# Review

In this chapter, we learned the following:

1.  A logic IC implements basic digital logic functions such as AND, OR, NOT, and so on.

2.  These logic functions refer to essentially the same ideas that they mean in ordinary language and exactly what they mean in formal logic.

3.  Logic ICs use different voltage levels for true and false—usually with true being near the supply voltage and false being near zero voltage.

4.  True is sometimes referred to as HIGH or 1. False is sometimes referred to as LOW or 0.

5.  The inputs of a logic function are usually designated as A and B, and the output is usually designated as Y or Q.

6.  If an input or output name has a line/bar printed on top of it, that means that the value is the logical *opposite* of what would be expected. So, if Y is the output value, then $\overline{Y}$ would be the opposite of the output value.

7.  A single digital logic function is called a gate. Most logic ICs have more than one gate on a single chip.

8.  Logic ICs require a supply voltage and a ground connection to power the logic.

9.  Most logic ICs provide powered logic outputs, so that a "true" value supplies both voltage and a small amount of current on its output. However, a current-limiting resistor is usually required.

10. If an input to a logic IC may be disconnected for its "false" state (as is common with button inputs), then it needs a pull-down resistor to connect it to ground when the button is not being pushed.

11. Logic ICs can usually be combined by wiring the output of one to the input of another to create more complex logical conditions.

12. Logic gates are often drawn in schematics using basic shapes to indicate their operation, rather than as connections to chips. In these cases, the power connections are not shown by schematics.

13. Every logic gate can actually be built from NAND gates wired together.

14. IC names are very confusing and take time and experience to get to know them well.

15. Many ICs require specific voltage levels to operate, often at 5 V or 3.3 V.

16. Many solutions are available for generating specific voltages, including voltage dividers, Zener diodes, voltage regulators, and add-on breadboard power units.

17. The LM7805 is a very common 5 V voltage regulator.

# Apply What You Have Learned

1. Draw the circuit in Figure 12-3 yourself. Identify the function of each resistor.

2.  Build the circuit in Figure 12-3 (don't forget that the power source should be 5 V).

3.  If you assume that a negligible amount of current flows through the inputs of the AND gate and that the output functions as a 5 V voltage source (and the LED is red), how much current flows through each resistor when all of the buttons are pressed? What, then, is the total current used by the circuit if you ignore the logic gate?

4.  Measure the actual current that flows through each resistor. If you are having trouble pushing the buttons while you measure the current, just replace the buttons with wires for this test.

5.  Measure the current that is used by the AND gate itself. You can do this by measuring the supply current of the AND gate. Measure it both when its output is true and false.

6.  Draw a schematic of a circuit that has two buttons (B1 and B2) which light up an LED if either button is pressed. Use the logic gate shapes for the schematic.

7.  Draw a schematic of a circuit that has two buttons (B1 and B2) which light up an LED if neither button is pressed. Use the logic gate shapes for the schematic.

8.  Draw a schematic of a circuit that has four buttons (B1–B4) which light up an LED either if B1 and B2 are pressed or if B3 and B4 are pressed. Use the logic gate shapes for the schematic.

9. Look at the construction of the different gates from NAND gates in Figure 12-11. Copy down the OR gate construction four times, and trace how the output is generated for each possible set of inputs (true/true, true/false, false/true, false/false). Show the inputs and outputs on each NAND gate. Compare the outputs to the truth table for the OR function in Figure 12-1.

10. Take the circuit in Figure 12-3 and draw a schematic to use pull-up resistors on the inputs rather than pull-down resistors. How will this change the behavior of the circuit?

11. Let's say that we want to create a door buzzer so that someone outside a door can push a button to be let in. However, the person inside also wants a switch to be able to disable the buzzer. The buzzer can be thought of as a simple device that buzzes when any positive voltage is applied. Draw a circuit diagram of this setup using logic gates. The buzzer can be drawn as a resistor labeled "buzzer" (don't forget to connect the other side to ground!).

# CHAPTER 13

# Introduction to Microcontrollers

In Chapter 12, we learned the basics of digital logic. However, I think we can all agree that those chips wound up taking up a lot of space on our breadboards. If we wanted to do a lot of complicated tasks, we would wind up needing a lot of chips, we would need more and more breadboards to put them on, and our project would get unwieldy very quickly. Additionally, as the number of chips increased, it would get very expensive to build such projects.

Additionally, when all of the logic of a circuit is hardwired into the circuit through logic chips, it is very difficult to change. If you need to change the logic (convert an AND gate to an OR gate or do anything else), you wind up needing to wade through masses of circuitry to make the change you want. Then, if you are mass-producing the circuit, you have to set up for mass production all over again.

To solve all of these problems (and more), the microcontroller was introduced. A microcontroller is essentially a low-power, single-chip computer. A "real" computer chip usually relies on a whole slew of other chips (memory chips, input/output chips, etc.) to operate. A microcontroller contains all of these (though usually on a smaller scale) in a single chip that can be added to an electronics project.

Unlike your typical computer, most microcontrollers can't be connected to a mouse, keyboard, or other typical inputs and can't be connected to a monitor, disk drive, or other typical outputs. Instead, microcontrollers usually communicate entirely through digital (true/false) electrical signals on their pins.

So, instead of wiring complex logic onto their boards, many people opt to have microcontrollers provide the bulk of their digital logic. One complication that this adds, however, is that since the microcontroller is essentially a computer, then just, like a computer, it has to be programmed. This means that not only must circuit designers be familiar with electronics, they must also be familiar with computer programming.

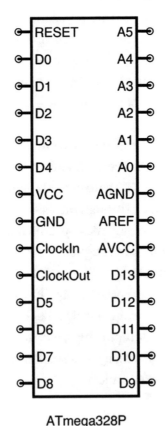

ATmega328P

**Figure 13-1.**  *A Simplified Pinout of the ATmega328/P*

# 13.1 The ATmega328/P Chip

The microcontroller we will be focusing on is the ATmega328/P. Actually, we will focus less on this specific chip than the overall environment surrounding it, known as Arduino (we will cover more of what this means in Section 13.2, "The Arduino Environment").

Even though the Arduino environment tries to minimize how much you have to know about the hardware itself, it is good to have a quick introduction to this chip and how it works.

The ATmega328/P is part of a family of microcontrollers developed by Atmel known as the AVR family. The AVR became popular because it was one of the first chips to use flash memory to store its programs, which allowed the onboard programs to be more easily changed.

Figure 13-1 shows a simplified pin configuration of the chip, focused on how it is used in the Arduino environment. The VCC pin and the GND pins are the primary power pins. The chip can run on a range of voltages, but 5 V is a very common and safe setting. AVCC and AGND power the chip's analog-to-digital converter unit.

All of the pins labeled "D" are digital input/output pins. They can be configured as inputs for buttons or other signals or as outputs for driving LEDs or other output devices. The pins labeled "A" are analog input pins (we will cover how to use these in Chapter 15). While the digital input pins can only read that a value is true/false, the analog pins can read voltages and convert them to numbers. AREF is a "reference voltage" used for setting the maximum voltage for analog inputs, but is usually unconnected (it should also not be a higher voltage than AVCC).

Microcontrollers, like most processors, control their operation by using a "clock." This is not a clock as you normally think of—it doesn't tell time. Instead of thinking of it as a clock, a better way to think of the "clock" is as a heartbeat. Basically, there is a continuous signal of pulses that are provided through the clock, and the pulses allow the chip to synchronize all of its activities. The ATmega328/P has an internal clock, but it can also be more efficiently operated by connecting an external clock (quartz crystals, for instance, provide a *very* steady pulse for this purpose).

As we have noted, the chip has a number of input and output pins. You might wonder, what does the chip *do* with its input and output pins? That is entirely up to you. It does *whatever you program it to do*. The ATmega328/P has **flash memory** on the chip which can store a computer program (flash memory means that it will remember the program even after the power turns off). You have to upload your program to the chip, and then after that, it will do whatever you like with its inputs and outputs. The D0 and D1 pins, in addition to providing input and output, can also be used to reprogram the chip. We will learn how to program the chip in Section 13.4, "Programming the Arduino."

# 13.2  The Arduino Environment

The chip itself is just one piece of the puzzle. In order to use the chip, you have to be able to program it. Programming requires the use of programming tools on your main computer. In addition, you also need some way to take the program that you built on your computer and load it onto the chip. That takes both software and hardware.

Then, once the program is on the chip, you have to build a circuit to properly power the chip. This requires voltage regulation for the VCC pin and several other recommendations from the manufacturer about how to set up the other pins. To make it run optimally, it would also be good to supply an external clock. All of this can be quite a lot of work, and a lot of pieces that need to be brought together.

Thankfully, most chips have what is called a **development board** that can be purchased. A development board is a prebuilt circuit that has a microcontroller chip pre-connected in its recommended manner. It is made to simplify the work of developing circuits. Likewise, most chips have a recommended **programming environment** as well. A programming environment is a set of tools for your computer that allow you to create programs for your microcontroller. Additionally, a device called an **in-system programmer** (ISP) connects your computer to your chip or development board and will transmit the program from your computer to the chip.

In 2005, a complete, simplified system for doing all of these tasks called **Arduino** was created, based off of an earlier system called Wiring. Arduino consists of (a) a simplified development environment for your computer to write software for microcontrollers, (b) a simplified development board to make it very easy to build electronics projects, and (c) integrating the in-system programmer into the development board so that all that is required to transfer the program to the microcontroller is a USB cable.

The Arduino environment supports a number of different microcontroller chips. Because it is a simplified environment, many of the special features of individual chips are not directly supported. However, for getting started and doing basic projects, the Arduino environment is excellent.

Even though there is a company behind Arduino, there are many Arduino-compatible boards made by other manufacturers. These boards use the same ATmega328/P microcontroller and often have very similar development boards and functions. Most importantly, they are compatible with the programming tools on the Arduino environment.[1]

---

[1] One important difference between "official" Arduino boards and most Arduino-compatible boards is the USB controller chip. Official Arduino boards use a chip from FTDI to do this, because the drivers for it are preinstalled on every operating system. To save on costs, many Arduino-compatible boards use a lower-cost chip to perform this function (often the CH340). Usually, the only disadvantage of this is that, on some operating systems, an additional driver is needed to communicate with these chips.

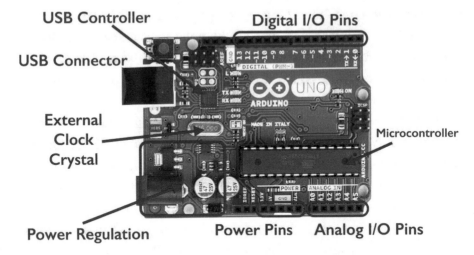

**Figure 13-2.** *The Major Components of the Arduino Uno*

# 13.3  The Arduino Uno

This book focuses on the Arduino Uno development board. Figure 13-2 shows what the board looks like, as well as a general idea of what the different areas of the board accomplish. The Uno is very nice because the USB port allows a whole slew of functions—not only can it be used to receive programs for the chip but you can also power the board through the USB, as well as send data back and forth to the computer through it. If you are not connected to a USB, there is a separate power plug that can be plugged into the wall or to a 9 V battery.

The Arduino Uno provides chips for power regulation, USB communication, as well as the ATmega328/P microcontroller itself. It also supplies an external clock for the microcontroller. Finally, it provides **headers** (places on the board to plug in wires) for the major pins on the microcontroller. Thus, everything you need to make use of the chip is provided for you in this development board. You simply connect the input and output pins to your own breadboard, and you can have a working project that you can program.

# 13.4 Programming the Arduino

Now that we have seen the pieces of the Arduino environment, let's tackle programming the Arduino. This book is not a book about programming, so we will only cover the absolute basics.

The programming tool for the Arduino is called the **Arduino IDE**. IDE stands for "Integrated Development Environment"—in other words, the thing that you develop with. The Arduino IDE is available for pretty much any computer—Mac, Windows, or Linux. You can download the IDE from `http://arduino.cc/`.

Depending on whether you purchased an "official" Arduino or a clone, you may also have to download an additional driver for the USB interface. If you have an Arduino-compatible clone, you can download the driver from `http://bplearning.net/drivers`. Once you have installed the Arduino IDE and the USB driver, you are ready to start!

We will begin by using an example program (called a "sketch" in Arduino terminology) that ships with the Arduino. First, connect your Arduino to your computer with a USB cable. Open up the Arduino IDE; then click "File," then "Examples," and then "01.Basics"; and finally click "Blink." This loads up a ready-made program for your Arduino. This program simply turns the D13 pin on and off. On an Arduino, the D13 pin already has an LED attached to it, so you don't even need to add any components!

Now that you have the program loaded up, click the button with the checkmark icon. This verifies that the program is written in a way that the computer can understand. If it has any errors, it will show them in the black panel on the bottom.

Now you need to make sure that the IDE is targetted at your board. Go to "Tools" and then "Board" and make sure that "Arduino/Genuino Uno" is selected. Then, click "Tools" and then "Port" and make sure your Arduino was detected and that it is selected. If you don't see your Arduino listed here, you may need to check the USB driver installation.[2]

Once your configuration is verified, click the button with the arrow icon to upload it to the Arduino. It should take about 2–5 seconds, and then the LED on your Arduino should start blinking. If there are any errors, they will display in the black status area below. Note that some Arduinos come with this program preinstalled. If this is the case, your Arduino may not have changed what it is doing much. You can verify that it is all working by changing the program slightly. If you change all of the numbers that say 1000 to 500, it should blink twice as fast. Remember, though, that you must verify it (click the checkmark button) and upload it (click the arrow button) to get your new code onto the board.

Now, let's take a look at the code and how it functions. The first part of the code should be grayed out. That's because it is a **comment**, or a note telling you about the program. This isn't read by the computer at all. Comments start with the characters /*, and they continue until they reach the characters */ (this can even span multiple lines). Shorter comments are sometimes made with the characters //. Those comments only continue until the end of the line.

After the comments, there are two **functions** defined—setup() and loop(). A function is simply a piece of code that is named. In the Arduino environment, the setup and loop functions are special. The setup function runs exactly once when the chip first turns on or resets or when a new

---

[2]You might try the following instructions with a device listed there even if you don't recognize it as your Arduino in case your computer had difficulty detecting the device type.

program is loaded. It is used for things such as telling the chip which pins will be used for input and which ones will be used for output and doing other setup-related tasks. After the setup function completes, the loop function runs continually over and over again for as long as the chip is on.

If you look at the code, the setup function contains one command:

```
pinMode(13, OUTPUT);
```

This tells the microcontroller that digital output 13 (D13) will be used for output. Note that this refers to the D13 pin in Figure 13-1 (usually just labeled 13 on the Arduino Uno), not to pin 13 of the chip itself (which would be D7). With the Arduino Uno, we don't actually need to worry about the pinout of the ATmega328/P, we just need to read the names of the pins next to the pin headers.

The loop function is the main part of the code. It looks like this:

```
digitalWrite(13, HIGH);
delay(1000);
digitalWrite(13, LOW);
delay(1000);
```

The first line, digitalWrite(13, HIGH);, says to turn D13 to HIGH, which is about 5 V. This provides the power for the LED attached to D13. This pin will remain high until we tell it to do something else.

The next line, delay(1000);, tells the chip to wait for 1,000 milliseconds (which is 1 second). During this time, nothing happens—the chip just waits. Changing this number changes the amount of time that the chip will wait for. Changing it to 500 will cause it to wait for half a second, and increasing it to 2000 (note that there are no commas in the number!) will cause it to wait for 2 seconds.

The next line turns D13 to LOW/false/off/0 V. This turns off the LED, because there is no longer any voltage supplied to it. D13 will stay in this state until told otherwise. The next line then waits for 1 second. Once this function finishes, the chip will simply run the loop function again from the start.

In Chapter 14, we will look at how to build projects with the Arduino that use additional components.

# Review

In this chapter, we learned the following:

1.  A microcontroller is a small computer in a single microchip that provides customizable logic for handling digital signals.

2.  A development board is a circuit board that simplifies the process of building circuits with a microchip by providing most of the standard connections for you, allowing you to focus your efforts on the things that make your project distinctive.

3.  In order to use a microcontroller, it has to be programmed from a computer.

4.  The Arduino environment is a combination of software and hardware meant to make building microcontroller projects easier.

5.  The Arduino Uno is a development board for the Arduino environment that includes a microcontroller, USB connection, power regulation, and headers for connecting the microcontroller's input/output pins to other circuits.

6.  The ATmega328/P is the microcontroller used in the Arduino Uno.

7.  An Arduino program (called a sketch) has two standard functions—setup (which is run once when the chip powers on) and loop (which runs over and over again as long as the chip is on).

8.  Once a program is uploaded to the Arduino Uno, it will be saved on the device until another program is loaded.

# Apply What You Have Learned

1.  Practice modifying and uploading the Blink program to the Arduino Uno. Change the numbers given to delay to different values, and see how that affects the operation of the program.

2.  The ATmega328/P is only one of many different microcontrollers available in the AVR family. Research online to find one or two other AVR chips and what different features they have.

3.  The AVR family is only one of many microcontroller families. Research one or two other microcontroller families and look at what features are claimed for each. Examples of other microcontroller families include PIC, STM32, MSP432, and the Intel Quark.

4.  Go to the arduino.cc website and look at the different types of Arduinos that are available. What makes them different? Why might you choose one for a project over another?

# CHAPTER 14

# Building Projects with Arduino

Chapter 13 covered the basics of what microcontrollers are, what the Arduino environment is, and how to load a program onto an Arduino board. In this chapter, we will go into more depth on how to include an Arduino Uno into a project.

## 14.1 Powering Your Breadboard from an Arduino Uno

The first thing to understand about the Arduino Uno is that one of its main jobs is power regulation. As we saw in Chapter 13, the Arduino can use a variety of power sources—USB, battery, or a wall plug. Additionally, there is a connection on the Uno's headers that allows for you to supply power from some other source.

If you have a power source that just has wires coming out of it—like a 9 V battery with a simple wire connector—the Uno has a place that you can plug it in. The pin labeled $V_{IN}$ is used for supplying an unregulated voltage supply (7–12 volts) to the Uno (*do not* use the one labeled 5 V—it is for *outputting* power). Therefore, if you plug the positive wire into $V_{IN}$ and the negative wire into any of the *GND* pins (it doesn't matter which one), then the Uno will spring to life.

© Jonathan Bartlett 2020
J. Bartlett, *Electronics for Beginners*, https://doi.org/10.1007/978-1-4842-5979-5_14

On the flip side, you can actually power the rest of your project from the Uno and take advantage of its voltage regulation, as well as its numerous methods for getting power. To do this, simply take a wire from the 5 V connection on the Uno and connect it to the positive rail on your breadboard. Then, take another wire from one of the GND connections on the Uno and connect it to the ground rail on the breadboard. Voilà! A very flexible 5 V power supply for your breadboard. Figure 14-1 shows how to use this to light a simple LED circuit.

Also note that there is also a 3.3 V connection if you need it, as many small devices are powered at that level.

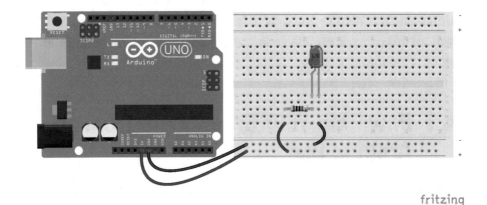

fritzing

*Figure 14-1.* *Powering a Simple Project from an Arduino Uno*

## 14.2 Wiring Inputs and Outputs to an Arduino Uno

Now that we know how to power a breadboard from an Arduino Uno, we can now see how to connect inputs and outputs to the Uno.

Wiring inputs and outputs to an Uno is actually very easy. Outputs of the Uno can be viewed as simple voltage sources, like a battery, which operate at either 5 V (if set to HIGH) or 0 V (if set to LOW). Remember that any of the digital I/O pins can be set to be input or output pins in your Arduino program with the pinMode command.

However, even though an output pin can act as a voltage source, the current needs to be limited to prevent damage to the Arduino. Each output pin should only be sourcing up to 20 mA of current, and the total amount of output of all pins combined should never exceed 100 mA. So, for instance, if you have an LED output, be sure to add a resistor to limit the amount of current. Microcontrollers generally cannot drive high-power devices such as motors directly and must rely on some method of amplifying the signal after it leaves them (we will cover amplification in Part 4 of the book).

Inputs to an Arduino are essentially voltage sensors. They will detect a HIGH (around 5 V) or LOW (near 0 V) signal on the pin. You can think of them as having a very large resistor attached to them (about 100 MΩ—100 million ohms), so they don't actually use up any serious amount of current (in other words, you don't have to supply a current-limiting resistor because it is already built in). However, because they use so little current, that means that, just like our inputs in Chapter 12, they cannot be left disconnected, or the results may be randomized from static electricity in the air. Thus, for inputs, you should always attach a pull-up or a pull-down resistor (usually a pull-down) to the input to make sure that the input is *always* wired into the circuit in a known-valid state.

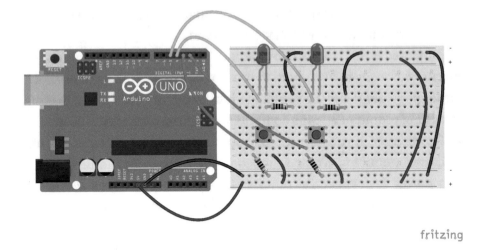

fritzing

***Figure 14-2.*** *Wiring a Simple Button-Based Arduino Project*

# 14.3  A Simple Arduino Project with LEDs

In this section, we are going to look at making a simple Arduino project ·
with two buttons, each controlling one of two LEDs. This would actually
be simpler to wire without the Arduino, but the goal is to make a baby
step to understanding how Arduino projects work. Later we can do more
complicated things, but, for right now, we will just see how we get an input
signal to the Arduino and send an output signal back out.

This project is going to have buttons wired into Digital Pin 2 and Digital
Pin 3 of the Arduino and LEDs wired into Digital Pin 4 and Digital Pin 5.
Let's think about what these need to look like. The LEDs will each need
a current-limiting resistor, and the buttons will each need a pull-down
resistor.

Figure 14-2 shows how this should be wired up. The breadboard is
being powered from the 5 V and GND terminals on the Arduino. The
wires on the right side make sure power is connected to both sides of the
breadboard. On the bottom, buttons are wired up with pull-down resistors

and connected to Digital Pins 2 and 3 on the Arduino. On the top, the LEDs are connected to Digital Pins 4 and 5, with current-limiting resistors making sure they don't draw too much current.

Now, of course, for an Arduino, this is not enough. The Arduino also needs a program to control it! Figure 14-3 shows the program you will need to type in to control the LEDs.

Note that, as usual, the project is divided into two pieces—setup(), which only occurs once when the chip starts up, and loop(), which continuously runs over and over again until the chip is turned off or reset:

```
void setup() {
    pinMode(2, INPUT);
    pinMode(3, INPUT);
    pinMode(4, OUTPUT);
    pinMode(5, OUTPUT);
}

void loop() {
    // Turn pin 4 on/off based on
    // the input from pin 2
    if(digitalRead(2) == HIGH) {
        digitalWrite(4, HIGH);
    } else {
        digitalWrite(4, LOW);
    }

    // Turn pin 5 on/off based on
    // the input from pin 3
    if(digitalRead(3) == HIGH) {
        digitalWrite(5, HIGH);
    } else {
        digitalWrite(5, LOW);
    }
}
```

*Figure 14-3.* *An Arduino Program to Control Two Buttons and Two LEDs*

setup() simply tells which pins should be in which mode. Note that, unless it includes the calls to the delay() function, the loop() function will literally run thousands of times per second (or more). The Arduino Uno can execute approximately 16 million instructions per second. Each line of code translates to many instructions, but nonetheless, it goes *really fast*. Just keep this in mind when you are writing programs.

Inside the loop() function, we have a new Arduino function—digitalRead(). The digitalRead function takes a pin number and returns whether that pin is HIGH or LOW. We have put this into a conditional—*if* the read from the button pin is HIGH, then the corresponding LED pin is turned HIGH. Alternatively (i.e., *else*), if the read from the button pin is not HIGH (i.e., it is LOW), then the corresponding LED pin is turned LOW. Note that there are *two* equal signs used in the comparison. In many programming languages, you use two equal signs to tell the computer to compare values. A single equal sign often means that you are *setting* a value (not comparing them).

This book is not a book on computer programming, so we are not going to cover all of the details. Because of this, most of the programs will be given to you, and you will only need to make minor modifications. However, if you are interested in learning more, the programming language being used in the Arduino environment is C++, and the Arduino focuses on the easier-to-understand portions of it. The book *Beginning Arduino Programming* by Brian Evans is a good place to start. If you want to learn more about programming in general (not related to Arduino), you can check out my own book, *New Programmers Start Here.* If you want to understand better how programming works from the perspective of the computer, you can check out my book *Programming from the Ground Up.*

# 14.4 Changing Functionality Without Rewiring

Now, you might reasonably be thinking, *Wouldn't this be a lot easier if we just directly attached the buttons to the LEDs to turn them off and on?* Indeed, it would. However, by having the inputs and outputs all wired to the Arduino, we can actually *change* the functionality of the project *without* having to do a single bit of rewiring! For instance, if we wanted to have the left button control the right LED and the right button control the left LED, then all we would have to do is swap all of the 2s for 3s in the program and vice versa.

Now imagine if we had spent time developing such a device and even had it sent off to manufacturing, but later decided that we wanted to change the functionality. If all of the logic of the device is implemented by hardware, then that means that you have to throw away all of your old inventory to modify your functionality. If, instead, you use software to connect your components, then oftentimes you can update your device merely by updating your software.

Other modifications we can think of to this simple device might include the following:

1. Making the LEDs turn off rather than on when the buttons are pressed

2. Making the LEDs blink when the buttons are pressed

3. Changing the buttons to be simple toggles, so that you don't have to keep on holding the buttons down to keep the LED on

4. Requiring that the buttons be pushed in a particular order in order to turn on the LED

5. Requiring that both buttons be pushed to turn on the LEDs

This list could go on and on. By routing all control processing through your microcontroller, you make your devices much more flexible. Additionally, at some point, they also become cheaper. When mass-producing, microcontroller chips like the ATmega328/P can be had for just over a dollar. Some chips, when purchased in bulk, cost less than 50 cents! So, if a microcontroller is replacing a complex sequence of logic gates and other control functionality, moving all of your control logic to a microcontroller can actually be much less expensive than hardwiring it, and you get added flexibility as a side bonus.

# Review

In this chapter, we learned the following:

1. You can power your breadboards using the 5 V and GND pins on the Arduino to simplify power regulation in your projects.

2. Input pins on the Arduino are high-impedance inputs (they act like they have a very large resistor attached, so they don't eat a lot of current).

3. Because input pins use so little current, buttons need to be sure they have a pull-up or pull-down resistor attached to make sure the input is always detecting real voltage values and not static electricity in the air.

4.  Care has to be taken when using output pins to make sure the current is never too much for the chip.

5.  Using a microcontroller allows you to rewrite the logic of the project without changing the wiring.

# Apply What You Have Learned

1.  Which Arduino pin do you use when supplying an unregulated voltage (i.e., a voltage above the 5 V that the Arduino runs at)?

2.  What Arduino pins would you use to extract power out from an Arduino connected to a power supply?

3.  What is the voltage of an output pin set to HIGH?

4.  What is the maximum current that should be sourced by any particular Arduino pin?

5.  If you have a red LED attached to an Arduino output pin, what is the minimum size of a resistor that you need?

6.  If an Arduino input pin is completely disconnected from a circuit, what state does the Arduino read it as?

7.  How much current does an Arduino input use?

8.  What is the best way to wire a button to an Arduino?

9.  What is an advantage of storing a program in a microcontroller even if the logic could be built directly in hardware?

# CHAPTER 15

# Analog Input and Output on an Arduino

In Chapter 14, we learned how to do basic digital input and output with an Arduino using its I/O pins. In this chapter, we will cover how to do analog input and output as well.

## 15.1 Reading Analog Inputs

So far we have been focusing on digital input and output—HIGH and LOW states. The Arduino Uno also supports some amount of analog input (through its analog pins) and a sort of "faked" analog output (through its pulse-width modulation (PWM) pins, which will be covered in the next section).

On the Arduino Uno, the analog input pins are grouped together in a section labeled "Analog In." These pins are voltage sensors similar to the digital I/O pins, but they can detect a range of values between 0 V and 5 V (you should never exceed 5 V on any Arduino pin). The analogRead() function is similar to the digitalRead() function in that it takes a pin number and returns an output value. The difference is that the pin number given to analogRead() corresponds to an analog input pin number, not a digital pin number, and the output, rather than being LOW or HIGH, is a number from 0 to 1023 (10 bits of resolution). 0 V will give you a 0, and 5 V will give you 1023. In-between values will give you an in-between result.

© Jonathan Bartlett 2020
J. Bartlett, *Electronics for Beginners*, https://doi.org/10.1007/978-1-4842-5979-5_15

Because of this, we can rework the darkness sensor we developed in Chapter 11 to use the Arduino. Since the photoresistor is just a resistor, we *still need* to make it part of a voltage divider to convert the resistance value to a voltage. However, we no longer need the voltage comparator to get it to work—we can just directly connect it to an analog port on the Arduino!

Figure 15-1 shows the darkness sensor rebuilt for the Arduino. Notice that we have a lot fewer custom components, because the control has been moved from hardware to the Arduino's software. We don't need a reference voltage, and we don't need a voltage comparator. We just have one voltage divider to convert the photoresistor's resistance to a voltage (with a wire going to the Arduino's Analog Input Pin 1) and an LED with a current-limiting resistor for the output (fed from Digital Pin 2). Everything else comes from software.

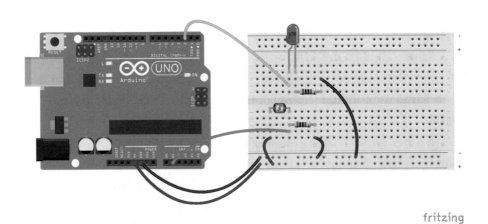

fritzing

***Figure 15-1.*** *The Darkness Sensor Rebuilt for Arduino*

```
void setup() {
    pinMode(2, OUTPUT);
}

void loop() {
    if(analogRead(1) < 450) {
        digitalWrite(2, HIGH);
    } else {
        digitalWrite(2, LOW);
    }
}
```

***Figure 15-2.*** *Code for the Arduino Darkness Sensor*

Figure 15-2 shows the code that will run the sensor. Note that in the loop() function, we are now using analogRead() rather than digitalRead(). Now, instead of it returning HIGH or LOW, it is returning a number. We can then compare that number to a baseline number to tell us whether we should turn the LED on or off.

Now, you may wonder where I got the value to compare against (i.e., 450). What I did was to test the sensor in a variety of conditions and see which value turned off the light when I wanted it to!

However, you may be wondering what exactly the values are that it is reading. Thankfully, the Arduino environment allows a way for us to get feedback from the device while it is running, if it is connected to the computer. To do this, we use what is known as the **serial** interface to the Arduino. This interface communicates over USB so that we can let our computer know how things are going in the program.

To use the USB serial interface, in your setup function, you add the following line:

```
Serial.begin(9600);
```

This tells the chip to initialize its serial interface at 9600 baud (**baud** is an old term meaning "bits per second"), which allows us to talk back to the computer. However, it is important to note that if you use the `Serial` functions, you should not have anything connected to Digital Pin 0 or Digital Pin 1 of the Arduino.

Now, in your program, you can do `Serial.println()` to output any value you want. We will do

```
Serial.println(analogRead(1));
```

to let us know what the current value of the analog input is reading at. The new program, with the added feedback, is shown in Figure 15-3. After uploading this code to the Arduino, to see your output, click the magnifying glass on the top right of the screen. You can also go to the "Tools" menu and select "Serial Monitor." Either way gets you to the same screen. When the code is running, it should be spewing out pages and pages of numbers. Each of these numbers is the current value of `analogRead()` when it is encountered in the code, which happens hundreds or thousands of times each second (it is slowed down a bit by the USB communication, and you could slow it down even further by adding `delay` commands at the end of the `loop` function). This outputting of data in order to better see what is happening within your program is known as **debugging** and is useful for tracking down problems within your code.

## 15.2  Analog Output with PWM

So we have discussed analog *input*, but what about analog *output*? Truthfully, the Arduino does not support analog output as such. However, analog output is *faked* on an Arduino using a technique known as **pulse-width modulation**, abbreviated as **PWM**. The Arduino only outputs 5 V on its output pins. But let's say we wanted to fake a 2.5 V signal. What might we do? Well, if we turned the pin on and off rapidly so that it was only on for half the time, that would give us about the same amount of electrical power as a continuous output of 2.5 V. That's what PWM does—it fakes lower voltages by just flipping the power to the pin on and off very rapidly so that it "looks" like a lower voltage. In Chapter 22, we will see how to actually convert this to a "true" voltage.

```
void setup() {
    pinMode(2, OUTPUT);
    Serial.begin(9600);
}

void loop() {
    Serial.println(analogRead(1));
    if(analogRead(1) < 450) {
        digitalWrite(2, HIGH);
    } else {
        digitalWrite(2, LOW);
    }
}
```

***Figure 15-3.*** *Darkness Sensor with Serial Feedback*

Arduino programs use the function analogWrite() to use a pin for PWM. This function is a little confusingly named because (a) it uses digital pins, not analog pins, and (b) the value is between 0 and 255, not 0 and 1023 like analogRead(). Other than that, it basically does what you might expect. analogWrite(3, 0); will turn off Digital Pin 3, analogWrite(3, 255); will turn it all the way on, analogWrite(3, 127); will flick it on and off pretty evenly, and analogWrite(3, 25); will keep Digital Pin 3 on only a short time relative to how long the pin stays off.

To get a flavor for PWM, we will do a very simple PWM project—a dimmed LED. Figure 15-4 shows what the connection will look like—just an LED with a current-limiting resistor attached to Digital Pin 3 (which is marked with a ~ to indicate that it is capable of PWM). Figure 15-5 shows the code to dim the output.

This code is a little more complicated. It's alright if you don't understand it fully, as this isn't a programming book. But I think if you think about it long enough, you can get it.

In short, it creates a **variable**, which is a named temporary storage location for a value (we are calling it i for a short name). It is declared an int, which means it will hold an integer, and we set it with a starting value of zero.

The while command means that this will repeat (or **loop**), executing everything within the block of code between { and } over and over again, as long as i is less than 255. Within this block, we write the value of i to pin 3 using analogWrite(). Then, we delay for 10 milliseconds to make sure the change is visible (you can adjust this value to the speed you want the brightness to change at). Then, we increase i by one to go to the next value.

The next while loop does the same thing but goes the other way. It starts at 255 and progresses down to 0. Then, when it is all the way to zero, the loop() function completes. Then, the Arduino runs the loop function over again.

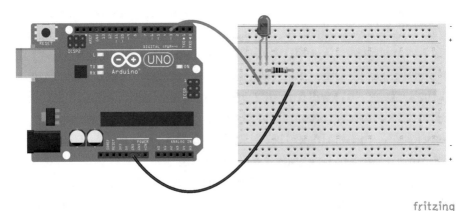

fritzing

***Figure 15-4.*** *A Simple Analog Dimmer*

Even though the Arduino is outputting "analog" by switching the pin on and off at different rates, it *looks like* the LED is dimming on and off. It is flickering so fast that we merely perceive it as a lower-energy light than as a pulsing light. In fact, when it gets to about 180 (about 70% on and 30% off), there is not a lot of difference between that and full brightness.

```
void setup() {
    pinMode(3, OUTPUT);
}

void loop() {
    // Slowly turn the LED all the way up
    int i = 0;
    while(i < 255) {
        analogWrite(3, i);
        delay(10);
        i = i + 1;
    }

    // Slowly turn the LED all the way back down
    while(i >= 0) {
        analogWrite(3, i);
        delay(10);
        i = i - 1;
    }
}
```

***Figure 15-5.*** *Code for the Analog Dimmer*

# Review

In this chapter, we learned the following:

1. The Arduino can read voltage values between 0 V and 5 V through the analog input pins, using the analogRead() function.

2. The values given from the analog input pins will be integers between 0 and 1023, where 0 represents 0 V, 1023 represents 5 V, and the numbers in between represent in-between voltages.

3. When using resistive sensors, you still need to incorporate the resistive sensors into a voltage divider circuit in order to convert the varying resistance into a varying voltage.

4. We can send debugging information back to the Arduino IDE with the USB serial interface, using the Serial object and its related commands.

5. Analog output on Arduino is done with the Arduino *digital* pins (not the analog pins), but only on the ones labeled with a tilde (˜), using the analogWrite() function.

6. Analog output on Arduino is done using pulse-width modulation (PWM), which switches the output pin on and off very rapidly to simulate a partial voltage.

7. The analog level of the analog output on the Arduino is specified by a number between 0 and 255, where 0 means no voltage, 255 means to keep the pin at 5 V the whole time, and the numbers in between cause the pin to switch back and forth rapidly to emulate a voltage between the two values.

8. In computer programming, a variable is a temporary storage location for a value.

9. In computer programming, a while loop repeats the inside of the while loop over and over again until its condition is no longer valid.

# Apply What You Have Learned

1. What do you have to do to a resistive sensor in order to read the value of the sensor on the analog input?

2. In the code that dimmed the lights, how would we slow down the dimming process?

3. Modify the darkness sensor circuit and code so that it will output a dimmed (analog) value to the LED.

4. Further modify the darkness sensor circuit so that, at different darkness levels, the LED has different levels of brightness.

5. Think of your own modifications to the circuits in this chapter. Come up with a new way of putting together the pieces to which you have learned to create some amount of modified functioning. Implement this new design.

# PART III

# Capacitors and Inductors

# CHAPTER 16

# Capacitors

In this chapter, we will start looking at the **capacitor.**

## 16.1  What Is a Capacitor?

Before we begin discussing the capacitor, we need to quickly review the concepts from Chapter 3 on the relationship between charge, current, and voltage. In fact, it might be helpful to reread that chapter if you find that you have forgotten how those terms related to each other.

To review

- Charge is essentially the amount of electrical "stuff" (positive or negative) that something contains, measured in coulombs.

- Current is the *movement* of charge, measured in coulombs per second, also known as amperes.

- Voltage is the amount of force that each coulomb will produce. You can think of it as the amount of electric energy that each coulomb is capable of producing or the amount of power that each ampere of current yields.

© Jonathan Bartlett 2020
J. Bartlett, *Electronics for Beginners*, https://doi.org/10.1007/978-1-4842-5979-5_16

A capacitor is a storage device which stores electric energy by holding two opposing charges (i.e., positive and negative). The amounts of charge that the capacitors that we will be working with can store is very small, but some capacitors can store very large amounts of charge. One way to think of a capacitor is as a very, very, very tiny rechargeable battery. However, unlike batteries, instead of storing a fixed voltage, a capacitor stores opposing charges. Unlike a battery, the actual voltage a capacitor yields when it discharges will depend on both the size of the capacitor and the amount of charge it is holding, and the voltage will decrease as the charge is reduced.

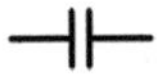

$$\dashv\vdash$$

**Figure 16-1.** *The Symbol for a Capacitor*

The size of a capacitor is known as its **capacitance**, and it is measured in **farads** (abbreviated with the letter F), named after the influential scientist Michael Faraday. A capacitance of 1 farad means that if a capacitor stores 1 coulomb of charge, it will discharge with a force of 1 V. Most capacitors, however, have a capacitance much lower than a farad. Capacitors are usually measured in microfarads (1 millionth of a farad, abbreviated as μF or uF), nanofarads (1 billionth of a farad, abbreviated as nF), or picofarads (1 trillionth of a farad, abbreviated as pF). Capacitors are rarely rated in millifarads (1 thousandth of a farad).

So, to convert from microfarads to farads, multiply the capacitance by 0.000001. To go back from farads to microfarads, multiply the capacitance by 1000000. To convert from picofarads to farads, multiply the capacitance by 0.000000000001. To go back from farads to picofarads, multiply the capacitance by 1000000000000.

# 16.2  How Capacitors Work

The symbol for a capacitor in a circuit is shown in Figure 16-1. This symbol provides a visual reference for how a capacitor works. Capacitors usually work by having two conductive plates or surfaces that are separated by some sort of nonconductive material. Since the two plates are *near* each other, having a charge in one of the plates will pull charge into the other plate due to the **electric field**. An electric field is generated any time a charge accumulates. Essentially, an electric field pulls an opposing charge closer in.

Electric fields influence nearby charges even though they don't directly touch. The field will pull opposite charges closer to itself. Therefore, having a charge in one plate will attract the opposite charge in the other plate. However, since the plates are not actually touching, the electrons cannot actually jump the gap. Therefore, the capacitor will accumulate a certain amount of charge and hold it in its plates.

To understand this better, imagine that you are a positive charge. You are moving through the circuit, but why? What are you moving toward? As a positive charge, you are trying to move to the negative charge. So then, moving along, you see this big swimming pool (i.e., a capacitor). At the bottom of the swimming pool, the barrier is so thin that you can see to the other side. And what do you see there? It's the negative charges—right there at the bottom of the swimming pool! The negative charges have their own swimming pool the size of your own, separated by a barrier so thin that you can see each other.

Because you can see them, you go down into the swimming pool to see if you can interact. A lot of other bits of positive charge see this too, and they go down to see what is going on. However, when you get there, you realize that no matter how hard you try, you can't get to the negative charge that you can see. As more and more charge fills up the swimming pool, it starts to get crowded in the swimming pool. This creates *pressure* in the swimming pool—also known as *voltage*. As the swimming pool gets more and more crowded, it is harder and harder to fit new charge into it, and so the rate that it gets filled goes down, and the voltage (the pressure pushing the charge out of the pool) goes up. The same thing is happening to the negatively charged swimming pool on the other side.

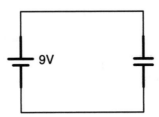

***Figure 16-2.*** *A Simple Circuit to Charge a Capacitor*

When the pressure (voltage) to push charge out of the swimming pool equals the pressure (voltage) of the pipe (wire) leading to the swimming pool (capacitor), then the capacitor is full. When the voltage on the wire goes down (i.e., the battery disconnects), then the pressure of the charges in the capacitor pushes them back out into the wire, discharging the capacitor.

So, if one terminal of the capacitor is connected to the positive side of a battery and the other terminal is connected to the negative side of a battery, charge will quickly flow into the capacitor, as happened in our example with the swimming pool. Figure 16-2 shows this circuit setup. The exact amount of charge that flows in depends on the voltage of the battery and the capacitance of the capacitor (i.e., the size of the swimming pool). Note that this is not a short circuit, because the two plates of the capacitor are *not actually connected.* They are just close enough to attract the opposite charge onto the opposite plate.

In a setup like Figure 16-2, there is an equation that tells you the amount of charge that can be stored in a capacitor for a given voltage:

$$Q = C \cdot V \qquad\qquad (16.1)$$

In this equation, $V$ is the voltage applied, $C$ is the capacitance (in farads), and $Q$ is the amount of charge (in coulombs) stored in the capacitor's plates.

> **Example 16.7** If I attached a 66 µF capacitor to a 9 V source, how much charge gets stored on the capacitor?
>
> Well, first, we need to convert the capacitance from microfarads to farads. 66 µF is 66 millionths of a farad, so it would be 0.000066 F. Now, we just need to plug the numbers into the equation:
>
> $$Q = C \cdot V$$
> $$= 0.000066 . 9$$
> $$= 0.000594 \text{ coulomb}$$
>
> Therefore, if I attached a 66 µF capacitor to a 9 V source, the capacitor would store 0.000594 coulomb of charge.

After my capacitor is charged up, I can use it as a very tiny battery. That is, I could disconnect it from the circuit in Figure 16-2 and reconnect it as the battery for another circuit. However, as I mentioned, this will be a very, very tiny battery. Additionally, as the charge leaves the capacitor, the voltage of the battery will decrease as well.

If we use the capacitor as a battery, if we know how much charge is stored in the capacitor, we can rearrange Equation 16.1 slightly to figure out how much voltage it will deliver when it begins to discharge:

$$V = \frac{Q}{C} \qquad (16.2)$$

Now, as the capacitor discharges, since the charge it is holding will decrease, so will the voltage it delivers. If we know how much charge is left at any given moment, we can calculate the present voltage.

> **Example 16.8** If I have a charge of 0.0023 coulomb stored in a 33 µF capacitor, if I discharge the capacitor, what voltage will it begin to discharge at?
>
> The first thing to do here is to convert the capacitance to farads. A microfarad is 1 millionth of a farad, so 33 µF = 0.000033 F. Now we can just plug numbers into the equation:
>
> $$V = \frac{Q}{C}$$
> $$= \frac{0.0023}{0.000033}$$
> $$\approx 69.7\,\mathrm{V}$$
>
> Therefore, when the capacitor discharges, it will discharge at 69.7 V.

Within a circuit, capacitors are typically used in places where voltages vary. Until the voltage in the capacitor equals the voltage in the circuit, the capacitor will pull charge out of the circuit. When the voltage in the capacitor exceeds the voltage in the circuit, the capacitor will put charge back into the circuit. This dynamic will serve as the core principle used when designing circuits with capacitors.

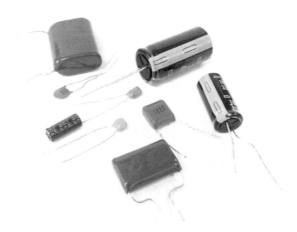

**Figure 16-3.** *Several Different Types of Capacitors (Shutterstock/ Muhammad Anuar bin Jamal)*

# 16.3  Types of Capacitors

There are numerous types of capacitors available, each varying in the types of materials they are made of, the internal geometry of the capacitor, and the packaging. Figure 16-3 shows many different types of capacitors that are available.

However, the most important feature of capacitors besides their capacitance is whether they are **polarized** or **non-polarized**. In a *non-polarized capacitor*, it doesn't matter which way you attach the leads. Either side can be the more positive or more negative side. The most common type of non-polarized capacitor is the circle-shaped ceramic disk capacitor. While ceramic disk capacitors are easy to use, they suffer from having limited capacitance.

In a *polarized capacitor*, however, one lead *must* stay more positive than the other lead, or you risk damaging the capacitor. The most common type of polarized capacitor is the electrolytic capacitor. Electrolytic capacitors look like little barrels with leads coming out of them. They usually have much higher capacitances than ceramic disk capacitors, but you have to be sure that the polarity is correct and never switches direction.

241

On polarized capacitors, it is important to know which lead is positive and which is negative. There are several different ways that a manufacturer might indicate this:

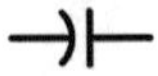

$$\dashv\vdash$$

**Figure 16-4.** *A Polarized Capacitor Symbol*

1. One or both of the leads can be marked with their respective polarities (+ or -).

2. The negative lead can be marked with a large stripe.

3. The positive lead can be longer than the negative.

Many manufacturers do all three.

In a circuit schematic, if a polarized capacitor is called for, it will use a special capacitor symbol as shown in Figure 16-4. The only difference is that one side is curved. In a polarized capacitor, the straight side is the positive side, and the curved side is the negative side. Sometimes polarized capacitors are marked with plus (+) and minus symbols (-) instead of (or in addition to) having a straight side and a curved side.

On any capacitor, it is important to know the capacitance of the capacitor you are looking at. On larger capacitors (especially on electrolytics), manufacturers can print the full capacitance including the units directly on the capacitors. However, many capacitors are extremely small and can't fit that much information on them.

For smaller-sized capacitors, the capacitance is described by three digits and an optional letter. The third digit is how many zeros to add to the end of the other two digits, and then the whole number is the capacitance in picofarads. So, if the number is 234, then the capacitance is 230,000 pF (23 followed by four zeros). If the number is 230, then the capacitance is 23 pF.

The letter at the end tells the *tolerance* of the capacitor—how much the capacitance is likely to vary from its markings. Common letters are J (±5%), K (±10%), and M (±20%).

# 16.4 Charging and Discharging a Capacitor

To charge up a capacitor almost instantly to a specific voltage, you can (as we also did earlier in the chapter) directly connect the positive and negative leads of the battery to the leads of the capacitor. Once it it charged, you can use the capacitor as a very tiny battery for a project.

In Figure 16-5, we see two simple circuits and an electrolytic capacitor. For this circuit to really work, it helps to have an electrolytic capacitor at least 100 μF and a resitor at least 10 kΩ. So, first, build the LED circuit on the right side of Figure 16-5 on a breadboard. However, don't connect any power to the power rails. Next, take the capacitor, and touch the positive lead of the capacitor to the positive terminal of the 9 V battery and the negative lead of the capacitor to the negative terminal. *Do not let the leads of the capacitor touch each other.* Hold it there for a second or two to allow the capacitor to fully charge. Now, *without touching the leads of the capacitor,* place the capacitor so that the positive lead goes into the positive rail of your breadboard and the negative lead goes into the negative rail of your breadboard. When you do this, the capacitor will power your LED project for a few seconds.

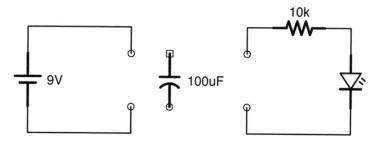

***Figure 16-5.*** *Using a Capacitor as a Battery*

Now, you will notice that the LED gets dimmer before it goes out. Why does this happen?

Remember that the voltage that the capacitor yields is based on the charge that is present in it. So, going back to Equation 16.2, we can see that the voltage is based on the charge that is in the capacitor. When the capacitor is connected, it will start with a 9 V discharge, since that is what the battery was able to put into the capacitor. However, the capacitor is using up its charge to power the project. This means that as soon as its charge starts leaving, the voltage starts going down, since the voltage is related to how much charge is inside the capacitor.

**Example 16.9** If we use the components listed in Figure 16-5, how much charge does the battery initially store in the capacitor?

We can use Equation 16.1 to determine this:

$$Q = C \cdot V$$
$$= 100 \mu F . 9V$$
$$= 0.000100F . 9V$$
$$= 0.0009 \text{coulombs}$$

**Example 16.10** After 0.0003 coulomb of charge has been discharged, what voltage is the capacitor discharging at?

To find this out, we first have to find out how much charge is *remaining* in the capacitor. So, to find this out, we just subtract the amount of charge that has been discharged from our starting charge. This gives $0.0009 - 0.0003 = 0.0006$ coulomb.

Now, we can use Equation 16.2 to find out what voltage the capacitor is discharging at:

$$V = \frac{Q}{C}$$
$$= \frac{0.0006}{0.000100}$$
$$= 6\,\mathrm{V}$$

Therefore, the capacitor is discharging at 6 V.

## 16.5 Series and Parallel Capacitances

Just like resistors, capacitors can be used either in series or in parallel. In fact, they use the same equations for series and parallel capacitance as do resistors. However, there is *one big difference*. The parallel and series versions of the equations are *reversed* for capacitors.

If we want to double resistance in a circuit, we simply add another resistor of the same size in series. If I want to double my capacitance, I can add in another capacitor of the same size. However, for the capacitor, we would add the capacitor *in parallel*. The following is the formula for adding capacitance in parallel:

$$C_T = C_1 + C_2 + \ldots \qquad (16.3)$$

If we want to put capacitors in series, we would use a formula that is exactly like the formula for resistors in parallel:

$$C_T = \frac{1}{\dfrac{1}{C_1} + \dfrac{1}{C_2} + \ldots} \qquad (16.4)$$

245

**Example 16.11** If I have a 100 μF capacitor in series with a 200 μF capacitor, how much total capacitance do I have?

To do this, we use Equation 16.4. It is best to convert our capacitances to farads first. It does not matter as long as the units are the same, but it is good practice to convert to farads so you don't forget when you start doing capacitances in different units. 100 μF is the same as 0.0001 F, and 200 μF is the same as 0.0002 μF.

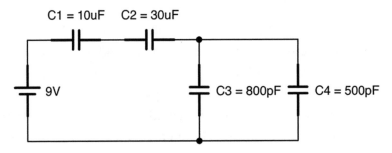

C1 = 10uF    C2 = 30uF

9V

C3 = 800pF    C4 = 500pF

*Figure 16-6.* *Capacitors in Series and Parallel*

Now, we will plug these values into the equation:

$$C_T = \cfrac{1}{\cfrac{1}{C_1} + \cfrac{1}{C_2}}$$

$$= \cfrac{1}{\cfrac{1}{0.0001F} + \cfrac{1}{0.0002F}}$$

$$= \cfrac{1}{10000 + 5000}$$

$$= \cfrac{1}{15000}$$

$$= 0.0000666F$$

$$= 66.6\,\mu F$$

**Example 16.12** Just as we did for resistors, we can combine a variety of parallel and series capacitances for a single capacitance value. For instance, take the circuit in Figure 16-6. What is the total capacitance of this circuit?

First, we can start by converting all of the capacitances to farads. This will make combining everything easier down the road. In that case, $C_1 = 0.00001$ F, $C_2 = 0.00003$ F, $C_3 = 0.0000000008$ F, and $C_4 = 0.0000000005$ F. C3 and C4 are in parallel, so we can combine them using the parallel formula (Equation 16.3):

$$
\begin{aligned}
C_T &= C_3 + C_4 \\
&= 0.000000000F + 0.0000000005F \\
&= 0.0000000013F
\end{aligned}
$$

Now, if we substitute that capacitance in for C3 and C4, we can use the series formula (Equation 16.4) to find the total capacitance of the circuit:

$$
\begin{aligned}
C_T &= \cfrac{1}{\cfrac{1}{C_1} + \cfrac{1}{C_2} + \cfrac{1}{C_{3\&4}}} \\
&= \cfrac{1}{\cfrac{1}{0.00001} + \cfrac{1}{0.00003} + \cfrac{1}{0.0000000013}} \\
&= \cfrac{1}{100000 + 33333.33 + 769230769.23} \\
&= \cfrac{1}{769364102.56} \\
&= 0.0000000013F \\
&= 1.3nF
\end{aligned}
$$

So the total capacitance of the circuit is 1.3 nF.

# 16.6  Capacitors and AC and DC

One important characteristic of a capacitor is that it *allows* the flow of AC (alternating current) but it blocks the flow of DC (direct current). To understand why this is, let's think about how capacitors operate.

Capacitors, when they are charging, essentially act as short circuits. As positive charge flows into the capacitor at one terminal, negative charge flows into the other side. An *inflow* of negative charge to that side means that there is a net *outflow* of positive charge on that side. So, *even though the physical electrons never cross the boundary between the plates*, the total charge *actually moves* from one side to the other.

However, this situation is *temporary* because, as the capacitor gets more full of charge, new charge is less likely to enter. Once the capacitor is fully charged (based on the voltage), no new charge can flow into one side to cause the charge to go out to the other.

Once the capacitor is charged, *current stops flowing through it*. If the voltage level on one of the leads *changes*, then charge will flow until the change is compensated for by the capacitor charging or discharging.

Thus, because there is a barrier between the two sides of a capacitor, it is only when the voltage *changes* that the current flows *through* a capacitor. If the voltage stays the same, then charge will stop flowing through the capacitor as soon as it reaches capacity for that voltage.

Because of this, we say that capacitors *allow* AC but *block* DC. This rule of thumb will help us use capacitors in a variety of circuits later on.

# 16.7 Using Capacitors in a Circuit

In this section, we will discuss the uses of capacitors in a circuit. We haven't discussed enough to actually use capacitors in these ways, but I thought it would be helpful to see why capacitors are used so you can see why you should care about these things.

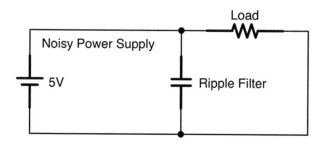

**Figure 16-7.** *A Capacitor Filtering a Noisy Power Supply*

The first thing that capacitors are used for is for filtering noisy signals, especially in power sources. Imagine that you had a power source which, instead of delivering a constant voltage, the voltage would wobble a bit. If you placed a capacitor in parallel with this circuit, the power source would charge the capacitor up. Then, if the power source dropped a bit, the capacitor would start discharging to compensate. Likewise, if the power source increased, the capacitor would absorb some of that increase by storing the charge.

Thus, by acting as a temporary location to store extra charge, the capacitor can smooth out ripples in a signal, as seen in Figure 16-7. This sort of usage is known as a *filtering* capacitor because it filters out noise.

This can be seen as another implementation of our rule that capacitors allow AC to flow but block DC. When the source voltage has a ripple, the *ripple itself* gets shunted to ground by the capacitor. However, under normal operation, the DC part of the current can't flow through the capacitor and just continues on to the load.

On many ICs that have fluctuating power requirements, you will find many of their spec sheets recommending one or more capacitors on their power supply or other pins in order to filter out the noise.

Another way of using capacitors is as a **coupling capacitor**. A coupling capacitor is used when you have *both* an AC signal and a DC signal combined. This will happen a lot when we talk about amplification. What happens is that we will have an amplified signal, but we *only* want the AC portion of the signal. We can do that by adding in a capacitor to join the segment of the circuit that has both AC and DC components to the segment of the circuit that only wants the AC component. Only the variations in the voltage, not the base voltage, will be transmitted through the capacitor.

Another way that capacitors are used is for filtering specific frequencies. Higher-frequency signals are easily transmitted through a capacitor, but low-frequency signals are essentially blocked as if they were DC. The frequencies that are allowed are based on the capacitance. If you put a capacitor in series with the signal path, then it will only allow higher frequencies. If you put a capacitor in parallel with the signal path, then it will ony allow lower frequencies (the higher frequencies will be shunted to ground).

## CAPACITOR SAFETY

If you see a capacitor in any sort of equipment, do not touch it, even with the power off. Because capacitors store charge, they can still hold onto the charge even after the power is off. If you need to touch a capacitor for some reason, use a resistor to discharge it. Placing a large (megaohm) resistor between the leads of a capacitor (without touching the leads yourself!) for a few seconds should drain most capacitors. You can also use a multimeter to determine that the capacitor is drained (0 volt).

# Review

In this chapter, we learned the following:

1. An electric field is generated wherever there is an accumulated charge.

2. A capacitor is a device that stores electric energy by holding two opposing charges.

3. Capacitors are sized by their capacitance which is measured in farads.

4. Because a farad is so large, capacitors are usually measured in microfarads, nanofarads, or picofarads.

5. Polarized capacitors (usually electrolytic capacitors) have distinct positive and negative terminals, while non-polarized capacitors (usually ceramic disk capacitors) can go either way.

6. When a battery is connected to a capacitor, it will store a charge on the capacitor.

7. The equation for the charge ($Q$) stored on the capacitor when a battery is connected is $Q = C \cdot V$ where $C$ is the capacitance in farads, $V$ is the voltage, and $Q$ is the charge in coulombs.

8. By rearranging the equation, we can determine, for a given amount of charge, how much voltage a capacitor will discharge when it is allowed to: $V = \dfrac{Q}{C}$.

9. As the capacitor discharges its charge through the wire to create current, the amount of charge remaining will decrease, which will also lower the voltage it is putting out.

10. Capacitors with small packages are often marked with a three-digit code, where the third digit is the number of zeros to add to the other two digits and the final number is in picofarads.

11. When multiple capacitors are used together, their capacitances can be combined similar to resistors, but with the series and parallel equations switched.

12. The series capacitance equation is as follows:

$$C_T = \frac{1}{\dfrac{1}{C_1} + \dfrac{1}{C_2} + \ldots}$$

13. The parallel capacitance equation is as follows:
$C_T = C_1 + C_2 + \ldots$

14. Capacitors allow the flow of AC through them but block the flow of DC.

15. Capacitors can be used to split AC (high-frequency) and DC (low-frequency) portions of a signal. The AC portion will travel through the capacitor, while the DC portion will remain on one terminal side.

16. Capacitors can be used to filter audio frequencies, filter power supply ripples, operate as voltage boosters, and couple together a combined AC/DC circuit with an AC-only circuit.

# Exercises

1. Convert 23 F to microfarads.

2. Convert 15 µF to farads.

3. Convert 35 pF to farads.

4. Convert 0.0002 F to microfarads.

5. Convert 0.0030 µF to farads.

6. If a voltage of 6 V is applied to a 55 µF capacitor, how much charge would it store?

7. If a voltage of 2 V is applied to a 13 pF capacitor, how much charge would it store?

8. If a 132 µF capacitor is holding 0.02 coulomb of charge, how many volts will it produce when it begins to discharge?

9. If a 600 pF capacitor is holding 0.03 coulomb of charge, how many volts will it produce when it begins to discharge?

10. A 121 µF capacitor is connected to a battery. After some fluctuation, the capacitor has 0.00089 coulomb of charge stored in it, and the battery is reading 8.9 V. Is the capacitor going to be charging or discharging at this point?

# CHAPTER 17

# Capacitors as Timers

In this chapter, we are going to learn how to measure the time it takes for a capacitor to charge. Once we learn this, we can use capacitors for timers—both for delaying a signal and for creating an oscillating circuit.

## 17.1  Time Constants

As we learned in Chapter 16, when a voltage is applied to a capacitor, it will store energy by storing a charge on its plates, the amount of charge being based on the voltage supplied and the capacitance of the capacitor (see Equation 16.1).

The cases we examined in Chapter 16 generally had the battery connected directly to the capacitor. In such cases, the capacitor charges to the source voltage almost immediately. However, if a capacitor charges through a resistor (instead of being directly connected to the battery), then it takes much longer to fill the capacitor to capacity than if it were connected to the battery directly. In fact, it never *fully* reaches capacity, though it gets close enough that we say that it does.

Having a resistor in series with a capacitor is a configuration known as an **RC (resistor-capacitor) circuit**. The amount of time it takes a capacitor to charge is based on both the resistance of the resistor and the capacitance of the capacitor. The actual equation for this is kind of complicated, but there is a simple trick that suffices for nearly every situation, known as the RC time constant.

© Jonathan Bartlett 2020
J. Bartlett, *Electronics for Beginners*, https://doi.org/10.1007/978-1-4842-5979-5_17

The RC time constant is merely the product of the resistance (in ohms) multiplied by the capacitance (in farads) which will yield the RC time constant in seconds. The RC time constant can be used to determine how long it will take to charge a capacitor to a given level (we will talk about what this level is in a moment). So, for instance, if I have a 100 µF capacitor and a 500 Ω resistor, the RC time constant is 0.0001 ∗ 500 = 0.05 second.

This constant can then be used with the table in Figure 17-1 to determine how long it will take to charge a capacitor to a given level.[1]

| # of Time Constants | % of Voltage | % of Current |
|---|---|---|
| 0.5 | 39.3% | 60.7% |
| 0.7 | 50.3% | 49.7% |
| 1 | 63.2% | 36.8% |
| 2 | 86.5% | 13.5% |
| 3 | 95.0% | 5.0% |
| 4 | 98.2% | 1.8% |
| 5 | 99.3% | 0.7% |

*Figure 17-1.* *RC Time Constants*

For instance, if I wait for 2 time constants (in this case, 0.05 ∗ 2 = 0.1 second), my capacitor will be charged to 86.5% of the supply voltage. The current flowing through it will be at 13.5% of what current would be flowing if there was just a straight wire instead of a capacitor.

---

[1]For those curious how these numbers are calculated, see Appendix D, Section D.7.3, "Time Constants."

While a capacitor is never really "fully charged" (because it never fully reaches 100%), in this book, we will use 5 time constants to consider a capacitor fully charged.

> **Example 17.13** I have a power supply that is 7 V and a capacitor that is a 100 µF capacitor. I want it to take 9 seconds to charge my capacitor. What size of a resistor do I need to use to do this?
>
> To solve this problem, we need to work backward. Remember, we are considering 5 time constants to be fully charged. Therefore, the time constant we are hoping to achieve is 9/5 = 1.8 seconds. The capacitance is 100 µF, which is 0.0001 F. Since the time constant is merely the product of the capacitance and resistance, we can solve for this as follows:
>
> $$RC \text{ TimeConstant} = \text{capacitance} \cdot \text{resistance}$$
> $$1.8 = 0.0001 * R$$
> $$0.0001 * R = 1.8$$
> $$R = \frac{1.8}{0.0001}$$
> $$R = 18000$$

Therefore, to make it take 9 seconds to charge the capacitor, we need to use an 18 kΩ resistor.

In the same way, if we connect the capacitor to ground through the resistor instead of to the voltage supply, the capacitor will discharge in the same way that it charged. It will begin discharging a lot, but then, as it gets closer to zero, it will level off the amount that it is discharging. You would then read Figure 17-1 to know what percentage of the voltage/current the capacitor has *discharged*.

**Example 17.14** Suppose a 100 μF capacitor has been charged up to 7 V and then is disconnected from the power supply, but the ground connection remains. We then connect the positive terminal of the capacitor to a 5 kΩ resistor that connects to ground. After 2 seconds, how much voltage is remaining in the capacitor?

To find this out, we first need to find the RC time constant of the circuit.

$$T = 5k\Omega * 100\mu F$$
$$= 5,000\,\Omega * 0.0001\,F$$
$$= 0.5 \text{ seconds}$$

So the RC time constant is 0.5 second.

So, after 2 seconds, we have performed 4 RC time constants. Looking at Figure 17-1, we have discharged 98.2% of the capacitor's voltage. This means that the amount of voltage *lost* should be 0.982 * 7 V = 6.874 V. If we have lost that much voltage, that means we should subtract it, so the remaining voltage is 7 V − 6.874 V = 0.126 V.

So the voltage after 2 seconds will be 0.125 V.

# 17.2 Constructing a Simple Timer Circuit

Let's say that we want a circuit that, when turned on, *waits* for a certain amount of time and then does something. How might we do it?

Think of it this way. We can use capacitor charging to give us a time delay. However, we need something that "notices" when the time delay is finished. In other words, we need a way to trigger something when a certain threshold is crossed.

What happens to the capacitor as it charges? The voltage across its terminals changes. When it is first connected to the circuit, there is zero voltage across its terminals. As it charges, the voltage across the capacitor's terminals keeps going up until it matches the supply voltage. Therefore, we know when we have hit our target time based on when the voltage is at a certain level. But how will we know when we are at the right voltage? Have we done a circuit so far that detects voltages? What component did we use?

If you remember back in Chapter 11, we used the LM393 to compare voltages. We supplied the LM393 with a *reference* voltage, and then it triggered when our other voltage went above that voltage. We can do the same thing here.

What we will construct is a circuit that waits for 5 seconds and then turns on an LED. In order to do this, we will need to choose (a) a reference voltage to use, (b) a resistor/capacitor combination that will surpass the reference voltage after a certain amount of time, and (c) an output circuit that lights up the LED.

There are virtually infinite combinations we could choose from for our reference voltage, resistance, and capacitance. In fact, the supply voltage doesn't matter so much since what we are looking at are *percentages* of the supply voltage, which will be the same no matter what the actual voltage is.

For this example, we will use a basic 5 V supply and make the reference voltage to be half of the supply voltage. This allows us to use any two equivalent resistors for a voltage divider to get our reference voltage.

Now, since the reference voltage is half of our supply voltage, we will use the table in Figure 17-1 to determine how many time constants that needs to be. The table says that for 50% of voltage, it will take 0.7 time constant (it is actually 50.3%, but we are not being that exact).

Therefore, the equation for our resistor and capacitor is

$$T = 5 \text{ seconds}$$
$$5 \text{ seconds} = 0.7 \cdot R \cdot C$$
$$\frac{5}{0.7} = R \cdot C$$
$$7.14 = R \cdot C$$

So we can use any resistor and capacitor such that the ohms multiplied by the farads equals 7.14. I usually use 100 μF capacitors for larger time periods such as this because they are larger and because being exactly 0.0001 F, it makes it easier to calculate with. Therefore, we can very simply calculate the needed resistor for this capacitor:

$$7.14 = R \cdot C$$
$$7.14 = R \cdot 0.0001$$
$$\frac{7.14}{0.0001} = R$$
$$71400 = R$$

Therefore, we need a resistor that is about 71, 400 Ω. We could choose a combination of resistors that hits this exactly, but for our purposes, we only need to get close. In my case, the closest resistor I have is 68,000 Ω (i.e., 68 kΩ). That is close enough (though I could get even closer by adding in a 3 kΩ resistor in series).

Figure 17-2 shows the full circuit. When building this circuit, don't forget that the comparator also has to be connected to the supply voltage and ground as well! As you can see, R2 and R3 form the voltage divider that provides the reference voltage for the comparator at half of the supply voltage. The values for R2 and R3 are arbitrarily chosen, but they must be equal to get the reference voltage. I chose medium-high values for these resistors so as to not waste current with the voltage divider. The circuit made by R1 and C1 is the timing circuit. When the circuit is first plugged in, C1 is at voltage level 0, essentially acting as a short circuit while it first begins to store charge. At 0 volt, this is obviously less than our reference voltage. However, as the capacitor charges, less and less current can flow into C1. Its voltage level increases under the rules of the RC time constant. After 0.7 time constant, the voltage will be above the voltage level set by the reference voltage, and our voltage comparator will switch on.

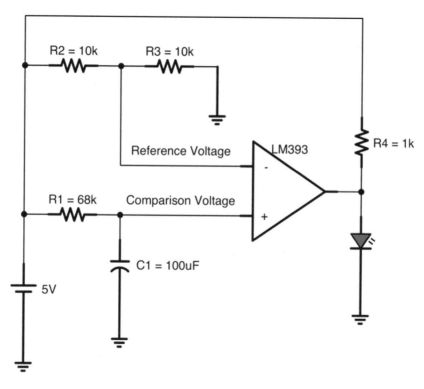

**Figure 17-2.** *A Simple Timer for an LED*

Remember, though, from Chapter 11, that the LM393 operates using a pull-up resistor. That is, the comparator doesn't ever source current. It will sink current (voltage level 0 when the + input is less than the – input) or disconnect (when the + input is greater than the – input). Therefore, R4 is providing a pull-up resistor to supply power to the LED when the LM393 disconnects.

Figure 17-3 shows this circuit laid out on the breadboard. We are using the second voltage comparator of the LM393 just because it was a little easier to show the wiring for it. If you need to see the pinout for the LM393 again, it was back in Figure 11-4.

Notice the prominence of our basic circuits from Chapter 9 on the breadboard. On the top, we have a combination pull-up resistor which is also acting as a current-limiting resistor (as they often do). On the bottom left, we have a voltage divider.

On the bottom right, we have our new timing circuit, which looks a lot like a voltage divider. In fact, it acts like one too, where the voltage varies by time! If you think about what the capacitor is doing, when we first apply voltage, it acts like a short circuit—in other words, no resistance. This means that there is 0 volt across the capacitor and the resistor is eating up all of the voltage. But, as the capacitor fills up, it increases voltage, which it is *dividing* with the resistor! Just like before where we had a sensor which created a sensor-based variable voltage divider, here we have what is essentially a time-based variable voltage divider.

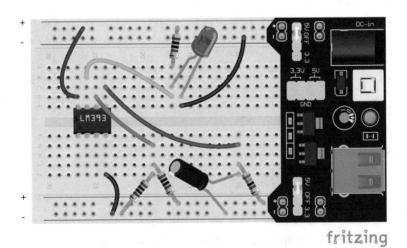

*Figure 17-3.* *The Capacitor Timer Circuit on a Breadboard*

# 17.3 Resetting Our Timer

The timer is great, except for one thing—how do we turn it off? You might have noticed that, even if you disconnect power to the circuit, when you turn it back on, it doesn't do any timing anymore! Remember, the capacitor is *storing* charge. When you turn off the circuit, it is *still* storing the charge.

Now, you can very simply get rid of the charge by putting a wire between the legs of the capacitor. However, for larger capacitors, you would need to do this with a resistor instead of a wire in order to keep there from being a dangerous spark (the resistor limits the current, which makes the discharge slower). But how do we do this with a circuit?

What we can do is add a button or switch that will do the same thing as putting a wire or resistor across the legs of the capacitor. Figure 17-4 shows how to do this.

Now let's look at how this circuit works. First of all, we added two components, the switch and the R5 resistor connected to it. To understand what this does, pretend for a minute that the resistor isn't there. What happens when we push the button? That would create a direct link from the positive side of the capacitor to ground. Since the negative side of the capacitor is also connected to ground, that means that these two points would be directly connected. Thus, they would be at the *same* voltage. This would be achieved by the charge suddenly rushing from one side to another to balance out.

If the capacitor were larger or the voltages greater, this might be somewhat dangerous. You would have a large current and a large voltage for a short period of time (which would yield a large wattage), which could blow something out. Therefore, it is good practice to use a small resistor between the button and ground. The resistor should be *much* smaller than the resistor used to charge the capacitor. The specific size doesn't matter too much—it needs to be small enough to discharge it quickly and large enough to prevent a spark when you push the button. You can use the same time constants for discharging the capacitor that you used for charging it. However, keep in mind that the charging circuit is still running! That's why the resistor has to be small—it has to discharge the capacitor *while* the other resistor is trying to charge it.

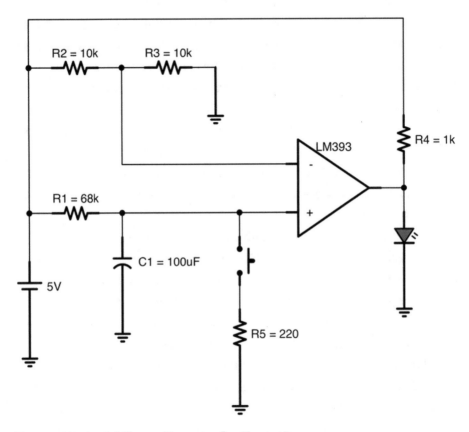

**Figure 17-4.** *Adding a Reset to the Capacitor*

Also notice R1 and R5. When the button is being pushed, what is happening to them? Think back to our basic resistor circuits. If we have two resistors, with a wire coming out of the middle, what is that? It's a voltage divider! So not only is R5 being a current-limiting resistor for the button, it is also acting as a voltage divider in concert with R1.

What this means is that the capacitor will only discharge down to the level of voltage division between these resistors. That's fine, as long as it is low enough. You will find that in electronics, "close enough" often counts. The trick is knowing how close is close enough and how close is still too far.

However, usually we can perform some basic calculations to figure this out. Since R1 is 68 kΩ and R5 is 200 Ω, what is the voltage at the point of division? If we use a 9 V supply, using the formula from Equation 9.1, then we can see that

$$V_{OUT} = V_{IN} \cdot \frac{R_5}{R_1 + R_5}$$
$$= 9 \cdot \frac{220}{68000 + 220}$$
$$= 9 \cdot \frac{220}{68220}$$
$$\approx 9 \cdot 0.00322$$
$$\approx 0.029\,V$$

So, as you can see, when the button is pushed, the final voltage of the capacitor, while not *absolutely* 0 volt, is pretty darn close.

Also note that, if we wanted, we can reverse the action of this circuit. By swapping our two inputs to the voltage comparator, we can make the circuit be on for 5 seconds and then switch off.

# Review

In this chapter, we learned the following:

1.  Having a resistor and capacitor in series with each other is known as an RC circuit.

2.  In an RC circuit, the amount of time it takes for a capacitor to charge to the supply voltage is based on the capacitance of the capacitor and the resistance of the resistor.

3.  The RC *time constant* is a convenient way to think
    about how long it takes for a capacitor to charge in
    RC circuits.

4.  The RC time constant is calculated by multiplying
    the resistance (in ohms) by the capacitance (in
    farads) with the result being the number of seconds
    in 1 RC time constant.

5.  The table in Figure 17-1 shows how long it takes to
    charge a capacitor to different percentages of supply
    voltage as a multiple of RC time constants.

6.  The RC time constant chart can also be used to
    calculate the amount of time it takes for a capacitor
    to discharge to ground if it is disconnected from
    its source and connected through a resistor to
    ground. In this case, Figure 17-1 is used to tell what
    percentage of the voltage has been *discharged*.

7.  A timer can be constructed by using a comparator
    and an RC circuit along with a reference voltage
    provided by a voltage divider. By tweaking the RC
    circuit, the timing can be changed.

8.  After charging a capacitor, a means needs to be
    provided to discharge it as well, such as a button
    leading to ground.

9.  Such discharge methods need to have resistance to
    prevent sparks and other failures, but not too much
    resistance as they can accidentally form voltage
    dividers with other resistors in the circuit and
    prevent full discharge.

10.  Even as our circuits get more advanced, the basic circuits we found in Chapter 9 are still dominating our circuit designs.

# Apply What You Have Learned

1.  If I have an RC circuit with a resistor of 10 Ω and a capacitor of 2 F, what is the RC time constant of this circuit?

2.  In the previous question, how many seconds does it take to charge my capacitor to approximately 50% of supply voltage?

3.  If I have an RC circuit with a resistor of 30,000 Ω and a capacitor of 0.001 F, what is the RC time constant of this circuit?

4.  In the previous question, what percentage of the capacitor's voltage is charged after 60 seconds?

5.  If I have an RC circuit with a resistor of 25 kΩ and a capacitor of 20 μF, what is the RC time constant of this circuit?

6.  Give a resistor and capacitor combination that will yield an RC time constant of 0.25 second.

7.  Reconfigure the circuit in Figure 17-2 to wait for 3 seconds. Draw the whole circuit.

8.  Redraw the previous circuit and circle each basic resistor circuit pattern and label it.

# CHAPTER 18

# Introduction to Oscillator Circuits

In Chapter 17, we learned how to use RC (resistor-capacitor) circuits to create timers. In this chapter, we are going to use our concept of timing circuits to move from one-time timer circuits to *oscillating* circuits.

## 18.1 Oscillation Basics

So far, most of the circuits we have made have been fairly directional. You do an action (i.e., press a button) and then something happens, but then the circuit just maintains a steady state after that. In Chapter 17, we at least added a delay—allowing the circuit to do something *later*.

However, if you want actions to continue on into the future, you need to not only have delays, you need to have *oscillations*. **Oscillation** means to go back and forth. An oscillating circuit is one that goes back and forth continually between two states—usually zero voltage and some positive voltage. Imagine blinking lights at Christmas. These lights go from a state of zero voltage (off) to a state of positive voltage (on). And they go back and forth between these states over and over again as long as there is power in the circuit. These are oscillating circuits.

© Jonathan Bartlett 2020
J. Bartlett, *Electronics for Beginners*, https://doi.org/10.1007/978-1-4842-5979-5_18

An oscillator is usually described by either its **period** or its **frequency**. The period of an oscillator is how many seconds it takes to go through one complete cycle. So, if I had lights that blinked on for 1 second and then off for 2 seconds (and continued repeating in that fashion), the period would be 3 seconds.

The frequency of an oscillation is the number of times that the system cycles every second, which is merely the reciprocal of the period (i.e., one divided by the period). So, in the example given, since the period was 3 seconds, the frequency is $\frac{1}{3}$ cycle per second. The "cycles per second" unit of frequency also has a special name—**hertz** (often abbreviated as Hz). Therefore, we would say that our blinking lights blinked at a frequency of $\frac{1}{3}$ Hz.

> **Example 18.15** Let's say that we have an oscillator that turns a light on for 4 seconds and then turns off for 4 seconds and repeats this continually. What is the period and frequency of this oscillator?
>
> The period is merely the total time it takes to go through one complete cycle. Therefore
>
> $$\text{period} = 4 \text{ seconds on} + 4 \text{ seconds off}$$
> $$= 8 \text{ seconds}$$
>
> So what is the frequency of this oscillator? Simple— just take the reciprocal of the period. That makes the frequency $\frac{1}{8}$ Hz.
>
> **Example 18.16** On a piano, the middle-C key plays a sound with a frequency of 261.6 Hz. What is the period of this sound?

Since the frequency is the reciprocal of the period, it works the other way around as well—the period is the reciprocal of the frequency. Therefore, the period is simply $\dfrac{1}{261.6}$ second. Or, as a decimal, this is 0.00382 second.

There are many other factors that are important to various kinds of oscillations, such as the speed of transition between states, what percentage of time each state is achieved, and so on. However, the period/frequency is a good way to summarize the behavior of an oscillator into a single number.

# 18.2  The Importance of Oscillating Circuits

Oscillating circuits are important in electronics for a number of reasons. First, obviously, is blinky lights. Who goes into electronics without being enamored by blinking lights? But, more importantly, the following are all applications of oscillators in circuits:

Sound Production: Sounds and tones are made by moving a speaker back and forth, which is moved back and forth by electricity oscillating between different voltages.

Time Clocks: Every clock on earth operates by an oscillator. The clock simply counts the number of oscillations that have occurred to know whether or not to advance another time step (second, minute, etc.).

Hardware Coordination Clocks: In computers and other advanced hardware, system events are coordinated based on signals from an oscillating circuit. When the clock changes state from off to on (or the reverse), then the circuit does the next step in the process. The clock keeps the various circuits synchronized and keeps them from stepping on each other.

Radio Transmissions: Oscillators are used in radios in order to encode signals onto "carrier waves," which are just oscillating signals run at a specific frequency.

Servo Motors: A servo is a motor which moves an arm to a specific angle (i.e., think of a car's steering wheel). Servos are usually operated by frequencies, where each frequency specifies a different angle to move.

Let's look in more depth about how sound is produced by oscillation. You hear sound through your eardrum, which communicates vibrations it detects to your brain which you interpret as sound. Therefore, any sound that you hear is merely the vibrations of your eardrum. In other words, your eardrum *oscillates* back and forth, which you interpret as sound.

What makes your eardrum move back and forth? The answer is oscillations in the air. What makes those oscillations happen? Oscillations in the sound speaker. When the speaker moves back and forth, it moves the air which produces sound that you hear.

But what moves the speaker back and forth? Oscillations in the voltage and current supplied to the speaker. The speaker has a magnet attached to it which responds to changes in voltage in the wire. As the voltage in the wire increases, it moves the speaker in one direction. As the voltage decreases, the speaker moves in the other direction. Thus, the oscillations in voltage eventually wind up as sound for your ears.

# 18.3  Building an Oscillator

Let's think for a moment of what it would take to build an oscillator. An oscillator has (at least) two different states—on and off.[1] Then, you have a time period of changing from one state to the other.

What sort of circuit have we looked at that provides a time period?

As we saw in Chapter 17, RC (resistor-capacitor) circuits can provide us with time delays. We can then use these time delays as the time periods between the states of the oscillation. What we need is a circuit that will give out a state (we'll called it S1) for a time period (we'll call it T1) and then move to another state (we'll call it S2) and stay there for another time period (we'll call it T2). After T2 is finished, the circuit moves back to state S1 and begins again.

Now, it is possible that we might be able to build such a circuit using multiple RC timers with multiple comparators. It is doable, but it is harder than it sounds. Thankfully, there is an integrated circuit that is built for making such timers—the NE555, often referred to as just a "555 timer" or just a "555." The NE555 is a very flexible component, and engineers are constantly finding new ways to make use of it. However, we will just focus on using it as a basic oscillator.

It is easiest to describe how a 555 works if we start out by showing a simple circuit with it. The circuit in Figure 18-2 blinks an LED on and off.

The order of the pins on the actual 555 chip is a little confusing (see Figure 18-1). In order to make understanding the circuit in Figure 18-2 easier, I have simply put tags for each pin in the diagram, so you can see where they each belong *functionally*.

---

[1]You can build an oscillator with more than two states, but we won't be concerned with those circuits in this book, though the setup is similar.

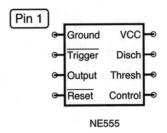

**NE555**

**Figure 18-1.**  *The 555 Pinout Diagram*

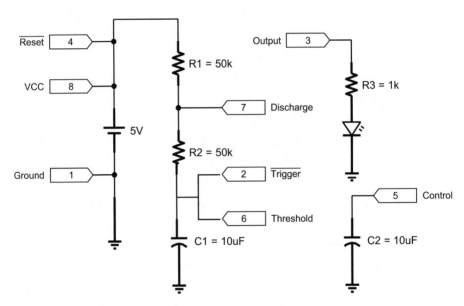

**Figure 18-2.**  *A Schematic of a Simple 555 Oscillation Circuit*

First, let's look at the pins on the left-hand side of Figure 18-1 that are directly connected to the power rails. Pin 1 (Ground) and pin 8 (VCC) are easy enough—they are connected to ground and positive voltage, respectively. Pin 4 ($\overline{\text{Reset}}$) gets connected to the voltage source too. That is a reset pin which is activated if the pin receives a *low* voltage signal. Pins that are activated by low-voltage signals are often shown with a line over them.[2] In our case, we never want to reset the chip, so we will just tie the reset pin to positive voltage which will prevent any accidental resets from changes in voltages in the environment.

Now, on the right-hand side at the top, you can see the LED connected to pin 3 (Output). Pin 3 is simply the output pin. It is an active output, meaning that it will supply current to the output on its own. We don't need a pull-up resistor as we did for the LM393. Instead, we just need a current-limiting resistor for the LED. The regular NE555 output yields a voltage that is about 1.7 V less than the supply voltage and sources up to 200 mA before it breaks.

Note that there are other, low-power versions of the 555 timer that have other output characteristics. For instance, the LMC555 has an output voltage that is equal to the input voltage, but can only source about 100 mA. For our purposes, either one would work, as we are not doing anything precise with our output, nor are we sourcing very much current. However, any calculations we do will assume a typical NE555 component.

On the bottom right, pin 5 (Control) is connected through a 10 µF capacitor to ground. This is just a standard part of using the chip. You can't effectively include capacitors in integrated circuits larger than a few picofarads, so many chips specify certain capacitors be attached to certain pins. The NE555 uses a 10 µF capacitor on pin 5 to provide voltage stability. In Chapter 16, we learned that capacitors act essentially like little batteries. This capacitor is doing just that. It is providing a short-term supply of charge in case there is a sudden change in current needs within the chip. For instance, when the output goes active, there may be a sudden need for charge. This capacitor supplies a quickly available reservoir of charge to the chip so that sudden changes in current needs will not affect other chip properties.[3]

---

[2]Since most pins are activated by a higher voltage, pins that are activated with a lower voltage get the special designator.

[3]For most of our uses of the NE555, you can actually leave pin 5 unconnected—our usage of the chip is not so precise or power-hungry as to be affected in this way. Nonetheless, I show it connected so that you can see how it is *supposed* to be connected.

Down the middle of the schematic is where all of the action happens. This is what controls the oscillation. It is essentially an RC circuit with (a) an extra resistor and (b) a few tie-ins to the chip. As we will see shortly, the capacitor will alternately charge and discharge. The capacitor itself is attached to two voltage sensors on the chip. The first sensor, $\overline{\text{Trigger}}$, watches the voltage on the capacitor and activates if the voltage falls below $\frac{1}{3}$ of the supply voltage (the line over the name of the pin indicates that it activates on a low value). The second sensor, Threshold, watches the voltage and will activate if the voltage goes above $\frac{2}{3}$ of the supply voltage.

The oscillator works by moving the capacitor voltage back and forth between $\frac{1}{3}$ and $\frac{2}{3}$ of the supply voltage. It is fairly obvious to see how the capacitor charges—it is a basic RC circuit using both of the resistors R1 and R2. So how does the capacitor discharge? The capacitor discharges through the action of the Discharge pin, pin 7. When the 555 starts up, pin 7 essentially acts as if it were not connected to anything, so you can basically ignore it. When the capacitor goes over the $\frac{2}{3}$ supply voltage and triggers the Threshold pin, the 555 will then connect pin 7 to ground.

Think about what will happen if pin 7 is connected to ground. Will the capacitor charge? No, the current coming in through R1 will immediately go to ground because it is the easiest path. If the capacitor is charged up, is it above or below ground? It is obviously above ground. Therefore, current will flow *out of* the capacitor, through R2, and to ground. Thus, the capacitor discharges, but at a *different* rate than it charged. The RC circuit for the charging of the capacitor used both R1 and R2 for the resistance. However, the discharge of the capacitor only uses R2. Therefore, the discharge from $\frac{2}{3}$ voltage down to $\frac{1}{3}$ voltage will be faster than the charge up.

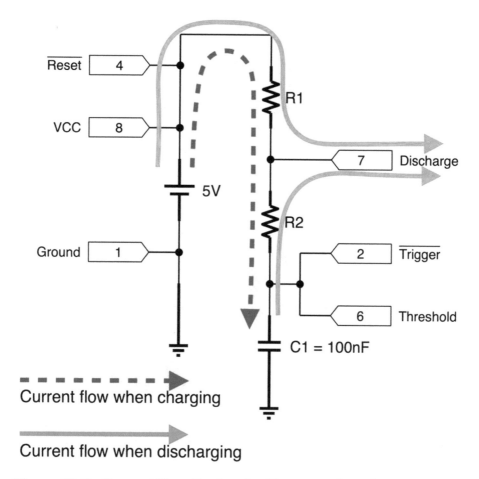

*Figure 18-3.* *Current Flow During the Charge and Discharge Phases*

Once the capacitor discharges down to $\frac{1}{3}$ of supply voltage, pin 2 ($\overline{\text{Trigger}}$) will detect this event and turn pin 7 off so that the capacitor can recharge again. Therefore, the capacitor will be continually charging and discharging from $\frac{1}{3}$ to $\frac{2}{3}$ of supply voltage, as the 555 turns pin 7 (connected to ground) on and off. This is also why having two resistors is so important. If we didn't have R1, when pin 7 connected to ground, it would make a short circuit between the supply voltage and ground.

Figure 18-3 shows the different current flows of this part of the circuit during the charging and discharging phases.

You may be wondering why there are two detectors connected to the capacitor and not just one. The reason for this is that having two different detectors allows for a *lot* of flexibility in how the 555 is wired. As mentioned earlier, there are a huge number of ways the 555 has been used, and some uses tie $\overline{\text{Trigger}}$ and Threshold to different parts of the circuit. For our purposes, both of these will always be used together.

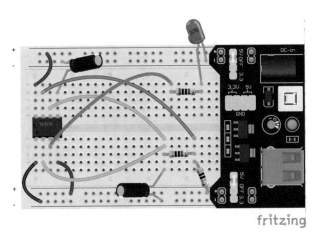

**Figure 18-4.**  *The 555 Oscillator Circuit on a Breadboard*

So how does this charging and discharging of the capacitor affect the output? Quite simply, when the capacitor is *charging*, the output is *on*. When the capacitor is *discharging*, the output is *off*. Note that when we first turn on the 555, the output will be on for a little bit longer than for the rest of the time. This is simply because when the circuit first starts up, it is charging all the way from 0 V instead of from $\frac{1}{3}$ of supply voltage.

You can see the completed 555 circuit on a breadboard in Figure 18-4. This should blink the light on for about two-thirds of a second and off for about a third of a second. This gives the total period of about 1 second and a frequency of about 1 Hz. In the next section, we'll see how to use RC time constants to calculate our own on and off times.

# 18.4 Calculating On and Off Times with the 555

Remember that the capacitor is charging and discharging through an RC circuit. Therefore, we can use what we know about RC circuits to determine how long the output circuit will be high and low.

When the capacitor is *charging*, the capacitor is charging through *both* R1 and R2. In this situation, what is the RC time constant? First, we need to know the resistance. Since the resistance here is a series resistance, we can simply add them together:

$$R_T = R_1 + R_2$$
$$= 50,000 + 50,000$$
$$= 100,000$$

So the resistance is 100,000 $\Omega$, and we are using a 10 µF capacitor (which is 0.00001 F). Therefore (based on Chapter 17), the RC time constant is 100,000 ∗ 0.00001 = 1. So our RC time constant is 1 second. However, we are charging/discharging the capacitor in a strange way. We are not starting from zero (except for the first time)—instead we are usually starting from $\frac{1}{3}$ of supply voltage.

Go back to Chapter 17 and look at Figure 17-1. While we don't have a time constant for *exactly* $\frac{1}{3}$ of supply voltage, we do have one for 39.3%, which is pretty close. So, in the table, that occurs as 0.5 time constants. In this case, that is our *starting* value. Our ending value is when the capacitor is $\frac{2}{3}$ charged. That is very close to 63.2%, which is at 1 time constant.

Therefore, the *difference* between the points where we are $\frac{1}{3}$ charged and $\frac{2}{3}$ charged is $1 - 0.5 = 0.5$ time constants.

Since we were using approximate values from the table, this is only an approximation to see how this idea works. The distance from $\frac{1}{3}$ to $\frac{2}{3}$ of supply voltage actually takes 0.693 time constant. This is an important number to remember when using the NE555, as it will be used in all of your time calculations. Since our time constant is 1 second, that makes the calculation really easy: $1 * 0.693 = 0.693$ seconds.

Now, for discharge, remember that the point that the capacitor is discharging to is pin 7. This is *between* R1 and R2. That means that it is *only* using R2 to discharge, so the RC time constant will be based only on R2 and the capacitor. So the RC time constant is $50,000 * 0.00001 = 0.5$ seconds.

Since the charge/discharge time between $\frac{1}{3}$ and $\frac{2}{3}$ is 0.693 time constants, the resulting time to discharge from $\frac{2}{3}$ down to $\frac{1}{3}$ is $0.693 * 0.5 = 0.347$ seconds.

The total period will be the total time for one cycle. This will be our charge time (0.693 second) plus the discharge time (0.347 second) which will give us a total of 1.04 seconds.

The value 0.693 looks like a strange number, but that will *always* be the value used for the number of time constants for charging/discharging between $\frac{1}{3}$ and $\frac{2}{3}$ of supply voltage. If you are going to use the 555 timer, it is best to just memorize it.

Also note that since the charging goes through *both* resistors while the discharge only goes through *one* resistor, the charge time (with the output on) will *always* be longer than the discharge time (with the output off).

> **Example 18.17** Let's say we have the basic oscillator circuit shown in Figure 18-2, but with a 2,000 Ω resistor for R1, a 6,000 Ω resistor for R2, and a 10 µF capacitor for C1. What will be the charge time, the discharge time, the period, and the frequency for our oscillator?

To find this out, it is easiest to first calculate the charge and discharge times separately and then use those to find period and frequency. The charge time will be calculated based on *both* resistors in our RC circuit. So the resistance will be 2,000 $\Omega$+6,000 $\Omega$ = 8,000 $\Omega$. The capacitance is 10 $\mu$F = 0.00001 F. This means that the RC time constant will be 8,000 $\Omega$ * 0.00001 F = 0.08 seconds.

The number of time constants it takes to charge from $\frac{1}{3}$ to $\frac{2}{3}$ is 0.693. This means that the charge time will be 0.08 * 0.693 = 0.0554 seconds.

The discharge happens only through R2. This means that the RC time constant will be 6,000 $\Omega$ * 0.00001 F = 0.06 seconds. Since we will use 0.693 time constants, the total time it takes to discharge from $\frac{2}{3}$ down to $\frac{1}{3}$ is 0.693 * 0.06 = 0.0416 seconds.

Now that we have the charging and discharging times, we find the period by merely adding them together. This means the period is 0.0554 + 0.0416 = 0.097 seconds.

The frequency is merely the reciprocal of this number, or $\frac{1}{0.097}$, which gives us 10.3 Hz.

**Example 18.18** Now let's say that we want to build an oscillator for which the LED stays on for 3 seconds and then goes off for 2 seconds. Assuming we keep our 10 $\mu$F capacitor, what values should we use for each resistor?

To do this, we need to solve for R2 first, since it is much easier. The discharge will be 2 seconds, which will be the same as 0.693 time constants. Therefore, we can write this as an equation:

$$2\text{seconds} = R \cdot C \cdot 0.693$$
$$2\text{seconds} = R \cdot 0.00001 \cdot 0.69$$
$$2\text{seconds} = R \cdot 0.0000069$$
$$\frac{2\text{seconds}}{0.0000069} = R$$
$$289,855\Omega \approx R$$

So the resistor, R2, needs to be 289,555 Ω.

The time to charge the capacitor, however, needs to be 3 seconds. This means the resistance (which will be *both* R1 and R2) will need to be calculated for this as well. Therefore, we will use a similar equation:

$$3\text{seconds} = R \cdot C \cdot 0.693$$
$$3\text{seconds} = R \cdot 0.00001F \cdot 0.693$$
$$3\text{seconds} = R \cdot 0.00000693$$
$$\frac{3\text{seconds}}{0.00000693} = R$$
$$434,783\Omega = R$$

So the resistance for charging the capacitor needs to be 434,783 Ω. However, this is the *combined* resistance for R1 and R2. Thankfully, though, we already know what we want for R2—289,855 Ω. Therefore, we can put these into an equation and solve for R1:

$$R_1 + R_2 = 434,783\Omega$$
$$R_1 + 289,855\Omega = 434,783\Omega$$
$$R_1 = 434,783\Omega - 289,855\Omega$$
$$R_1 = 144,928\Omega$$

So now we know our values for R1 and R2—144,928 $\Omega$ and 289,855 $\Omega$. Depending on our application, we would probably simply choose resistors that were close to that amount (like 150 k$\Omega$ and 300 k$\Omega$) rather than trying to find a combination of resistors that hit that precise resistance. But, for solving equations, it is best to use exact values.

## 18.5  Choosing the Capacitor

Ultimately, there are no hard-and-fast rules for choosing capacitors. As long as the RC time constant yields the right value, then you can compensate for pretty much any size capacitor with the right size of resistor. However, sometimes just having a little guidance helps people get started, and there are a few situations that you need to watch out for.

First of all, the size of the capacitor will affect the size of the resistor you need for a given time constant. If all you have are smaller-sized resistors, then you should probably use a larger capacitor to compensate.

However, using a smaller capacitor with larger resistors gives a very large advantage in the amount of wasted current. If you are using smaller resistors, then Ohm's law indicates that we will have larger currents for a given voltage. Since $V = I \cdot R$, if you lower the $R$, you will increase the $I$. So having a higher resistance means that your RC circuit will use much less current.

Remember that we aren't actually *using* the current to *do* anything except keep time. The current in our RC circuit is not used to power the LED (the 555 does that through the power source), and it isn't used for anything else; it is just used to keep time. Therefore, pretty much all current used by the RC circuits is wasted. We have to use it, but any smaller currents we can get away with, we should!

This gets even more pronounced when the capacitor is discharging. When pin 7 (Discharge) switches to ground, not only does it discharge the capacitor but it also creates a useless waste of current going from the voltage source through R1. In our oscillator configuration, you can't get rid of this, but having larger resistors will reduce the amount of waste.

So, in short, if you have higher-valued resistors to compensate, your circuit will waste much less current by using smaller capacitors.

# Review

In this chapter, we learned the following:

1. Because this material is based so heavily on RC circuits, you may want to review the material in Chapter 17.

2. When something oscillates, it moves back and forth between a set of values.

3. In electronics, oscillators usually refer to circuits whose output voltages go back and forth between two different values.

4. Oscillations are usually described by their period or frequency.

5. The period of an oscillation is the time that it takes to go through one entire cycle (usually in seconds).

6. The frequency of an oscillation is the number of times that an oscillation occurs per second, which is simply the reciprocal of the period (i.e., $\frac{1}{\text{period}}$), with a unit of hertz (cycles per second).

7. Oscillating circuits are used in a number of circuit applications, including sound production, time keeping, coordinating activities, radio transmissions, and motor control.

8. Oscillating circuits are often built with RC time circuits which control the time periods of the oscillations.

9. The NE555 (often referred to as a 555 timer or just the 555) is an integrated circuit which allows for several timing applications including making oscillating circuits.

10. The NE555, when set up as an oscillator, is controlled by two resistors and a capacitor.

11. The NE555 can be set up to monitor the charge of the capacitor. It has two pins for monitoring the voltage, $\overline{\text{Trigger}}$ (which checks for the capacitor to drop below $\frac{1}{3}$ of supply voltage) and Threshold (which checks to see when the capacitor is charged above $\frac{2}{3}$ of supply voltage).

12. The NE555 cycles between charging and discharging the capacitor from $\frac{1}{3}$ of supply voltage to $\frac{2}{3}$ of supply voltage and back (using $\overline{\text{Trigger}}$ and Threshold to check the voltage level).

13. The Discharge pin of the NE555 acts like it is disconnected when the capacitor is charging and is connected to ground to allow for a path for the capacitor to discharge when in the discharge part of the cycle.

14.  The Output pin of the NE555 is turned on (higher
     voltage level) while the capacitor is charging
     and off (low voltage level) when the capacitor is
     discharging.

15.  The NE555 output operates at about 1.7 V less
     than the source voltage when on and can source a
     maximum of 200 mA to the output circuit.

16.  The $\overline{\text{Reset}}$ pin can be given a low voltage to reset the
     whole device. If it is unused, it should just be tied to
     a positive voltage line.

17.  The Control pin is attached to a capacitor in order
     to regulate and stabilize the circuit operation.

18.  The RC circuit takes 0.693 time constants to charge
     from $\frac{1}{3}$ voltage to $\frac{2}{3}$ voltage or to discharge the
     other way. Therefore, once you have the RC time
     constant, multiply by 0.693 to find the actual time it
     will take.

19.  The RC circuit utilizes *both* resistors when charging,
     but only *one* resistor when discharging. This means
     that charging and discharging each have their own
     RC time constants.

20.  Because the charge circuit uses two resistors while
     the discharge circuit only uses one, the charging
     portion of the oscillation period will always be at
     least a little longer than the discharging portion.

21.  The period of the oscillation is the combination of
     both the charge time and the discharge time.

22.  When calculating for resistors for an RC time circuit, it is best to calculate the discharge resistance first, since it only uses one resistor (R2). Then you can calculate the combined resistance for the charge circuit, which allows you to deduce what the R1 resistor should be.

23.  When choosing components for a given RC time constant, you can choose a variety of combinations of capacitor/resistor values for the same result. Choosing a smaller capacitor and a larger resistor will save power in the circuit.

24.  An equation for determining the frequency of a 555 oscillator circuit can be found in Appendix D, Section D.4, "555 Timer Oscillator Frequency Equation."

# Apply What You Have Learned

Figure 18-2 will be used as the basis for the problems in this section:

1.  Copy Figure 18-2 to a piece of paper including the current flows on charge and discharge.

2.  Why is R1 important? What would happen if we just replaced it with a wire?

3.  Why are there two different pins on the NE555 connected to the capacitor? What type of circuit (that we have discussed in this book) do you think they are connected to inside the chip?

4.  Why is the charging time of the NE555 always at least a little longer than the discharging time?

5. Why does the NE555 stay in the on state a little longer when the circuit is first turned on?

6. Let's say that we wanted our circuit to be on for 2 seconds and off for 1 second. Keeping the same capacitor, what values should we use for R1 and R2 to accomplish that?

7. Let's say that we wanted our circuit to be on for 10 seconds and off for 3 seconds. Keeping the same capacitor, what values should we use for R1 and R2 to accomplish that?

8. The factory called and said that they were out of the capacitor we wanted for the circuit and instead only had a 23 µF capacitor that we could use. Recalculate the previous problem using this new capacitor value.

9. How much current is our output sourcing from the chip?

10. When the chip first turns on (and thus the capacitor is empty and at 0 V), how much current is the RC circuit in Figure 18-2 using?

# CHAPTER 19

# Producing Sound with Oscillations

In Chapter 18, we learned to make an oscillator circuit. Oscillations affect a lot of areas of electronics, but the one that is most directly usable (well, besides making blinky lights) is in making sounds.

## 19.1  How Sound Is Produced by Speakers

As we mentioned in Chapter 18, sound is the result of vibrations (i.e., oscillating motions) in the air. These vibrations are produced in electronics with a speaker when the speaker oscillates back and forth. The speaker oscillates back and forth because it is connected to a magnet and a coil. When the electricity in the coil oscillates between more positive and more negative charges, the magnet is attracted to and repelled from the coil, moving the speaker back and forth.

The frequency of this oscillation will determine the pitch of the sound (i.e., how high or low the sound is). If the frequency is higher (shorter periods), then the pitch is higher. If the frequency is lower (longer periods), then the pitch is lower.

© Jonathan Bartlett 2020
J. Bartlett, *Electronics for Beginners*, https://doi.org/10.1007/978-1-4842-5979-5_19

Now, compared to the blinking lights we worked with in Chapter 18, sounds that you can hear are all of a much higher frequency. The bottom end of the hearable audio is about 20 Hz—that is, 20 cycles per second. The top end is about 20 kHz (i.e., 20,000 Hz). These values vary by individual, but this is a pretty good guide for most people. If we tried to blink an LED that fast, we just would not be able to see it—it would just look like a dimmer-than-normal light.

# 19.2  Graphing Electricity

Now, when we deal with circuits that are oscillating quickly, we need to have a way to visualize what is happening. With circuits that have one or two states, we don't need to visualize much—we just need to calculate what the values are. However, with circuits that are continually oscillating (such as sound circuits), it is helpful to be able to graph what the voltages are at different points in time.

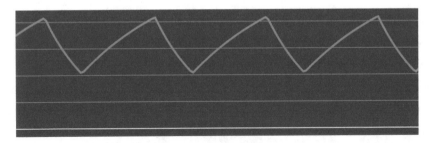

***Figure 19-1.***  *A Graph of the Capacitor Voltage in a 555 Oscillator*

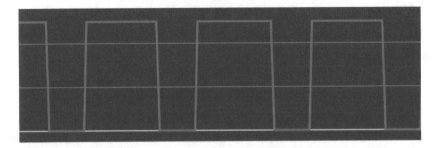

***Figure 19-2.***  *A Graph of the Output Voltage in a 555 Oscillator*

There are several ways to graph electricity. One of the most common ways is to plot *time* on the *x*-axis and *voltage* on the *y*-axis. This gives a visible representation of how the voltage is varying within the circuit. Now, because each point on a circuit has a different voltage, you have to specify *which point* on the circuit you are graphing. For instance, if you take the 555 oscillator circuit from Chapter 18 (i.e., Figure 18-2), the two places whose voltages you might want to graph are (a) right before the capacitor and (b) right after the output pin.

These will give *very* different graphs, but both of them are instructive. The graph of (a) will show you what the input side of the circuit looks like, and the graph of (b) will show you what the output side of the circuit looks like.

Notice that Figure 19-1 changes fairly smoothly (except when it changes directions). This is because capacitor charging causes the voltage to change smoothly over time. It charges up until it reaches $\frac{2}{3}$ of supply voltage and then discharges down to $\frac{1}{3}$ of supply voltage. It does this over and over again as you can see on the graph.

The output, however, is either *on* or *off*. Therefore, Figure 19-2 shows a very jagged graph. This is known as a **square wave**, because it is basically rectangular. The voltage just goes from zero to the target voltage almost instantly, and then after it stays there a bit, the voltage goes back down again just as instantaneously as it rose.

In addition to graphing voltage, we can also graph current in the same way, though it is harder to measure. Because voltage can be measured with simple probes and measuring current requires replacing a wire, most of the time, people just focus on voltage measurements.

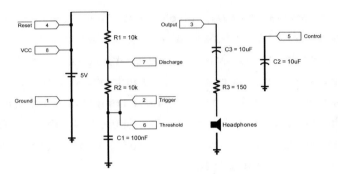

**Figure 19-3.** *Schematic for a Simple 555-Based Tone Generator*

Special devices known as **oscilloscopes** can be used to measure voltage changes over time. Graphs such as those in Figures 19-1 and 19-2 can be made by hooking up an oscilloscope to the circuit while it is in operation.[1] Oscilloscopes used to cost thousands of dollars, but now you can pick up a small handheld oscilloscope for under $50.

Usage of an oscilloscope is outside the scope of this book, but the basics are simple enough. An oscilloscope usually has an active probe and a ground probe. You hook up the ground probe to the ground on your circuit, and you hook up the active probe to the point on the circuit that you want to measure. Then, you look at the screen, and it will graph for you what the voltage is at that point over a period of time. Most oscilloscopes have all sorts of adjustments, such as how wide of a voltage range you want to measure and how long of a time window you want to show on the screen. In any case, oscilloscopes provide graphical views of oscillating voltages.

# 19.3  Outputting a Tone to Headphones

In this section, we are going to modify the circuit in Figure 18-2 to add in a headphone output. Figure 19-3 shows the final circuit, and Figure 19-4 shows how to build it. This circuit has several changes to our original circuit that we will discuss in this section.

---

[1]The graphs depicted in the figures are actually idealizations, however, not actual output from an oscilloscope.

The first changes to this circuit are to the RC time circuit. Because we want the circuit to be in audio range, we are making a much higher frequency (i.e., a shorter period). To do this, we swapped out the electrolytic capacitor for a ceramic disk capacitor of 100 nF. Then, we dropped the resistors down to 10 kΩ each. This will make a tone with a period of 0.003 seconds. Taking the reciprocal gives us a frequency of about 333 Hz. This is well within hearing range for most people. You can adjust the resistors and capacitors how you wish for different tone frequencies. We are merely using the equations from Chapter 18 to determine the period and frequency.

The strange change is in the output circuit. When we were blinking the LED, we just used a medium-sized resistor to limit output current. Here, however, we are using a combination of a capacitor and a resistor. This *looks like* an RC time circuit—and it would be, if it had a constant voltage going to it. However, in this circuit, the voltage going to the RC circuit is fluctuating, and that introduces a whole host of new considerations.

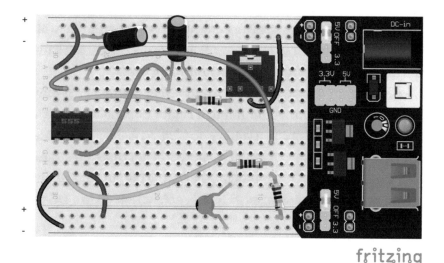

***Figure 19-4.*** *Breadboard Layout for a 555-Based Tone Generator*

# 19.4  AC vs. DC

In Chapter 3, we introduced the ideas of *direct current* (DC) and *alternating current* (AC). In DC circuits, the circuit has a more-or-less constant voltage. Our power supply is at a certain voltage, our output is at a certain voltage, and so on. In AC circuits, however, the voltage oscillates back and forth. These oscillations introduce a whole new set of considerations.

In pure AC circuits, voltage and current actually swing both to positive and negative values. What is a negative current? A negative current happens when the electricity flows in the *opposite* direction. Thus, in a *pure* AC circuit, electricity flows back and forth, switching between directions while it is running, spending about even time in each direction.

Some components, such as speakers, assume that they are going to receive or process pure ACs. That is, they *expect* the current to switch direction at some point. As mentioned earlier, the speaker is driven by changing voltages in a coil, which alters the attraction of the coil to a magnet. These variations in attraction and repulsion move the coil back and forth, which moves the speaker cone, which vibrates the air, which vibrates your eardrum, which you hear. Speakers expect the oscillating current to go back and forth each direction about evenly.

However, in our circuit, the voltage only swings between a positive voltage and 0 V. If you look at the graph in Figure 19-2, notice that while the voltage goes up to a positive voltage, the *lowest* that it ever goes is zero. Therefore, it is not a pure AC circuit, because it is not centered around 0 V. Instead, the AC has a **DC bias voltage**. That is, the output voltage can be thought of as a combination of an AC voltage signal added to a DC voltage.

# 19.5 Using Capacitors to Separate AC and DC Components

Sometimes having a DC bias is good, and sometimes we need to separate out our AC and DC signals. Capacitors are excellent at this. Capacitors are said to *allow* AC to flow and to *block* DC. This is a simplistic view, and we will get a little more nuanced in future chapters, but it works for now.

To understand why this happens, let's remember what a capacitor does physically. It stores charge—like a small battery. Remember, even though the pathway between the plates of a capacitor is blocked, when a positive charge accumulates on one side, it pulls electrons onto the other side, which means that the other side beyond the capacitor gets more positive as well. Do you remember what happens when the capacitor *first* starts charging? The capacitor basically acts as a short circuit. As the capacitor fills up, it starts acting more and more like a resistor, preventing current from flowing.

Thus, when given a constant voltage, once the capacitor is nearly full, it essentially stops getting more charge (or comes very close to it). Therefore, once it is full, it is basically *blocking* any more current from flowing. Since what goes onto one side of the capacitor affects what is on the other side, this same blockage will block the *transmission* of the current to the other side as well. Thus, in the long run, if you have a DC voltage, the capacitor will eventually block current flow. Thus, the current on the *other* side of the capacitor will be *zero*.

However, now consider what happens if the voltage *changes*. If the voltage changes, then the capacitor will allow current to flow through. If the voltage goes up, then the capacitor has more storage available (since the amount of storage depends on voltage). While it is charging to the new level, current will be flowing. If the voltage goes down, then the capacitor will actually have to discharge back into the circuit.

Now, if the capacitor discharges back into the circuit, *which way is the current flowing*? Well, that means the current from the capacitor is now flowing in the *opposite* direction!

Thus, what ends up happening is that the capacitor winds up only sending *changes* in voltage to the other side of the circuit! While the capacitor is charging and discharging, charge is moving through both sides of the capacitor. Thus, when the voltage (and therefore the charge) on the capacitor is changing, current is indeed flowing. Now, when the voltage stays the same, no electrons move, no matter what the voltage is. Therefore, even though you have a positive voltage on one side, if the voltage is not changing, no current is flowing. Therefore, on an unchanging current, the voltage on the other side of the capacitor will be zero.

Since the changes go up and down, but the DC bias voltage does not go up and down, this has the effect of sending AC through the capacitor, but blocking the DC bias voltage.

Therefore, capacitors are often used in series in a circuit to couple together parts of the circuit that are pure AC with other parts of the circuit that have a DC bias. Since the output of the 555 is DC biased and speakers generally are optimized for pure AC output, the capacitor in our output circuit filters out the DC bias and gives a pure AC signal.

A capacitor used in this way is known as a **coupling capacitor**.

Alternatively, if for some reason you wanted *only* the DC component, you could wire the capacitor to go to ground. This sends the AC part of the signal to ground, leaving only the DC component in the circuit. In such a scenario, the capacitor is being used as a **filter capacitor**.

Now, using a coupling capacitor does add in a small amount of distortion, both because DC bias voltage does have some effect on the signal and because different capacitor values are optimal for coupling different frequencies. For audio applications, a capacitor somewhere between 10 nF and 10 µF should be used.

# 19.6 Speaker Wattage

Next in the circuit is the R3 resistor. The R3 resistor is there to limit the output signal to the headphones. Headphones and speakers are all a little strange—there is very little standardization. Different headphones have different resistances in the speakers and different tolerances for how much wattage can be put through them. Speakers are usually rated by (a) how much resistance they normally add to the circuit, (b) how loud they are at a given wattage of power, and (c) what their maximum wattage is. Even though there is quite a bit of variance, for headphones, you can be fairly safe by estimating that the headphones will act as 16 Ω resistors and that they can consume a maximum of 20 mW.

The output of the 555 timer is 1.7 V less than my supply voltage. So, for a 5 V source, the output will be 3.2 V. However, since we have now centered it on 0 V, the output will actually only be half of that—1.6 V. We can use the formula $P = \dfrac{V}{(R^2)}$ from Chapter 10 to determine how many watts this will supply. If the speaker is 16 Ω, then the power used by the headphone without the extra resistor will be $\dfrac{(1.6^2)}{16} = 0.16$ W = 160 mW. Therefore, the R3 resistor pulls out some of that power.

With the resistor, the combined power usage of the resistor and the headphone speaker is 166 Ω. Therefore, the power here is $\dfrac{(1.6^2)}{166} = 0.015$ W = 15 mW. Remember, though, that this is the *combined* power of both the resistor and our speaker. The speaker is only supplying about $\dfrac{1}{10}$ of the resistance, so it is only using up to $\dfrac{1}{10}$ of the power, or 1.5 mW.

Now, the calculation for this is relatively easy because we are working with square waves. The calculation becomes harder for different types of output, because you have to take into account the *shape* of the wave.

However, we won't go into that in this book. This calculation using the peak voltage provides a simple method which will give you a good starting point, and you can judge for yourself if you need more or less resistance for your own circuits.

# 19.7  Sound Control

Now, as I mentioned, all headphones are different, and, with the exception of *having* a coupling capacitor, they all have different ranges and need different amounts of power. Usually this is accommodated by having a volume control.

This is usually done with a **variable resistor**. On a variable resistor, you usually turn a knob and the resistance changes. Variable resistors go by different names—variable resistor, adjustable resistor, rheostat, and trimming resistors, though they each have slight differences. Trimming resistors are the easiest to use for this, but probably the hardest to find.

*Figure 19-5.*  *The Potentiometer Symbol*

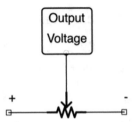

*Figure 19-6.*  *The Potentiometer as a Voltage Divider*

To use a variable resistor, you would need to find one with the right range of values and then simply replace the output resistor R3 with your variable resistor.

A more common type of component which can be used as a variable resistor is a potentiometer. A potentiometer is basically a variable voltage divider. The symbol for the potentiometer is shown in Figure 19-5. It has three leads—input, ground, and output. When you turn the knob, it adjusts the relative resistance of each side of the voltage divider to vary what is coming out of the output.

Potentiometers were built for working as a variable voltage divider. Figure 19-6 shows what this looks like. Essentially, the user controls a knob which alters the voltage coming out by changing the voltage division between the resistors.

However, you can also use a potentiometer as a simple variable resistor by just hooking up one side of the potentiometer. Figure 19-7 shows this configuration.

The simplest way of using the potentiometer for a volume control is simply setting it up like Figure 19-7, with the input coming from the coupling capacitor and the output going to the speaker. Potentiometers vary widely in how much resistance they offer, so if we were to add one as a volume control, we would need to make sure its resistance range approximately matches what is needed (around 150 Ω).

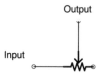

**Figure 19-7.** *The Potentiometer as a Variable Resistor*

# Review

In this chapter, we learned the following:

1. Sound is the result of oscillations in the air that is picked up by your eardrums.

2. Sound can be generated by an oscillating speaker cone vibrating against the air.

3. The oscillations in a speaker cone are made by a magnet being drawn and repelled to another magnet by oscillations in electrical power.

4. Sound generally has higher frequencies (i.e., shorter periods) than what we use for flashing lights.

5. Audible sound frequencies range from 20 Hz to 20 kHz.

6. On circuits where voltage and/or current changes with time, it is often helpful to plot their changes at specific points on a graph to help visualize what is happening.

7. The output of the 555 timer is known as a square wave because it has steep changes in voltage at specific points, making a rectangular-shaped graph.

8. An oscilloscope can be used to measure and record these types of graphs.

9. Voltages that oscillate quickly with time are known as alternating current or AC voltages.

10. Oscillating voltages that do not spend roughly equal amounts of time on either side of 0 volt are said to have a DC bias voltage.

11.  The DC bias voltage is how much voltage you would have to subtract from the voltage in order for the voltage to be centered on 0 volt.

12.  Most circuits have DC bias voltages, but most output devices (such as speakers) need the DC bias voltage removed and only use the AC component of the signal.

13.  DC bias voltage can be removed by placing a coupling capacitor in series with the output signal. The capacitor will only transmit voltage *changes*, thus removing the DC bias voltage.

14.  Speakers and headphones vary considerably in their properties.

15.  The most important considerations are how many ohms of resistance they have and how many watts are needed to drive the sound.

16.  For headphones, a good starting assumption is that the speaker is 16 Ω and needs under 20 mW of output.

17.  If your output signal is larger than this, be sure to add a resistor in series to consume some of the output signal's power.

18.  The output resistor can be replaced with a variable resistor or a potentiometer to have a user-controlled output setting, also known as a volume control.

19.  A potentiometer is a variable voltage divider. However, by using only the positive and output terminals, it can be used as a variable resistor instead.

# Apply What You Have Learned

1.  Why is the input voltage signal to the 555 timer smooth, but the output is square?

2.  Will increasing the resistance of R1 and R2 make the pitch higher or lower?

3.  Can you think of a way to modify the circuit so that the pitch of the sound can be adjusted while the circuit is on?

4.  Given the circuit in Figure 19-3, what power would be delivered to your headphones if you were using an 8 Ω speaker instead of the 16 Ω speaker? What about a 100 Ω speaker?

5.  The frequency of the A note above middle-C on the piano is 440 Hz. Design a modification to this circuit that will yield this frequency.

6.  The output of the 555 is 1.7 V less than the power supply used. What is the effect on the wattage to the headphones if we change the power supply to be a 9 V power?

# CHAPTER 20

# Inductors

In this chapter, we will begin our study of **inductors** and **coils**.

## 20.1 Inductors, Coils, and Magnetic Flux

In Chapter 16, we learned that capacitors stored charge by using an electric field. We also learned that capacitors continued to hold their charge even after they were disconnected from the rest of the circuit. We learned in Chapter 19 that capacitors blocked DC signals but allowed AC signals to pass through.

### 20.1.1 What Is an Inductor?

An inductor is kind of like the capacitor's evil twin. It behaves in some ways that remind us a lot of capacitors, but it is operating on a different aspect of electrical behavior. Capacitors store charge and release it in response to voltage changes. Inductors, instead, store **magnetic flux** and release it in response to current changes. Thus, capacitors tend to even out voltages, and inductors tend to even out currents.

Figure 20-1 shows what an inductor looks like in a schematic. Inductors are non-polarized, so they can be wired in either direction. The symbol loosely represents a coil of wire, because that is what inductors are essentially made of.

**Figure 20-1.** *The Symbol for an Inductor*

## 20.1.2  What Is Magnetic Flux?

When current moves in a wire, it creates a very tiny magnetic field. It's not large enough to pick up anything, but it is present. Flux is the total amount of magnetism present in an inductor. Since this is an engineering book, not a physics book, we won't spend a lot of time trying to come to grips with what flux is and how it works. We will simply understand that it is the total size of the magnetic field of a component, and it is measured in Webers (Wb). To get a feel for what a Weber is like, a small bar magnet has a flux of around $\dfrac{1}{1000}$ Wb.

As a sidenote, when we say that something is magnetic, we are usually not talking about the total flux of something, but of the *density* of that flux—the amount of flux in a given area. Flux density is measured in Teslas (1 Tesla is $\dfrac{1\,\text{Wb}}{1\,\text{meter}^2}$), but we will not concern ourselves with Teslas or flux densities for this course.

## 20.1.3  What Is the Difference Between Electric and Magnetic Fields

Now, when we talked about capacitors, we talked a little bit about electric fields. Electric fields and magnetic fields are related, but different. An electric field is generated by a difference in charge between two surfaces. Electric fields can exist even when no current is moving at all—there just has to be two differently charged surfaces. Basically, any charged object will induce a force on another charged object for a certain distance, and this is the electric field.

The magnetic field, however, only exists when a charge is moving. When a charge is in motion, in addition to the electric field, it also creates a *magnetic* field surrounding itself, going perpendicular to the wire. This field also exhibits a force on charged objects within a small distance, but a much larger distance than the electric field. Additionally, when the current in the wire slows down, the magnetic field will convert its own energy into current in the wire.

The size of a magnetic field within a single wire is very, very small and can be ignored. However, the strength of the magnetic field of a wire can be increased by wrapping (coiling) it around a cylindrical core. This aligns the magnetic fields of the wires so that the fields can each be added together to produce a combined magnetic field. Each turn around the core adds an additional bit to the magnetic field. Devices based on this principle are called coils or **inductors**.

When an inductor is first turned on, most of the current goes into creating the inductor's magnetic field. Then, as the magnetic field is setting up, it allows more and more current to flow, until it hits a steady state. Then, if the current flow reduces, the energy from the magnetic field gets transformed into current and goes out to try to make up the difference.

While a capacitor stores energy as a charge and releases it when there is a voltage change, an inductor stores energy as magnetic flux and releases it when there is a current change. An inductor's inductance is measured using the Henry (H). The core equations of capacitors and inductors are related as well. The defining equation of a capacitor is $Q = C \cdot V$, where $Q$ is the charge in the capacitor. The defining equation of an inductor is just as simple:

$$\phi = L \cdot I \qquad\qquad (20.1)$$

In this equation, $\varphi$ is the magnetic flux in the inductor (in Webers), $L$ is the inductance (in Henries), and $I$ is the current (in amperes). The **Henry** is the primary unit of inductance and has an abbreviation of H.

**Example 20.19** If I have a 50-microhenry inductor and have a constant current of 2 milliamps, how much magnetic flux is being stored?

$$\phi = L \cdot I$$
$$L = 50\mu H = 0.00005 \text{ H}$$
$$I = 2mA = 0.002 \text{ A}$$
$$\phi = 0.00005 \cdot 0.002$$
$$= 0.0000001\,Wb = 0.1\ \mu Wb$$

Therefore, we have 0.0000001 Weber of flux, or 0.1 microweber of flux.

Therefore, when a relatively constant amount of current flows, it is easy to calculate the amount of flux in the magnetic field.

# 20.2  Induced Voltages

Changes in the flux of a magnetic field induce voltages. The amount of voltage induced depends on how fast the flux changes. The induced voltage is essentially the change in the flux divided by the number of seconds that it took for the change to occur. If the flux decreases, the energy is converted into voltage, which goes up. If the flux increases, the energy is taken from the voltage, which goes down. So, if there was a decrease of 10 Wb over the course of 2 seconds, then the amount of voltage induced would be $\dfrac{10Wb}{2seconds} = 5V$ .

The formal statement of this is known as Lenz's law. It is given as follows:

$$V_{average} = -\frac{\text{change in}\phi}{\text{change in time}} \qquad (20.2)$$

The average voltage produced by the change in a magnetic field over a given time period is the same as the amount of flux that was reduced by the field divided by the same time period.

Now, the amount of flux in the inductor will change with the current, as indicated by Equation 20.1. When the current decreases, it will cause the flux to be converted into voltage. When the current increases, it will add more flux into the magnetic field, using up voltage.

When the amount of flux changes, it creates a voltage. The amount of flux change (in Webers) divided by the amount of time it took to change (in seconds) will yield the voltage produced by the change. Therefore, when the current drops, the flux will be converted to voltage. If we add in voltage, it will also increase the current.

# 20.3  Resisting Changes in Current

Ultimately, what an inductor is doing is resisting changes in current. When the current goes up, the current is first used to construct the magnetic field, and therefore it takes some time to allow the full amount of current through. When the current goes down, the flux of the magnetic field decreases, which gets converted back to voltage, which induces more current.

The inductor, with regard to current, is the opposite of the capacitor. With direct current, the capacitor, when first connected to the circuit, acts as a short circuit—the current basically flows right through until the capacitor starts to fill up. When the capacitor is full, then it acts like an open circuit—blocking any more current from flowing.

The inductor is the opposite. When first connected to the circuit, the inductor acts like an open circuit—the current is basically being used to construct the magnetic field. As the magnetic field strength increases, more and more current is allowed to flow. Once the magnetic field flux matches what it should be for the given current, the current flows freely, as if the inductor were not even there, like a short circuit.

In summary, we can say that a capacitor acts as an open circuit for sustained DC and as a short circuit for alternating current. The inductor acts as a short circuit for sustained DC and as an open circuit for alternating current.

# 20.4 Analogy from Mechanics

If you are into mechanics, you can think of an inductor as a flywheel. Flywheels store mechanical energy into the motion of a large or heavy wheel. It takes energy to get the wheel spinning, but once it is spinning, the wheel itself can continue to drive the mechanism. The wheel is used to even out the drive of the other components of the mechanism.

For instance, an engine driven by pistons will have somewhat irregular motion, because the force of the pistons is not constant through their motion. However, attaching a flywheel will even out the energy output. When the pistons are delivering more power, most of the excess will be going to the flywheel, and when the pistons are delivering less power, the mechanism can be driven by the force of the flywheel.

# 20.5 Uses of Inductors

Inductors are used in a very wide variety of applications—much more so than capacitors. Capacitors are used primarily for their effects *within* electronic circuits—filtering noise, blocking DC, coupling DC-biased circuits, and so on. However, the electric field created on the plates of the capacitor is fairly useless on its own because the field fades so quickly with distance. Inductors are used for similar things as capacitors within circuits (their operation being largely the counterpart of what a capacitor would do), but additionally, the magnetic field of the inductor has innumerable uses because its effects are stronger further away. These uses include the following:

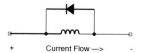

+    Current Flow —>    -

**Figure 20-2.**  *A Snubber Diode*

- Inductors are used to make **electromagnets**, for picking up and setting down large objects.

- Inductors are used to make **transformers**, which use the magnetic field in one inductor to generate a current in another inductor.

- Inductors are used to make motors, where the electromagnetic coils are used to turn a shaft.

- Inductors are used to make speakers, which use the magnetic field to move the speaker diaphragm back and forth.

- Inductors are used to make relays, which use the magnetic field to open and close switches.

These are just some of the uses of inductors. In short, the magnetic field created by the inductor is what allows many of the interfaces between electronic devices and the real world.

## 20.6  Inductive Kick

One important thing to keep in mind when using inductors is the concept of inductive kick. Lenz's law (Equation 20.2) shows that decreases in the magnetic flux will induce a voltage. Since the magnetic flux is divided by time to get the voltage, that means that a shorter timespan will generate a larger voltage. Thus, a sudden decrease in magnetic flux will cause a voltage spike.

But what controls the flux? If you go back to Equation 20.1, we can see that a decrease in current will decrease the magnetic flux. Therefore, a sudden decrease in current will cause a sudden decrease in the magnetic flux which will then cause a large voltage spike within the inductor itself. This spike is known as an **inductive kick** and can damage nearby electronic components. To avoid an inductive kick, a **flyback diode**, also called a **protection diode** or a **snubber diode**, can be used.

A flyback diode is a regular diode (*not* a Zener diode) wired backward across the terminals of an inductor. Under normal operation, the diode won't conduct. However, when the diode is shut off, it provides a safe path for the generated voltage to pass through (back through the other side of the inductor) and allows the inductor to bleed off voltage in a much more controlled manner.

Figure 20-2 shows how this is wired up. As you can see, under normal operation, the current flows in the direction of the arrow. Since the left-hand side is more positive than the right-hand side, no current can flow through the diode. However, when the current is shut off, the right-hand side becomes more positive very quickly, and the diode feeds the excess current back through the inductor to allow the extra energy to dissipate more slowly.

You might be wondering why the voltage doesn't just shift back to the left side on its own once the right-hand side is more positive. The answer is that the magnetic field that is generating the voltage is itself directionalized within the inductor. The field's movement is such that it is essentially pushing current to the right (which is why a voltage is being produced). Therefore, the flyback diode carries this excess voltage back to the left-hand side of the diode.

Flyback diodes are used with all sorts of inductors (motors, electromagnets, etc.) anywhere where there are components that could be damaged by an inductive kick. For basic applications, nearly any type of diode will work for a flyback diode. However, diodes differ in their speed in reacting to voltage changes. In some circuits, the speed at which a diode reacts to changes in voltage can be important.

# Review

In this chapter, we learned the following:

1.  Inductors are electronic components that are made of winding wire around a core which allows them to store charge in their magnetic fields.

2.  The strength of a magnetic field is the magnetic flux and is measured in Webers (Wb).

3.  While an *electric* field is made from the *presence* of charges, the *magnetic* field is made from the *movement* of charges (i.e., the current).

4.  When the current going into an inductor increases, the extra current is first used to build up the flux of the magnetic field before achieving a new steady state.

5.  When the current going into an inductor decreases, the flux of the magnetic field is converted into a voltage, which increases the output current, resisting the change in current.

6.  Inductors oppose changes in current. They act as resistors to AC and as short circuits to DC.

7.  An inductor can be thought of similar to a flywheel in mechanics, which stores energy in a rotating wheel.

8.  Inductors are useful because not only do they have interesting electric properties, their magnetic field also allows them to interface into the real world because magnetic field effects have a much longer reach than electric field effects.

9. When current to an inductor is suddenly shut off, it creates a large voltage, known as an inductive kick.

10. A snubber diode is used to mitigate against the negative effects of an inductive kick.

# Apply What You Have Learned

1. If I want a circuit to block DC but allow AC, should I use an inductor or a capacitor?

2. If I want a circuit to allow DC but block AC, should I use an inductor or a capacitor?

3. Why are inductors used so much in systems that interact with the outside world?

4. Why does inductive kick happen?

5. Draw a schematic of an inductor where the positive side of the inductor has a switch and the negative side is connected to an LED and a resistor. Add in a snubber diode to protect the LED from the effect of turning off the switch.

6. What is the purpose of the snubber diode?

7. If I have an inductor that is 5 H and has a steady current going through it of 2 A, what is the size of the magnetic flux in the inductor's magnetic field?

8. If I have an inductor that is 7 µH and has a steady current going through it of 3 mA, what is the size of the magnetic flux in the inductor's magnetic field?

9. If I have a 4 H inductor with 0.3 Wb of flux in its magnetic field, how much current is flowing through it?

10. If an inductor's magnetic field has 5 Wb of flux and it decreases to 3 Wb of flux over 2 seconds, what is the average voltage produced over that timeframe?

11. If an inductor's magnetic field has 1 µWb of flux and it increases to 2 µWb of flux over 0.4 second, what is the average voltage produced over that timeframe?

12. If the current flowing through a 3 H inductor drops from 7 mA to 1 mA over a period of 0.01 second, what is the average voltage produced over that time period?

# CHAPTER 21

# Inductors and Capacitors in Circuits

In this chapter, we will look at a few of the basic uses of simple inductors.

## 21.1  RL Circuits and Time Constants

Just as we had an RC circuit for capacitors, there is a similar circuit for inductors—the RL circuit. Just as inductors are the alter ego of capacitors, RL circuits are the alter ego of RC circuits.

An RL circuit is a circuit consisting of a resistor (R) and an inductor (L) in series with each other. They are similar in construction and usage to the RC circuits we looked at in Chapter 17, but have some important differences.

In RC circuits, the RC time constant was the amount of time it took to charge a capacitor to 63.2% of full voltage when coupled through a resistor. That is, after 1 time constant has passed, the voltage between the legs of the capacitor will be 63.2% of supply voltage.

In RL circuits, the RL time constant is the amount of time it takes to charge the inductor's magnetic field 63.2% of its final value. Since the size of the magnetic field and the current are directly related to each other, this is also the amount of time it takes to get the current up to 63.2% of its final rate.

© Jonathan Bartlett 2020
J. Bartlett, *Electronics for Beginners*, https://doi.org/10.1007/978-1-4842-5979-5_21

The way that the RL time constant is calculated *is different from* the way that RC time constants are calculated. The RL time constant is found by *dividing* the inductance in Henries (L) by the resistance in ohms (R).

$$\tau = \frac{L}{R} \tag{21.1}$$

Figure 21-1 shows the relationship between the number of time constants, the current through the inductor, and the voltage across the inductor. This is the same table as the one for RC time constants (Figure 17-1) except that current and voltage are swapped with each other.

| # of Time Constants | % of Current | % of Voltage |
| --- | --- | --- |
| 0.5 | 39.3% | 60.7% |
| 0.7 | 50.3% | 49.7% |
| 1 | 63.2% | 36.8% |
| 2 | 86.5% | 13.5% |
| 3 | 95.0% | 5.0% |
| 4 | 98.2% | 1.8% |
| 5 | 99.3% | 0.7% |

*Figure 21-1.*  *RL Time Constants*

> **Example 21.20** Let's say that we have a 2 H inductor in series with a 500 Ω resistor connected to a 5 V source. How long will it take before the inductor has 2.5 V across its terminals?
>
> To solve this, recognize that 2.5 V is basically half of the voltage source. Therefore, we need to look at Figure 21-1 and find the one which is closest to having 50% of the voltage. That is 0.7 time constant.

Now, we need to figure out what the time constant for this circuit is. The inductance is 2 H, and the resistance is 500 Ω. Therefore, according to Equation 21.1, we divide the inductance by the resistance:

$$\tau = \frac{2}{500}$$
$$= 0.004 \text{second}$$

Therefore, the time constant is 0.004 second. We are wanting 0.7 time constants, so the final answer is 0.004 · 0.7 = 0.0028 seconds.

## 21.2 Inductors and Capacitors as Filters

As we have mentioned, a general way of thinking about capacitors and inductors is that capacitors allow AC but block DC and inductors are the other way around. Inductors allow DC but block AC.

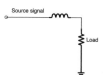

***Figure 21-2.*** *Removing High Frequencies Using an Inductor*

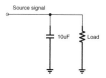

***Figure 21-3.*** *Removing High Frequencies Using a Capacitor*

This can also be thought of in terms of frequency response. When dealing with signals (audio circuits, radio circuits, etc.), you oftentimes want to deal with certain frequencies and not others. With an inductor, the lower the frequency is, the easier it is to pass through from one side to the other. With a capacitor, the higher the frequency is, the easier it is to pass through from one side to the other.

Many audio systems have different speakers optimized for different frequencies. A common setup is to have two speakers—a woofer which handles the low pitches and a tweeter which handles the higher pitches. By using capacitors and inductors, circuit designers can customize which frequencies go to which speakers.

Radio systems also utilize capacitors and inductors. Each radio station operates on a specific carrier frequency. A **carrier frequency** is the dominant frequency used to carry a signal. When building a radio receiver, capacitors and inductors are used to isolate the specific frequency from all of the frequencies being transmitted over the air.

Chapter 22 will discuss the mathematics behind this further.

# 21.3  Parallel and Series Capacitors and Inductors

Capacitors and inductors can each often take on the role of the other in frequency filtering. As we have mentioned, you can use a capacitor to allow AC signals and block DC and low-frequency signals. Inductors do the opposite—they allow DC and low-frequency signals and block AC signals. However, in a pinch, you can actually get each one to do the job of the other.

Imagine that you want to get rid of noise in a circuit. Noise is essentially high-frequency AC. Using the previously defined rules, we might want to put an inductor in series with the circuit to remove noise. Figure 21-2 shows what this looks like. There is, however, another option.

Instead of putting an inductor in series with the circuit, we can instead wire a capacitor that goes to ground in parallel with the circuit. Figure 21-3 shows this configuration. The way to think about this is that, since AC signals travel through a capacitor, the capacitor is shunting off AC signals to ground before they get to the load.

Likewise, the same can be done for low-frequency filtering. Normally a capacitor is used to block low-frequency or DC signals when wired in series. However, an inductor can be used in parallel to pass off low frequencies to ground while letting high frequencies pass through.

In both of these situations, if the currents going to ground will be significant at all, you might also consider putting a small resistor in the parallel circuit as well. This will lessen the ability of the circuit to pass signals off to ground, but will also prevent short circuit behavior if you get significant signals being shunted off to ground.

Additionally, when you switch from the inline to the parallel version of these circuits, you wind up wasting the power that gets shunted off to ground. In the series versions of the circuit, any unused power is either blocked or stored. Therefore, it doesn't really waste much power. However, in the parallel versions, the filtered power is simply sent to ground, essentially wasting it.

# Review

In this chapter, we learned the following:

1.  A resistor-inductor series circuit is known as an RL circuit.

2.  RL circuits have time constants very similar to RC circuits.

3.  The time constant for an RL circuit is given by *dividing* the inductance by the resistance.

4. For RL circuits, the voltage and current values for each time constant are swapped.

5. Inductors and capacitors can be used to filter specific frequencies.

6. Capacitors allow high frequencies to go through, while inductors allow lower frequencies to go through.

7. Using capacitors and inductors together allows a person to define a specific range of frequencies that they wish to either block or allow.

8. Radios use this feature which allows people to filter only the specific radio station frequency they want.

9. Capacitors and inductors can be used for the other's job in filters by wiring them in parallel so that they carry their type of current (AC or DC) to ground instead of letting it pass to the load.

# Apply What You Have Learned

1. What is the time constant of a series circuit consisting of a 50 Ω resistor and a 2 H inductor?

2. What is the time constant of a series circuit consisting of a 10 Ω resistor and a 5 µH inductor?

3. If I have a 9 V battery and I connect it to a series circuit consisting of a 1 kΩ resistor and a 23 µH inductor, how much time will it take before the current through the inductor reaches approximately 87% of its maximum value?

4. If I have a 5 V source and I connect it to a series circuit consisting of a 2 kΩ resistor and a 6 μH inductor, how much time will it take before the voltage across the inductor falls below 0.25 V?

5. If I have a circuit that has unwanted high-pitched noise, what component can I wire in series with the circuit to remove the noise?

6. If I have a circuit that has unwanted high-pitched noise, what component can I wire in parallel with the circuit to remove the noise?

7. What types of currents does an inductor (a) block and (b) allow?

8. What types of currents does a capacitor (a) block and (b) allow?

9. If I am building a radio, I need to allow through only very specific frequencies. What component or combination of components would I use to do this?

# CHAPTER 22

# Reactance and Impedance

## 22.1 Reactance

We have discussed resistance quite a bit in this book. Resistance is specifically about the ability of a component to be a good conductor of electricity. When a circuit encounters resistance, power is lost through the resistor.

However, another way of preventing current from flowing is known as *reactance*. With reactance, the power isn't dissipated, but rather the current is *prevented from flowing altogether.*

Let's think again about what happens when a voltage is connected to a capacitor in series. The capacitor starts to fill up. As the capacitor gets more and more full, there is less charge that can get onto the plate of the capacitor. This prevents the other side from filling up as well, and current cannot get through the capacitor. This acts *in a similar way to resistance*—it is preventing (impeding) the flow of current. However, it is not dissipating power because it is actually preventing the current from flowing. This is known as **reactance**. For capacitors, it is called **capacitative reactance,** and for inductors, it is called **inductive reactance**.

© Jonathan Bartlett 2020
J. Bartlett, *Electronics for Beginners*, https://doi.org/10.1007/978-1-4842-5979-5_22

Reactance is usually frequency dependent. Again, going to the capacitor example, with high frequencies, the capacitor is continually charging and discharging, so it never really gets full, so it never impedes the current flow very much. Therefore, capacitors add very little reactance with high-frequency AC. The lower frequencies, however, give the capacitors time to get full, and when they are full, they impede the current flow. Therefore, for capacitors, lower frequencies create more reactance.

Reactance is measured in ohms, just like resistance. However, they cannot be simply added to resistances, so they are usually prefixed with the letter $j$. So 50 ohms of reactance is usually labeled as $j50\ \Omega$ so that it is understood as a reactance. Reactances can be added to each other, and resistances can be added to each other. We will see how to combine them in Section 22.2, "Impedance." Reactances are usually denoted using the letter $X$.

The reactance of a capacitor ($X_C$) is given by the following formula:

$$X_C = -\frac{1}{2\pi \cdot f \cdot C} \qquad (22.1)$$

In this formula, $f$ is the AC frequency of the signal (in hertz), and $C$ is the capacitance. It might seem strange that this produces a negative value. The reason for this will make sense as we go forward. However, it is *not* producing negative impedance—we will see this when we combine reactance with resistance.

> **Example 22.21** What is the reactance of a 50 nF capacitor to a signal of 200 Hz? To find this, we merely use the formula:

$$X_C = -\frac{1}{2\pi \cdot f \cdot C}$$

$$= \frac{1}{2\pi \cdot 200 \cdot 0.00000005}$$

$$\approx \frac{1}{2 \cdot 3.14 \cdot 200 \cdot 0.00000005}$$

$$= \frac{1}{0.00000624}$$

$$\approx -j160256\Omega$$

You can see from this formula why it is said that a capacitor blocks DC. DC is, essentially, current that does not oscillate. In other words, the frequency is zero. Therefore, the formula will reduce to $\frac{1}{0}$, which is infinite. Therefore, it has infinite reactance against DC.

Also note what happens as the frequency increases. As the frequency increases, the denominator gets larger and larger. That means that the reactance is getting smaller and smaller—closer and closer to zero. As the frequency goes up, the reactance is essentially heading toward zero, but will never get there because the frequency can't be infinite.

The formula for **inductive reactance** $(X_L)$ is very similar:

$$X_L = 2\pi \cdot f \cdot L \qquad (22.2)$$

In this equation, $f$ is the signal frequency, and $L$ is the inductance of the inductor in Henries.

> **Example 22.22** Let's say that I have an 3 H inductor with a 50 Hz AC signal. How much reactance does the inductor have in this circuit?
>
> $$X_L = 2\pi \cdot f \cdot L$$
> $$= 2 \cdot 3.14 \cdot 50 \cdot 3$$
> $$= j9420\Omega$$

The reactance in this circuit is $j9,420\ \Omega$.

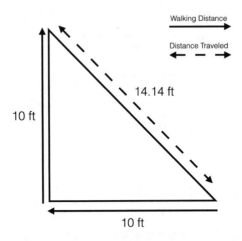

***Figure 22-1.*** *Total Distance Traveled vs. Total Displacement*

## 22.2 Impedance

In fact, resistance and reactance are usually combined together in a circuit to get a quantity known as **impedance**, which is simply the combination of resistive and reactive quantities. Impedance is often designated using the letter $Z$.

Resistance and reactance aren't added together directly; instead, you can think of them acting at angles to each other. Let's say that I start at my house and walk 10 feet out my front door. Then, I turn 90 degrees right and walk another 10 feet. While I have walked 20 feet, I am *not* 20 feet from my door. I am, instead, a little over 14 feet from my door. I can call this my displacement. Figure 22-1 shows what this looks like visually.

Since this is a right triangle, the distance from the start to the end is found on the hypotenuse of this triangle. We can calculate the total displacement using the Pythagorean theorem ($A^2 + B^2 = C^2$). If we solve for $C$ (total displacement), we get

$$C = \sqrt{A^2 + B^2} \qquad (22.3)$$

So, in our distance example, if I went forward 10 feet, turned left, and went another 10 feet, the total distance traveled would be

$$
\begin{aligned}
C &= \sqrt{A^2 + B^2} \\
&= \sqrt{10^2 + 10^2} \\
&= \sqrt{100 + 100} \\
&= \sqrt{200} \\
&\approx 14.14
\end{aligned}
$$

The total impedance is like the total distance from your door. Resistance and reactance are like different walking directions (at right angles to each other), and impedance is the total displacement. That's why we use the letter $j$ to signify reactance—it is just like resistance but in a different direction.

So how do we calculate impedance? In fact, it is calculated *precisely like* the displacement calculation in Equation 22.3:

$$\text{impedance} = \sqrt{\text{resistance}^2 + \text{reactance}^2} \qquad (22.4)$$

Or, using their common abbreviations, we can say:

$$Z = \sqrt{R^2 + X^2} \qquad (22.5)$$

Let's see how we can use Equation 22.4 to calculate total impedance. If I have a circuit that has 30 Ω of resistance and $j$20 Ω of reactance, then the formula for total impedance is

$$\text{impedance} = \sqrt{\text{resistance}^2 + \text{reactance}^2}$$
$$= \sqrt{30^2 + 20^2}$$
$$= \sqrt{900 + 400}$$
$$= \sqrt{1300}$$
$$\approx 36.1\Omega$$

As you can see, when using this formula, we are calculating a total impedance, so the $j$ drops away.

**Example 22.23** If I have a 1 kΩ resistor in series with a 100 nF capacitor with a 800 Hz signal, what is the total impedance to the signal that my circuit is giving?

To find out impedance, we need both resistance and reactance. We already have resistance—1 kΩ. The reactance is found by using Equation 22.1:

$$X_C = -\frac{1}{2\pi \cdot f \cdot C}$$
$$= \frac{1}{2\pi \cdot 800 \cdot 0.0000001}$$
$$\approx \frac{1}{0.0005024}$$
$$\approx -j1990\Omega$$

So the reactance is about $-j1990$ Ω.

So, if the resistance is 1000 Ω and the reactance is $-j1990$ Ω, what is the impedance? The impedance is found by using Equation 22.4:

$$\begin{aligned}
\text{impedance} &= \sqrt{\text{resistance}^2 + \text{reactance}^2} \\
&= \sqrt{1000^2 + (-1990)^2} \\
&= \sqrt{1000000 + 3960100} \\
&= \sqrt{4960100} \\
&\approx 2227\,\Omega
\end{aligned}$$

## 22.3 RLC Circuits

So far we have discussed RC (resistor-capacitor) and RL (resistor-inductor) circuits. When you combine all of these components together, you get an RLC (resistor-inductor-capacitor) circuit.

When you calculate the impedance of such circuits, you have to be sure you include the reactance of *both* the capacitive and the inductive components. While inductors and capacitors both offer reactance to certain frequencies, their reactances actually oppose each other. That is, the reactance of one cancels out the reactance of the other. This is why the capacitive reactance is negative and the inductive reactance is positive.

Therefore, when calculating reactances that include *both* inductance and capacitance, you can add the reactances just like you would add resistances. However, since the capacitive reactances are negative and the inductive reactances are positive, they wind up canceling each other out to some degree.

> **Example 22.24** If I have an inductor of 5 mH and a capacitor of 5 μF in series with a 200 Ω resistor, what is the impedance of the circuit for a frequency of 320 Hz?
>
> To solve this problem, we need to first find the capacitive reactance $(X_C)$ and the inductive reactance$(X_L)$. To get the capacitive reactance, we use Equation 22.1:

$$X_C = -\frac{1}{2\pi \cdot f \cdot C}$$

$$= \frac{1}{2\pi \cdot 320 \cdot 0.000005}$$

$$\approx \frac{1}{0.01}$$

$$\approx -j1990\Omega$$

The inductive reactance is found using Equation 22.2:

$$X_L = 2\pi \cdot f \cdot L$$

$$= 2\pi \cdot 320 \cdot 0.005$$

$$\approx j10\Omega$$

Now, we can just add these reactances together:

$$X_{total} = X_L - X_C$$

$$= j10\Omega + -j100\Omega$$

$$= -j90\Omega$$

The fact that this is negative is not a problem because it will be squared (which will get rid of the negative) in the next step. Now that we know the resistance (200 Ω) and the reactance ($-j90$ Ω), we just need to use Equation 22.4 to calculate the total impedance:

$$\text{impedance} = \sqrt{\text{resistance}^2 + \text{reactance}^2}$$

$$= \sqrt{200^2 + (-90)^2}$$

$$= \sqrt{40000 + 8100}$$

$$= \sqrt{48100}$$

$$\approx 219\Omega$$

So the total impedance (opposition to current) in this circuit is 219 Ω.

# 22.4 Ohm's Law for AC Circuits

In an AC circuit, the current and voltage are continually varying. Therefore, using the traditional Ohm's law, you would have to calculate Ohm's law over and over again in order to find out the relationships between voltage, current, and resistance.

However, there is a form of Ohm's law that works directly on AC circuits of a given frequency. That is, it is essentially a *summary* of the voltages and currents that happen on each cycle. Ohm's law for AC circuits is basically identical to the previous Ohm's law, but the terms are slightly different:

$$V_{RMS} = I_{RMS} \cdot Z \qquad (22.6)$$

Here, the voltage we are referring to ($V_{RMS}$) is an *average* voltage through one cycle of AC. This average is known as the **RMS** average. It is a little different than the typical average you might think of. If an AC voltage is swinging back and forth from positive to negative, the actual average voltage is probably around zero. However, RMS voltage is about calculating the average amount of push in any direction—positive or negative. Therefore, the RMS voltage will always yield a positive answer.[1]

Likewise, the current refers to the RMS current ($I_{RMS}$). Just like the RMS voltage, the RMS current will always be positive, because it is the measure of the average amount of flow in *any* direction.

Finally, the impedance $Z$ is calculated as we have noted in this chapter—by combining resistances and reactances together into an impedance.

---

[1]RMS stands for "root mean square." It is obtained by (a) squaring every data point, (b) averaging the squares, and then (c) taking the square root of the average. This is why it will be positive—it deals in squares.

Thus, Ohm's law for AC circuits can be used to express summary relationships about average voltage, average current, and impedance in an AC signal.

> **Example 22.25** I have an AC circuit whose RMS voltage is 10 V. I have calculated the impedance of this circuit to be 20 Ω. What is the RMS current of this circuit?
>
> To find this out, we just rearrange Ohm's law a little bit:
>
> $$V_{RMS} = I_{RMS} \cdot Z$$
> $$I_{RMS} = \frac{V_{RMS}}{Z}$$
>
> Now I just use the values given to fill in the blanks:
>
> $$I_{RMS} = \frac{V_{RMS}}{Z}$$
> $$= \frac{10}{20} = 0.5 \text{ A}$$

In this circuit, we would have an average of half an amp (500 milliamps) flowing through the circuit.

> **Example 22.26** I have an AC voltage source with an RMS voltage of 5 V running at 200 Hz. It is connected in series with a 50 kΩ resistor and a 50 nF capacitor. What is the current in this circuit?
>
> To find this out, we have to first find the total impedance of the circuit. That means we have to use Equation 22.1 to find the reactance of the capacitor:

$$X_C = -\frac{1}{2\pi \cdot f \cdot C}$$

$$= \frac{1}{2 \cdot 3.14 \cdot 200 \cdot 0.000005}$$

$$= \frac{1}{0.00000628}$$

$$\approx -j159236\,\Omega$$

Now that we have the resistance (50 kΩ) and the reactance ($-j159236\,\Omega$), we can use them in Equation 22.5:

$$Z = \sqrt{R^2 + X^2}$$

$$= \sqrt{50000^2 + 159236^2}$$

$$= \sqrt{2500000000 + 25356103696}$$

$$= \sqrt{27856103696}$$

$$\approx 166901\,\Omega$$

Now we can use Ohm's law for AC circuits (Equation 22.6 to find the current):

$$I_{RMS} = \frac{V_{RMS}}{Z}$$

$$= \frac{5}{166901}$$

$$\approx 0.00003\,\text{A}$$

This means that the average current ($I_{RMS}$) will be approximately 0.00003 A, or 30 μA.

# 22.5 Resonant Frequencies of RLC Circuits

As we have seen, the capacitative reactance goes closer to zero when the frequency goes up. Likewise, the inductive reactance increases when the frequency goes up. Additionally, the capacitative reactance and the inductive reactance have opposite signs—negative for capacitative reactance and positive for inductive reactance.

What is interesting is that if you have a combination of inductors and capacitors, there is always some frequency at which their reactances exactly cancel each other out. This point is known as the **resonant frequency** of the circuit.

When a capacitor and an inductor are in series with each other, it is termed an LC series circuit. Because the inductor inhibits high frequencies and the capacitor inhibits low frequencies, LC circuits can be used to let through a very specific frequency range. The center of this range is known as the **resonant frequency** of the circuit.

Now, if you are good with algebra, you can combine Equation 22.1 and Equation 22.2 to figure out the resonant frequency of a circuit (i.e., set them to add up to zero and then solve for the frequency $f$). However, to spare you the trouble, there is a formula that you can use to find the resonant frequency of a circuit:

$$f = \frac{1}{2\pi\sqrt{L \cdot C}} \qquad (22.7)$$

At this frequency, there is no total reactance to the circuit—the only impedance comes from the resistance.

> **Example 22.27** Let's say that you have a 20 µF capacitor in series with a 10 mH inductor. What is the resonant frequency of this circuit?
>
> To find the resonant frequency, we only need to employ Equation 22.7:

$$f = \frac{1}{2\pi\sqrt{L \cdot C}}$$

$$= \frac{1}{2\pi\sqrt{0.01 \cdot 0.00002}}$$

$$= \frac{1}{2\pi\sqrt{0.0000002}}$$

$$\approx \frac{1}{2\pi \cdot 0.000447}$$

$$\approx \frac{1}{0.00279}$$

$$\approx 358\text{Hz}$$

Therefore, this circuit has a resonant frequency of 358 Hz. This means that, at this frequency, this circuit has no reactive impedance.

Resonance frequencies are important in signal processing. They can be used in audio equipment to boost the sound of a specific frequency (since all other frequencies will have resistance). They can be used to select radio stations in radio equipment (since it will be the only frequency allowed through without resistance). You can also remove a specific frequency by taking a resonant frequency circuit to ground, thereby having a specific frequency short-circuited to ground with no resistance.

## 22.6 Low-Pass Filters

As mentioned, capacitors allow AC and block DC. If you wanted to remove the AC component of a signal, a capacitor can be connected to take the AC portion of your signal to ground. This is known as a low-pass filter, because, since the high-frequency (AC) component of the signal is being sent to ground, the low-frequency (DC) component of the signal is being allowed to pass.

How do you know what size of capacitor to use? Well, a rule of thumb is to have a capacitor whose reactance to the signal that you want to *keep* is greater than the resistance coming in to the capacitor (we want a larger resistance because we don't want that signal coming through the capacitor). Therefore, we can modify Equation 22.1 to say

$$f = \frac{1}{2\pi \cdot R \cdot C} \tag{22.8}$$

or

$$C = \frac{1}{2\pi \cdot R \cdot f} \tag{22.9}$$

If you know the incoming resistance, you can use that last equation to just solve for the size of capacitor you will need (if you don't have any incoming resistance, then you can simply add a resistor of your choosing and calculate for $C$).

## 22.7 Converting a PWM Signal into a Voltage

In Chapter 15, we talked about how the Arduino microcontroller can't emit an analog voltage, but can mimic it with a PWM signal, where it turns its 5 V signal on and off to mimic in-between voltages. We can use a low-pass filter to transform a PWM signal into a voltage.

The circuit to do so is fairly straightforward and is given in Figure 22-2. The resistor and capacitor serve to tune the lower end of the frequency of the signal that gets removed.

According to the specs, the PWM frequency is about 490 Hz. In theory, we could find the reactance of the capacitor using Equation 22.1. However, in practice, because the PWM is a square wave (it has very sharp edges), it requires a larger capacitor. In any case, this filter removes the AC component of the PWM and just leaves the residual voltage that it represents.

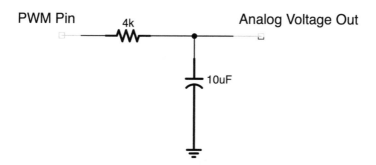

**Figure 22-2.** *Converting PWM to Analog with a Capacitor*

# Review

In this chapter, we learned the following:

1.  Reactance ($X$) is a property of some electronic components that is similar to resistance, but it *prevents* the flow of current instead of *dissipating* the flow (i.e., converting it to heat).

2.  Reactance, like resistance, is measured in ohms. A $j$ is placed in front of the reactance to specify that it is a reactance value.

3.  Reactance is frequency dependent—the amount of reactance depends on the frequency of the signal.

4.  Capacitors and inductors each have formulas that can be used to calculate the reactance of the components.

5.  Capacitors yield negative reactance and inductors yield positive reactance. This means that their reactances will oppose and cancel each other out to some degree.

6.  Impedance ($Z$) is the total inhibition of the flow of current, combining both resistive and reactive elements.

7.  Reactance and resistance are combined into impedance in the same way that walking two different directions can be combined into a total distance from your originating point—using the Pythagorean theorem.

8.  RMS voltage ($V_{RMS}$) is the average voltage of an AC circuit, regardless of the direction (positive or negative) of the voltage. This can be used to summarize the effects of an AC voltage.

9.  RMS current ($I_{RMS}$) is the average current of an AC circuit, regardless of the direction (positive or negative) of the voltage. This can be used to summarize the effects of an AC current.

10. Ohm's law for AC circuits yields the summary relationship between RMS voltage, RMS current, and impedance in an AC circuit. It is identical to the previous Ohm's law, but uses the summary values for the circuit at a particular frequency, rather than the values at a particular point in time.

11. The resonant frequency of a circuit is the frequency at which inductive reactance and capacitative reactance cancel each other out.

12.  Resonant frequencies can be used in any application where isolating a frequency is important, because the resonant frequency will be the only frequency not encountering resistance.

13.  Low-pass filters remove AC signals and allow lower-frequency signals to pass.

14.  A low-pass filter can be used to convert an Arduino PWM signal into a voltage.

# Exercises

1.  As the frequency of a signal goes up, how does that affect the reactance from a capacitor? What about with an inductor?

2.  As the frequency of a signal goes down, how does that affect the reactance from a capacitor? What about with an inductor?

3.  What is true about the relationship between the capacitative reactance and the inductive reactance at the resonant frequency?

4.  Why is power not used up with reactance?

5.  How are reactance and resistance combined to yield impedance?

6.  Calculate the capacitative reactance of a 3 F capacitor at 5 Hz.

7.  Calculate the capacitative reactance of a 20 µF capacitor at 200 Hz.

8. Calculate the inductive reactance of a 7 H inductor at 10 Hz.

9. Calculate the inductive reactance of a 8 mH inductor at 152 Hz.

10. Calculate the impedance of a circuit with a 200 Ω resistor in series with a 75 µF capacitor with a signal of 345 Hz.

11. Calculate the impedance of a circuit with a 310 Ω resistor in series with a 90 nF capacitor with a signal of 800 Hz.

12. Calculate the impedance of a circuit with no resistor and a 60 mH inductor with a signal of 89 Hz.

13. Calculate the impedance of a circuit with a 50 Ω resistor in series with a 75 µH inductor with a signal of 255 Hz.

14. If I have an AC circuit with an RMS voltage of 6 V and an impedance of 1 kΩ, what is the average (RMS) current of this circuit?

15. If I have an AC circuit and I measure the AC voltage as 10 V RMS and I measure the AC at 2 mA RMS, what is the impedance of this circuit?

16. If I have an 80 Hz AC circuit that has an 8 V RMS voltage source in series with a 500 Ω resistor, a 5 H inductor, and a 200 nF capacitor, what is the RMS current flowing in this circuit?

17. Calculate the impedance of a circuit with a 250 Ω resistor in series with a 87 µH inductor and a 104 µF capacitor with a signal of 745 Hz.

18.  What is the resonant frequency of the circuit in the previous question?

19.  What is the reactance of a circuit at its resonant frequency?

20.  If I have a 10 µF capacitor, what size inductor do I need to have a resonant frequency of 250 Hz?

# CHAPTER 23

# DC Motors

A **DC motor** is a device that converts DC electrical power into mechanical power. It operates by rotating a shaft using electromagnetism. DC motors are fairly simple to use, though they require slightly different reasoning from the way we have been examining circuits so far.

## 23.1 Theory of Operation

While there are more than one kind of motor, the "typical" DC motor is known as a **brushed electric motor**. This motor has a fixed outside container (called a **stator** because it is stationary) that contains magnets with opposite poles. Within the stator is an armature with electromagnets that is connected to the **shaft** (the shaft is the thing that turns). The electromagnets on the shaft's armature are then energized to be the same pole of the current magnetic orientation.

If you have ever tried to push two magnets together that have the same pole, you know that the magnetic fields exhibit a lot of physical force to try to prevent this from happening. Therefore, the fixed magnets' magnetic fields push on the temporarily created electromagnets' fields on the shaft's armature. When the shaft turns to align itself with the fixed magnets, it also turns the connector that connects the shaft to the electricity. When it is turned, the connectors on the shaft are now connected to the *opposite* polarity than they were, so their fields are no longer aligned again! Thus, the shaft continues rotating on.

© Jonathan Bartlett 2020
J. Bartlett, *Electronics for Beginners*, https://doi.org/10.1007/978-1-4842-5979-5_23

A certain type of motor, called a **brushless motor**, has a similar operation, except that instead of having the rotating shaft change the polarity of the current, it uses fixed magnets on the shaft and uses electromagnets for fixed magnets. Then, by pushing AC through the electromagnets, it changes the polarity of the fixed magnets back and forth, moving the shaft through the magnetic field. Brushless motors tend to be more expensive, but can rotate faster and have fewer parts which can wear out.

Even though brushless motors use AC internally, they are operated just like DC motors from the outside. Brushless motors have internal circuitry that converts the DC into an AC waveform for energizing the electromagnets appropriately.

## 23.2  Important Facts About Motors

Motors require a lot of current, especially to start up. Starting up, they require even more current (often ten times their normal current). This is also the amount of current they require if they ever stop rotating (known as stalling).

Motors are rated according to their most efficient operating voltage. If a motor is rated at 5 V, then it's not that you can't operate it at a different voltage, but that operating it at different voltages will change some of its characteristics and probably won't be as efficient.

Motors generate a negative voltage called *back EMF* that is in opposition to the voltage provided to them. Motors generate more back EMF the faster that they spin. At the point at which the back EMF is equal to the voltage provided, the motor will no longer spin faster. There is also some voltage drop by the internal resistance of the motor's coils, but it is relatively minor compared to the back EMF drop.

If there is nothing attached to the shaft, the amount of current the motor operates with is known as the **no load current**, and the speed at which the motor spins is known as the **no load RPM** (**RPM** means "revolutions per minute").

However, the most difficult thing that a motor does is to *start* rotating. When the motor isn't moving and is exhibiting its maximum rotational power (known as **torque**) to try to move, this is known as a **stall** condition. This is the most strenuous thing a motor can do, and many motors can't survive more than a few seconds in stall conditions. The amount of torque that a motor supplies in stall conditions is known as the **stall torque**, and the amount of current that the motor uses in these conditions is known as the **stall current**. Oftentimes, if you think you have a circuit that is properly sized for a motor, but it won't start spinning, this is because it isn't getting enough current for stall conditions. You can sometimes even check this by spinning the shaft by hand and seeing if the motor then springs to life.

Note that when a motor first turns on, it is always in stall conditions.

# 23.3  Using a Motor in a Circuit

DC motors are nice because they basically self-regulate. They spin fast enough to match whatever voltage is given to them and draw enough current to manage the proper torque for the load. If you want to know the details and calculations behind these things, see Appendix D, Section D.3, "Motor Calculations." However, if you stick with the voltage listed in the specs, the RPM of the motor generally gets fairly close to the specifications. In general, lower voltages lead to lower RPMs, and higher voltages lead to higher RPMs.

It is pretty rare to add series resistance to a motor circuit. There are several reasons for this. The first is that, as mentioned, motors basically self-regulate. This means that

1.  They will draw the amount of power they need to draw for the given torque and no more. Thus, a current-limiting resistor is not needed. Additionally, if you calculate the current-limiting resistor for steady-state conditions, it will provide too little current for stall conditions.

2.  They will utilize the given voltage to achieve the
    RPM that balances it out. Therefore, there will not
    be any excess voltage to consume.

Additionally, series resistance can actually cause problems. The amount of current a motor can draw can vary very widely. As mentioned, the stall current can sometimes be ten times the steady-state current. With series resistance, the voltage drop across the resistor will then vary up to ten times as well, which will affect the voltage available to the motor and thus alter the performance specifications of the motor. Under stall conditions, it will decrease the performance of the motor at precisely the wrong moment.

Therefore, while you might want to down-step voltage for a motor to get the proper RPM, you want to do so in an essentially non-resistive way, using diodes, transistors, or other components that are not likely to add significant series resistance to the motor.

However, you may want to prevent problematic conditions as well. You don't want a short circuit in your motor to fry your whole circuit. Because of this, you may want to add a fuse (instead of a current-limiting resistor) that will trip if it experiences excessively high current to protect the rest of your circuit.

Additionally, since motors contain electromagnets, they utilize induction. As mentioned in Chapter 20, when current to an inductor stops, it creates a voltage spike due to the collapsing of the electromagnetic fields. Therefore, we have to provide a snubber diode to prevent that current from blowing out our sensitive equipment. You can refer back to Figure 20-2 to see how this is wired.

Because motors are operated through induction, they are often represented with the same symbol as an inductor.

# 23.4 Attaching Things to Motors

Motors just spin a shaft. What happens after the shaft starts spinning is, technically, outside the scope of this book and entirely up to you. Nonetheless, I thought I would take just a moment to talk about attaching things to motors.

The first thing that comes up is, *how* do you attach something to a motor's shaft? There are several common options:

1. Some items are built to have a **mechanical fit** onto a shaft. That is, you can push them onto the shaft with some force, but they are unlikely to just fall off on their own.

2. Some items are attached with a **set screw**. This is similar to the previous method, except that what keeps the attachment in place is not the pure fit, but an extra screw that applies the force after your attachment is in position. This allows for a little wider range of variance in size, so if the sizes are off slightly, the set screw will make up for the lack of mechanical force.

3. Finally, some items need to be glued, welded, or in some other way permanently affixed to the shaft. The problem with this method is that, once attached, you can't really use your motor for anything else.

So what are we attaching to our motor?

Well, you *can* directly attach things such as wheels to the shaft of the motor. For free-spinning things such as propellers, this is exactly what you do. It works for wheels too, kind of. The problem is that small DC motors often can't generate the kind of torque you need for typical usages. Therefore, you need gears to translate the low torque/high RPM of the motor into a high-torque/low-RPM output to the wheels.

Many places sell gearboxes which handle all of this for you. In fact, you can even buy motors with the gearboxes inside the motor packages as well. Then, you connect your gearbox to the axle of the wheels using a gear or a belt, and the wheel is what performs the final actions.

I find it interesting that all of these are just a series of conversions. We first convert electrical power into mechanical power. We then convert low-torque/high-RPM power into high-torque/low-RPM power. This is actually very similar to the operation of a transformer in electronics, which converts low current/high voltage into high current/low voltage and vice versa. Then, the wheels convert rotational power into linear power, by driving your project along the ground or driving a belt around and so on. We have a source of power (the battery) and the thing we want to do (moving things), and what we have to figure out is the best way to convert the kind of power we have into the kind of power that we need.

# 23.5  Bidirectional Motors

Oftentimes we want motors to spin both forward and backward. Most motors can spin backward just by reversing the positive and negative leads to the motor. However, we need to be able to do that electrically instead of forcing someone to go and reverse wires on our circuit board whenever they want to back up instead of go forward.

Creating a circuit that can have current go either direction is hard enough, but added to that is the problem of positioning the snubber diodes—they will be needed in *both* directions! However, if we just attached snubber diodes in each direction, we would wind up with a short circuit no matter what (the current would prefer to just go through the diode pointing our way rather than through the motor).

A type of circuit to manage these considerations has been developed, known as an **H-Bridge**. We will not delve into the details of how H-Bridges work or how to use one, but I thought I should mention them.

If you are interested in H-Bridges, a popular chip is the L293.

# 23.6  Servo Motors

A **servo motor** (usually just called a servo) is a motor that, instead of spinning, creates an angle. Think about a remote-controlled car. To turn the car, the wheels have to be at an angle. A regular DC motor is what spins the wheels, but a servo motor is what causes the wheels to turn to a specific angle.

Servos are operated by sending an oscillating signal, much like the output of a 555 timer (see Chapter 18). Servos expect a signal every 20 milliseconds, and the length of the signal will determine the angle of the servo:

- If the signal is 1.5 milliseconds, the servo will be in the middle (neutral) position.

- If the signal is 1.0 millisecond, the servo will rotate 90 degrees counterclockwise.

- If the signal is 2.0 milliseconds, the servo will rotate 90 degrees clockwise.

- Between these positions, the servo will rotate in a proportional way.

As you can see, the servo can swing through 180 degrees of rotation. The servo expects to continually receive signals while it is on in order to maintain its position, but that position can be changed at any time with a change in the length of the signal. The behavior of a servo when no signal is applied depends on the particular servo you are using.

Servo motors have separate inputs for their voltage supply and their signal. The signal does not have to power the motor—it is powered through its supply voltage. Instead, the servo motor just needs to receive a small signal to know its rotation, and the actual power is supplied through its voltage input.

# 23.7 Stepper Motors

Stepper motors are motors that rotate in very precise increments. If you need something that can freely rotate, but need an *exact* number of revolutions or even half-revolutions, quarter-revolutions, and so on, a stepper motor supplies this capability. Stepper motors are often used in 3D printers, where the print head needs to move a precise distance. The integrity of the generated structure depends on the print head being in the exact correct location. Therefore, the rotation of the shaft must be precisely controlled.

The control of stepper motors is far outside the scope of this book and usually requires additional hardware (known as a stepper motor driver circuit), but I wanted to be sure you are aware of what they are and why they are important.

# Review

In this chapter, we learned the following:

1. A DC motor converts electrical power into mechanical rotational power by either changing the magnetization of the shaft (in brushed motors) or of the fixed magnets (in brushless motors).

2. Rotational mechanical power is known as torque.

3. Motors tend to require a lot of current, especially at startup.

4. The rated voltage of a motor is related to the motor's RPM—decreasing the voltage decreases the RPM and increasing the voltage increases the RPM. This is due to the negative voltage (back EMF) generated by the movement of the motor.

5.  The current flowing through a motor is related to the torque needed to spin the motor—more required torque draws more current.

6.  When a motor is not spinning (either because it is just starting or because its load is too high), it is in a stall condition.

7.  Stall current is the amount of current the motor draws in stall conditions (usually about ten times more than in a steady state).

8.  Stall torque is the amount of torque generated in stall conditions.

9.  Loading a motor so that it stays in stall conditions for any significant amount of time can damage the motor.

10. Series resistance is almost never added to a motor circuit.

11. Snubber diodes are used to mitigate against inductive spikes that happen when the electromagnetic field of the motor shuts off.

12. Gears can convert the low torque/high RPM of a motor into a high-torque/low-RPM output.

13. Motors can be used bidirectionally using an H-Bridge.

14. A servo motor is a motor that, instead of spinning, creates a fixed angle based on the length of a signal that is sent to it every 20 milliseconds.

15. A stepper motor is a motor that provides precise control over the amount of rotation of the shaft.

# Apply What You Have Learned

1.  If you wanted to prevent too much current from going through a motor, what should you use for this?

2.  What happens to the RPM of a motor when I reduce the voltage to my motor?

3.  What should be attached to a motor to protect the other parts of the circuit when a motor is shut off?

4.  List one reason why a series resistor should not be used with a motor.

5.  If I was building a robot and wanted to control the angle of a robot's arm, what type of motor could I use?

6.  If I was building a machine to place components into a precise position onto a board, what type of motor should I pick to achieve that?

# PART IV

# Amplification Circuits

# CHAPTER 24

# Amplifying Power with Transistors

**Amplification** is the conversion of a low-power signal to a higher-power signal. Normally when we think of amplification, we think of sound amplifiers for musical instruments. Indeed those are amplifiers, and we will build a sound amplifier later in this book. However, *anytime* you convert a low-power input to a higher-power output, you have amplified the signal, whether that was a DC signal or an AC signal. In this chapter, we will focus on amplifying DC signals.

Many devices have limits to the amount of power they can output or even the amount of power we want them to output. Microcontrollers, for instance, are generally very sensitive with the amount of power they can source. The ATmega328/P (used in the Arduino Uno), for instance, has a maximum current rating of 40 mA, which is actually quite generous for a microcontroller. Other types of microcontrollers, such as many PIC microcontrollers, are rated for current outputs of 25 mA or less. Additionally, the voltage is more or less fixed at the operating voltage of the chip, which is usually 3–5 V.

However, numerous applications require more output (whether current, voltage, or power) than these can provide. A typical toy DC motor, for instance, needs about 250 mA for operation. So, if you want to control the motor with a microcontroller, then you have to have some way to convert your small output current into a larger output current to drive your motor.

© Jonathan Bartlett 2020
J. Bartlett, *Electronics for Beginners*, https://doi.org/10.1007/978-1-4842-5979-5_24

Another scenario to consider is a situation where we want to control a high-power motor or another device from a button or switch. Sometimes it can be problematic to have a switch for a device to have high power run through it. It could be dangerous, or it could cost money. Let's say that we had a switch that we wanted to control a high-power device that was 1,000 feet away. If we had the full power running through the switch, that means that we have to run larger cables and will have to account for the large resistance in the wires. Running power across that distance will result in power loss because of the resistance in the wires, which will increase the cost for running the unit! However, if we instead use a low-power circuit to run the switch, we don't get nearly as much power loss. We just need to *amplify* the power output of the switch to control our device once the signal reaches it. The amount of amplification that occurs is known as the **gain** of an amplifier.

# 24.1 An Amplification Parable

As we noted in Chapter 10, physics tells us that we can't actually increase the power of something. What we can do, though, is use a smaller power signal to control a larger power source, and that is what we refer to as amplification.

Let's say that we have a dam on a river. The river wants to go downstream, but it is blocked by the dam. Let's say that we have a giant named Andre, which is able to lift the dam using his strength. If Andre lifts the dam a little bit, a little bit of water flows. If Andre lifts the dam a lot, all of the water can flow. The power of the water itself is actually more than Andre's power. Therefore, Andre can "amplify" his power by raising and lowering the dam.

Let's say that at the end of the riverbed was a structure that Andre wanted to destroy, but Andre himself isn't strong enough to do it. However, the river is strong enough to do it. Therefore, rather than try to destroy the structure on his own, Andre decides to raise the dam and let the river's power do it.

Note that Andre didn't actually increase the amount of power in the river. Instead, he (a being with lesser power) *controlled* the operation of the river (a higher-powered entity) by adjusting the dam (the physical resistance against the water). Thus, he *amplified* the effects of his actions by controlling the resistance on the higher-powered current.

# 24.2 Amplifying with Transistors

A very common method of amplifying power output in projects is with **transistors**. The term "transistor" is short for "transconductance varistor," which means that it is an electrically controlled variable resistor. In other words, it helps you amplify a signal in your project the same way that the dam allowed Andre to amplify his power. The transistor operates as a controllable electric dam, allowing a smaller-powered electric signal to control a higher-powered electric signal by adjusting resistance.

Another way you can think of it is like an outdoor faucet—the water going through the faucet is controlled by the wheel knob on the top, which provides a variable amount of resistance to the flow. The faucet can be fully on, fully off, or somewhere in between, all based on where the knob is set. The knob setting is like the input current—a specific level of input current will control the amount of flow that comes out.

There are many different types of transistors, with a wide variety of ways in which they work. What they all have in common is that they have three (sometimes four) terminals, and one of the terminals acts as a control valve for the flow of electricity between the other two.

The main way that the types of transistors differ is in whether the knob on the faucet is controlled by voltage or by current. The transistors operated by current are known as **bipolar junction transistors** (BJTs), and the ones operated by voltage are known as **field effect transistors** (FETs).

As a gross overgeneralization, FETs are most useful for lower-power switching applications, while BJTs are most useful for power amplification. This chapter will cover BJTs.

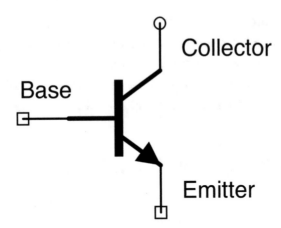

***Figure 24-1.*** *The Schematic Symbol for a Transistor*

BJTs come in two basic forms based on whether the knob is normally closed but turned on by positive current (an NPN transistor) or whether the knob is normally open but closed off by positive current (a PNP transistor). Here we will focus on NPN transistors.

## 24.3  Parts of the BJT

A BJT has three terminals—the collector, the base, and the emitter. In BJT NPN transistors, a small positive current comes in at the base (which you can think of as the knob of a faucet), and it controls the current moving from the collector to the emitter. The more current that comes through the base, the more current is allowed to flow between the collector and the emitter.

Figure 24-1 shows what an NPN BJT looks like in a schematic. The collector is at the top right of this diagram. The emitter is the line with the arrow pointing out. The current being controlled is the current between the collector and the emitter. The base is the horizontal line coming into the middle of the transistor. The base acts as a knob which can limit the flow of current between the collector and emitter.

Figure 24-2 shows a conceptual picture of how the transistor operates. The connection from the base to the emitter operates as a diode, and the connection from the collector to the emitter operates as a variable resistor, offering resistances from zero (completely open dam) to infinity (completely closed dam). The resistance of the variable resistor is based on the current flowing through the base. The variable resistor is adjusted so that, under certain conditions, the *current* flowing from the collector to emitter is a certain multiple of the current flowing from the base to the emitter.

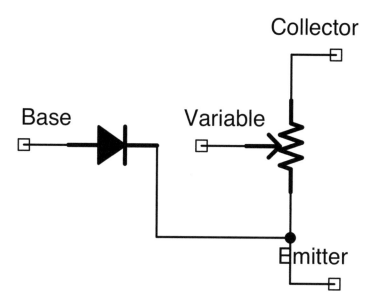

**Figure 24-2.** *A Conceptual View of Transistor Operation*

**Figure 24-3.** *A 2N2222A Transistor in a TO-92 Package*

When we talk about the voltages and currents flowing through the resistor, there are special names you need to remember and keep in mind. Each of the legs of the transistor is named by the first letter of its role. The collector is C, the emitter is E, and the base is B. Then, each of the voltages/currents is labeled based on which leg it is going from and to. Therefore, $V_{BE}$ is the voltage difference between the base and the emitter, $V_{CE}$ is the voltage difference between the collector and the emitter, and $V_{CB}$ is the voltage difference between the collector and the base. $I_{BE}$ is the current flowing between the base and the emitter, and $I_{CE}$ is the current flowing between the collector and the emitter. The total current coming out of the emitter is $I_{BE} + I_{CE}$. Take time to think about these designations as we are going to be using them extensively when we talk about transistors and their usage in a circuit.

A photo of a transistor can be seen in Figure 24-3. This is the transistor we will focus on in this chapter—the 2N2222A (sometimes called the PN2222A). It is important to read the datasheet to find out information about your transistor—especially to know which transistor leg is which! For the picture in Figure 24-3, the collector is on the right, the base is in the middle, and the emitter is on the left. Note that some other transistors have *different* pin configurations, which is why it is so important to check the datasheets. For instance, the P2N2222A (very similar name!) has the collector and emitter pins reversed!

Transistors can also come in a variety of shapes and sizes, known as **packages**. The package depicted in Figure 24-3 is known as a TO-92 package. Other packages you might see are a TO-18 package (which looks like a tiny metal cylinder) or a package similar to an integrated circuit.

# 24.4  NPN Transistor Operation Basics

To fully understand NPN transistor operation requires a lot of complicated mathematics. However, you can get a "good enough" understanding of it just by remembering a few simple rules.

## Rule 1: The Transistor Is Off by Default

By default, if there is no current flowing in the base, there will be no current flowing from the collector to the emitter. NPN transistors default to an "off" state.

## Rule 2: $V_{BE}$ Needs to Be 0.6 V to Turn the Transistor On

Remember that there is essentially a diode connecting the base to the emitter. Diodes have a voltage drop of about 0.6 V. Therefore, once the base voltage rises to 0.6 V *above* the emitter voltage, the transistor will turn on, and current will start to flow.

## Rule 3: $V_{BE}$ Will Always Be Exactly 0.6 V When the Transistor Is On

This is a corollary of the previous rule. Remember from Chapter 8 that we used diodes to give us fixed voltage differences between points on a circuit. This is the same in a transistor. Because the BE junction acts as a diode, the base will always be 0.6 V above the emitter while the transistor is turned on.

# Rule 4: The Collector Should Always Be More Positive Than the Emitter

While technically you can have the collector go below the voltage of the base or the emitter, it is generally a bad idea with NPN transistors. It makes the circuit much harder to analyze. This book will assume that the circuit is set up in this manner.

# Rule 5: When the Transistor Is On, $I_{CE}$ Is a Linear Amplification of $I_{BE}$

So, when the transistor is on, the transistor amplifies the *current* flowing from the base to the emitter by adjusting the floodgates between the collector and the emitter. The multiplier that the transistor amplifies by is known as the transistor's **beta**—this is the current gain that an NPN transistor provides. The symbol for this value can be either $\beta$ or $h_{FE}$. The problem with a transistor's beta is that it isn't very exact or very constant. A batch of "identical" transistors can have betas that vary quite a bit. And, while they are operating, their temperature and other environmental factors will affect the beta as well. There are things you can do to compensate for this, but for now just realize that it happens. While there are transistors with a wide variety of ranges of their betas, the most common NPN transistors have a beta of around 100.

The exceptions to this are in Rules 6 and 7.

# Rule 6: The Transistor Cannot Amplify More Than the Collector Can Supply

This is mostly a reminder that the amplification comes *from* the collector current. If the collector can't supply the amplification, it won't happen. Basically, we need to think of the transistor as controlling a resistor from

the collector to the emitter which will adjust itself to maintain the ratio
(beta) between the base-emitter current and the collector-emitter current.
Thus, it can't provide less resistance than no resistance.

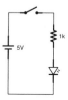

***Figure 24-4.*** *Using a Switch at the Start of a Circuit*

***Figure 24-5.*** *Using a Switch at the End of a Circuit*

# Rule 7: If the Base Voltage Is Greater Than the Collector Voltage, the Transistor Is Saturated

If the base voltage rises above the collector voltage, this causes the
transistor to behave as if there was no resistance going from the collector
to the emitter. This is known as **saturation mode**.

Using these rules, thinking about transistor action is fairly
straightforward. In the next section, we are going to put these rules into
practice.

# 24.5 The Transistor as a Switch

One of the issues with transistors is that it takes a while before using a transistor becomes intuitive. Transistors, as we will see in the forthcoming chapters, wind up needing a lot of special considerations. Because of this, many people don't use transistors directly and instead choose to only use integrated circuits (see Chapter 11). Integrated circuits, since they are based on the needs of a circuit instead of simple physical properties, tend to be much easier to work with. Most of the guess work has been taken out, and the chips are built so that they can be inserted into a circuit in a straightforward way. Even though some people opt to use integrated circuits instead of using transistors directly, it is worthwhile to understand their operation. It is always better to choose an option because you understand your available alternatives instead of choosing an option because that choice is the only one you understand.

Now, when we think of buttons and switches, most people naturally put the switch at the *beginning* of the circuit that is being turned on or off. Figure 24-4 shows what this looks like. However, it is just as valid to place the switch at the end, as shown in Figure 24-5.

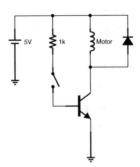

*Figure 24-6.*  *Using a Transistor as a Switch for a Motor*

When using transistors as a switch, we almost always place them at the *end* of a circuit. The reason for this should become clear as we examine circuits.

The first circuit we will look at is Figure 24-6. In this circuit, there is no real *need* for a transistor—we could just as easily have put the switch where the transistor is. However, understanding how this setup works will help us understand other transistor circuits. In this circuit, the base is controlled by a small signal (the size of the signal is set by the size of the resistor). When the base turns on, it switches on the connection from the collector to the emitter, which controls current to the motor (the diode is simply a snubber diode as described in Chapter 20).

---

## VISUALIZING INDUCTIVE KICK

If you wanted to see inductive kick in action, you can replace the snubber in the circuit in Figure 24-6 with an LED. Every time you turn of the switch, the LED will light up for a moment.

---

If the emitter of a transistor is simply connected directly to ground as it is in this example, the easiest way to analyze the circuit is by looking at the flow of current through the base. When the switch is closed, current will flow from the voltage source, through the resistor, across the transistor to ground. How much current? Well, this is actually a simple question. Remember that the junction from the base to the emitter can be treated as a simple diode (Rules 2 and 3). Therefore, we have a very simple circuit to analyze—voltage source to resistor to diode to ground. The voltage source is 5 V, and we have a diode (0.6 V) in the circuit path, so the voltage going through the resistor will be 4.4 V. Since the resistor is a 1 kΩ resistor, then, using Ohm's law, the current will be $I = \dfrac{V}{R} = \dfrac{4.4}{1000} = 0.0044\text{A}$ , or 4.4 mA.

Since the current going through the base ($I_{BE}$) is 4.4 mA, how much current is flowing from the collector to the emitter? We will assume for our exercises that the beta of transistors is exactly 100. According to Rule 5, that means that the current going from the collector to the emitter is 100 times the base current. Therefore, the current going from the collector to the emitter can be determined by $I_{CE} = \beta \cdot I_{BE} = 100 \cdot 4.4 = 440mA$. Therefore, the current going from the collector to the emitter is 440 mA. Because the current at the collector is 440 mA, that means that the current going through the motor is also 440 mA.

Depending on the current we *wanted* flowing through the motor, we could choose other resistor values to set the current to the appropriate level. However, because of Rule 6, the collector current will be limited by the motor's characteristics as well.

So why did we put the transistor at the end of the circuit? Let's imagine that we added one component to the circuit—a resistor after the emitter before the ground. All of a sudden, the circuit is a lot harder to analyze. Why? Well, we can no longer determine the base current by simply looking at the current path through the base. The voltage across that final resistor will *not* be based on the base current, but based on the *combined* current from both the base and the collector. Thus, when there are components after the emitter, in order to analyze the base current, you have to analyze how the components after the base respond to the *combined* current of the base and collector, but we won't know that until *after* you calculate the base current. It is *possible* to do this, but the math isn't fun. Instead, by connecting the emitter *directly* to ground, we simplify our calculations because we *know* the voltage after the emitter—since it is connected to ground, it will be zero.

Thus, by connecting the emitter directly to ground, we can analyze the current flow from the base *independently* of the current flow from the collector. Additionally, connecting the emitter to ground will automatically make sure our DC circuits follow Rule 4 and make it easy to analyze when the transistor turns on and off by Rule 2.

Just as we have looked at several common resistor circuit patterns, there are also several common transistor circuit patterns. The transistor pattern we are looking at in this chapter is known as a **common emitter** circuit. This is because the "interesting" parts of the circuit are at the base (which provides the current to be amplified) and the collector (where the preceding circuit enjoyed the amplified current) and the emitter is connected to a common reference point (the ground in this case).

# 24.6  Connecting a Transistor to an Arduino Output

To understand *why* we would use a transistor for a switch in the first place, let's imagine that we have a motor just like in Figure 24-6, but in this case we want it to be controlled by an output pin from an Arduino running on an ATmega328/P.

Now, on this chip, output pins put out 5 V, but their current rating maxes out at 40 mA. However, motors usually require much more current than that. If we wanted our motor to use as much current as in Figure 24-6, it would blow out the chip if we tried to connect it directly to the output.

However, we can instead wire the output of the Arduino to the base of a transistor. Then, the current coming out of the Arduino will be *much smaller* than the current used by the motor.

Figure 24-7 shows how this is configured. The schematic for this setup is almost identical to that of Figure 24-6. The only difference is that the electrical output of the Arduino is being used to control the base current instead of a mechanical switch. We can even calculate exactly how much current will be used. Since there is a diode (in the transistor), the resistor will be using 4.4 V. Therefore, since $I = \dfrac{V}{R}$, then $I = \dfrac{4.4}{1000} = 4.4\text{mA}$. With a beta of 100, that means that our motor can source 440 mA.

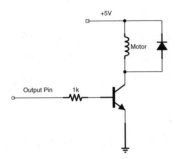

***Figure 24-7.*** *Using a Transistor to Control a Motor with a Microcontroller*

# 24.7 Stabilizing Transistor Beta With a Feedback Resistor

As we mentioned earlier, the transistor's beta is not a very stable parameter. If we mass-produced something with a transistor, each device would wind up having a transistor with a different beta. Additionally, as the device was used, the beta would *drift,* meaning that things such as the temperature of the transistor would affect the beta, so it wouldn't even have the same value the entire time it was turned on!

In order to get around this, engineers have developed ways of stabilizing the *actual* gain of a circuit even when the transistor's beta shifts. The way that this is achieved depends greatly on the type of circuit used. In a common emitter circuit like the one we have been looking at in this chapter, we can add a resistor to the emitter to stabilize the transistor's gain. I know that I *just said* not to do this because it is hard to analyze the effects. However, if you add a single resistor to the emitter, other people have worked out the math for you in order to make this work easily.

Now, to imagine *why* adding a resistor to the output stabilizes the transistor beta, we have to think about what happens when you do this. Without the resistor, when the transistor beta increases, it simply increases the current flow at the collector. Since the emitter is connected to ground, there aren't any more real effects. However, if I add a resistor to the emitter, then increasing the current flow at the collector will *also* increase the voltage at the emitter. Now, since the voltage between the base and the emitter ($V_{BE}$) *must* be at 0.6 V, this will actually *reduce* the current in the base.

This is known as **feedback**—where the *output* of the circuit comes back in some way to affect the input. Sometimes, feedback occurs because the output is wired back to the input, but in this case, the resistor simply increases the voltage at the emitter, causing the base to pull back.

What the final effect of adding a resistor to the base will do is to *limit* the gain of the transistor to a *fixed* value that won't change either due to manufacturing issues or due to changes during operation as the transistor beta changes due to temperature. Additionally, the computation for this is very simple. If your transistor beta varies between 50 and 200, you can add a resistor to the emitter which will limit the actual transistor gain below 50, and it will keep this value very stable even as the transistor's beta drifts. In such a configuration, the most stable gain you can get for a given transistor beta is about $\frac{1}{4}$ of the transistor's lowest beta.

The equation for the effect that a feedback resistor has on a transistor circuit depends on the circuit design itself—there isn't a one-size-fits-all rule. However, feedback resistors are usually fairly small compared to the rest of the circuit.

For most circuits, simply start with a small feedback resistor (10–100 Ω). The feedback resistor will usually improve the stability of your design, even if you can't calculate exactly how that affects the beta of the transistor. It means that your design will likely continue to work even with different transistors and operating at different temperatures. Just know that while you add stability, this will also limit the gain (which is sometimes problematic with motors).

# 24.8  A Word of Caution

One thing to keep in mind with transistors is that they can get very hot! Transistors have a maximum current rating, and that often is based on the amount of heat that they are able to dissipate. Transistors that are able to handle large currents are called **power transistors**, and usually have an attachment for a **heatsink**, which helps them dissipate heat to the air more efficiently.

If you build a circuit similar to the one in this chapter, be sure to keep in mind both the specs of the motor (how much voltage and current is required for it to operate) and the specs of the transistor (how much current the transistor can handle). If the motor doesn't have enough voltage or current, it might not turn on, and if the transistor can't handle the current, it could easily burn out.

# Review

In this chapter, we learned the following:

1.  It is often beneficial to be able to control a high-power signal using a low-power signal.

2.  The two major types of transistors are bipolar junction transistors (BJTs) and field effect transistors (FETs).

3.  BJTs are current-controlled devices and FETs are voltage-controlled devices.

4.  The terminals of a BJT are the base (B), the collector (C), and the emitter (E).

5. Voltages and currents going through a transistor are labeled using the terminals that the current is passing through. For instance, $I_{BE}$ refers to the current flowing between the base (B) and the emitter (E), and $V_{CE}$ refers to the voltage difference between the collector (C) and the emitter (E).

6. BJTs come in two main configurations—NPN and PNP.

7. With NPN transistors, a small positive current at the base causes a larger current to flow from the collector to the emitter.

8. With PNP transistors, current at the base reduces the current flow from collector to the emitter.

9. NPN transistors can be analyzed using these seven rules:

   • The transistor is off by default.

   • $V_{BE}$ needs to be 0.6 V to turn the transistor on.

   • $V_{BE}$ will always be *exactly* 0.6 V while the transistor is turned on.

   • The collector should always be more positive than the emitter.

   • When the transistor is on, $I_{CE}$ is a linear amplification of $I_{BE}$.

   • The transistor cannot amplify more than the collector can supply.

   • If the base voltage is greater than the collector voltage, the transistor is saturated (it will offer no resistance from the collector to the emitter).

10. The amount of current amplification a transistor provides is known as the transistor's beta (also known as $\beta$ or $h_{FE}$).

11. The actual beta of a transistor is not very stable and fluctuates quite a bit both because of manufacturing differences between transistors and even within a single transistor due to environmental changes such as temperature.

12. When used as a switch, transistors are usually placed at the *end* of a circuit in order to make the circuit analysis easier.

13. Transistors are often used to couple the outputs of devices with low current limits (such as a microcontroller) with devices that require higher output currents (such as motors).

14. To stabilize a transistor circuit's gain so that it doesn't vary with the transistor's beta, you can add in a small emitter resistor.

# Apply What You Have Learned

Unless otherwise specified, assume that the transistor is a BJT NPN transistor and that the beta is stable:

1. If the base of a transistor is at 3 V and the transistor is on, what will be the emitter voltage?

2. If the base of a transistor is at 45 V and the emitter is on, what will be the emitter voltage?

3. If the base of a transistor is at 5 V and the emitter, if conducting, would have to be at 4.5 V, is the transistor on or off?

4. If the base of a transistor is at 0.6 V and the emitter is at ground, is the transistor on or off?

5. If the base of a transistor is at 0.4 V and the emitter is at ground, is the transistor on or off?

6. If a transistor has a base current ($I_{BE}$) of 2 mA and the transistor has a beta of 55, how much current is going through the collector ($I_{CE}$)?

7. In the previous problem, how much total current is coming out of the emitter?

8. If a transistor has a base current of 3 mA and the transistor has a beta of 200, how much current is going through the collector?

9. If the base voltage is greater than the collector voltage, what does this mean for our transistor operation?

10. The output of your microcontroller is 3.3 V and supports a maximum output current of 10 mA. Using Figure 24-7 as a guide, design a circuit to control a motor that requires 80 mA to operate. Assume that the transistor beta is 100.

11. Redesign the previous circuit so that it utilizes a stabilizing resistor on the emitter to prevent variations in the transistor beta.

## CHAPTER 25

# Transistor Voltage Amplifiers

In Chapter 24, we started our study of the BJT NPN transistor. We noted that what the transistor actually amplified was *current*, so that the current coming into the collector was a multiple (known as *β*) of the current coming into the base.

Even though what a transistor does is provide *current* amplification, in this chapter, we will learn how to transform that into voltage amplification.

## 25.1 Converting Current into Voltage with Ohm's Law

If the transistor provides us with current amplification, how might we translate an amplification in the amount of current into an amplification in the amount of voltage? The answer is simple—Ohm's law describes the relationship between current and voltage: $V = I \cdot R$. Therefore, a current amplification can be transformed into a voltage amplification if we use a resistor! The larger the resistor, the larger the change in voltage drop that a given change in current will induce for that resistor.

To see that happening, take a look at the circuit in Figure 25-1. Note that this circuit on its own is rather useless, but it is helpful for illustrating how the calculations work. In this circuit, the current at the

© Jonathan Bartlett 2020
J. Bartlett, *Electronics for Beginners*, https://doi.org/10.1007/978-1-4842-5979-5_25

base is controlled by the resistor $R_B$. This current will be amplified into an increased current from the collector. However, the current at the collector is driven through a resistor, $R_C$. Because this is through a resistor, that means that Ohm's law will take effect, and the size of the voltage drop across $R_C$ will depend on the current running through it.

Remember Ohm's law states that $V = I \cdot R$, so any increase in current will increase the voltage drop across $R_C$, at least until the voltage at the collector is equal to the base voltage (which, in this circuit, is 0.6 V). If that happens, there is nothing more the transistor can do—it will just treat the collector-emitter junction as a short circuit.

Let's calculate what our circuit is actually doing. The voltage across the base is 5 V − 0.6 V = 4.4 V (remember we have to account for the diode-like voltage drop in the transistor from the base to the emitter). Therefore, using Ohm's law, we can calculate the base current at I = V/R = 4.4/10000 = 0.0004 A.

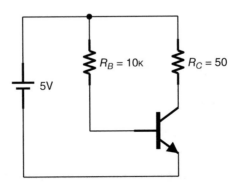

***Figure 25-1.*** *A Simple Current-to-Voltage Amplifier*

Let's assume the transistor beta is 100. Therefore, the current flowing at the collector will be 0.0004·100 = 0.040 A. So the voltage drop across the resistor can be calculated using Ohm's law. $V = I \cdot R = 0.040 \cdot 50 = 2$ V.

Now, let's say that we change $R_B$ so that we have more current running in the transistor. Let's decrease $R_B$ from 10 kΩ to 6 kΩ. Now the base current will be $I = V/R = 4.4/6000 = 0.000733$ A. Now the current flowing at the collector will be $100 \cdot 0.000733 = 0.0733$ A. So the voltage drop across the resistor is now $V = I \cdot R = 0.0733 \cdot 50 \approx 3.67$ V.

When we increase the current, we increase the voltage drop across the resistor. You may be wondering what happens to the extra voltage. That is, since the emitter of the resistor is at ground and the voltage across $R_C$ keeps changing, where is the remainder of the voltage? The transistor essentially swallows it up.

Remember, in our model of the transistor in Figure 24-2, the transistor acts as a variable resistor for the collector current. Therefore, the rest of the voltage drop happens *within* the transistor.

So, in effect, what we are doing is to translate changes in current at the base into changes in the voltage drop across $R_C$ (and likewise the $V_{CE}$ of the transistor).

As you might have noticed, when dealing with transistors, the place where the "action" occurs is not always right where you might expect it. In this circuit, the location where the voltage amplification *actually occurs* is at a resistor $(R_C)$ connected to the *collector*. So the transistor, acting as an amplifier, is not sending the amplified signal to the emitter. Instead, you can think of it as sending the amplified signal to the collector, where the resistor at the collector converts the amplified current into a corresponding voltage drop.

> **Example 25.28** In the circuit given in Figure 25-1, what is the voltage across the resistor $R_C$ if the base resistor $R_B$ goes up to 20 kΩ?

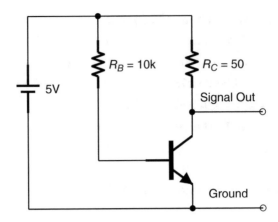

**Figure 25-2.** *Reading the Amplified Signal from a Voltage Amplifier*

$$I_B = 4.4 / 20000 = 0.00022 \, \text{A}$$
$$I_C = 100 \cdot I_B = 100 \cdot 0.00022 = 0.022 \, \text{A}$$
$$V_{RB} = I_C \cdot R_B = 0.022 \cdot 50 \approx 1.1 \, \text{V}$$

Just to see where we are going, eventually we will use small voltage changes in the base to trigger current changes in the base which will then be amplified into a larger change in the voltage across $R_C$.

# 25.2  Reading the Amplified Signal

So we have managed to create a voltage drop which changes in response to changes in current at the base. But how do we read this voltage drop? It is rather difficult to read it directly, but we can read its *inverse* directly.

Take a look at Figure 25-2. In this figure, we added some output signal line to show where we would read the output of the amplifier (i.e., where we would connect the rest of the circuit that receives the amplification). We put the output line *between* the collector resistor $R_C$ and the transistor. What this will do is give us the voltage of the source voltage (5 V) *minus* the voltage across $R_C$. So, when we have a large voltage across $R_C$, that will be reflected in a low voltage in our output. Likewise, when there is a low voltage across $R_C$, that will be reflected in a high voltage in our output.

This sort of an output is known as an **inverted output**, because the output voltage is essentially reverse-amplified. That actually works just fine for audio signals, as it does not matter to the listener if the signal is inverted or not. However, if we needed to get it back to the non-inverted form, we could just add another amplification stage onto the end (we will see how to do this in Section 25.4, "Adding a Second Stage").

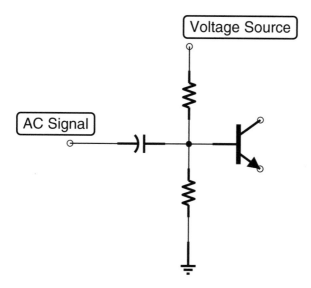

**Figure 25-3.** *Components of a Transistor Biasing Circuit*

Having said all that, I should point out that we still don't know how to amplify an audio signal—yet. That is coming in the next section.

# 25.3 Amplifying an Audio Signal

What we really want to do is to amplify an audio signal. Imagine that someone is singing into a microphone, and we want to amplify the signal we get so that we can send it to a speaker. How would we do that?

There are a number of problems that you have to solve in order to get this done. You might imagine that you could just connect a microphone to the base of the transistor and just amplify directly. That's a good idea, but sadly life is not always that easy. To understand why, remember that audio signals are basically alternating current. That means that the signal will swing both positive *and* negative. Also remember that the base voltage has to remain *above* the emitter voltage and the emitter is tied to ground. Therefore, if we tried to do this, we would lose the bottom (negative) half of the signal. In fact, if it was a small signal, we might lose the *entire* signal if it never reached the required 0.6 V above ground.

Therefore, the signal coming into the transistor needs to be **biased**. We basically need to bring the voltage of the incoming signal up so that it keeps the transistor on, but doesn't overwhelm the signal coming in.

If you remember in Chapter 19 when we built the tone generator, we had to unbias the signal. We did that by taking the signal and coupling it through a capacitor. That allowed the two sides to exist at different base voltages, but transmit the *changes* in the voltage through the capacitor. This will be the same idea, but where the input is unbiased and the output is biased.

Figure 25-3 shows what this looks like in general terms. A simplistic way to think about this is to think of it as a voltage divider. The resistors are basically setting a bias voltage, and that voltage is varied based on the current that comes in through the capacitor.

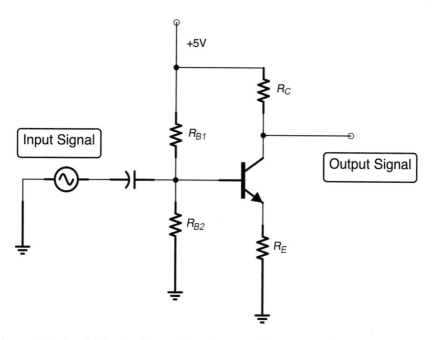

**Figure 25-4.** *A Single-Stage Transistor Voltage Amplifier*

While that is somewhat true, the details get more complicated as
we add more components, especially the transistor. The emitter of the
transistor will be connected to ground though through a resistor, $R_E$. This
means that, for the transistor to be on, the actual voltage coming in to the
base of the transistor must always be 0.6 V (or above, based on $R_E$). That
means that the voltage divider itself must always be 0.6 V (or slightly above,
due to $R_E$) as well.

Figure 25-4 shows all of the parts of our simple transistor amplifier. The
main question is, what do we set the values of each of these resistors to?
There are many considerations, and they affect both the amount of gain
you will get in your amplifier and whether or not the signal is clipped.

Clipping will happen if the base voltage goes below 0.6 V because
the transistor will simply stop conducting (and actually a little above that
because of $R_E$). Clipping will also happen if the $R_C$ resistor is too large,

because if the current going through $R_C$ causes the voltage at the collector to get too low, the transistor will have reached its saturation point and therefore will stop amplifying. Since $R_C$ is converting the current into voltage, it also needs to be large enough to yield a wide voltage swing with the amount of current expected.

For the base resistors ($R_{B1}$ and $R_{B2}$), you need to keep in mind how much current you expect the input source to have. Remember that this current is going to be going to be alternating between the positive and negative directions. Therefore, when the input source swings negative, there has to be enough current coming through $R_{B1}$ to keep the voltage positive and keep the transistor on. When the input source swings fully positive, $R_{B2}$ can prevent clipping as well, as it provides an alternate path for incoming current that isn't through the transistor.

You may be wondering what the resistor at $R_E$ is doing. $R_E$ is a feedback resistor. The gain ($\beta$) of a transistor varies both within manufacturing and based on temperature. A feedback resistor, by raising the voltage at the emitter of the transistor, will limit the amount of gain that the transistor can deliver based on its source input.

**Feedback** means that the output of a circuit is affecting the input in some way. Sometimes, feedback occurs because the output is wired back to the input. However, in this case, the resistor simply increases the voltage at the emitter, causing less current to flow in through the base and more current to flow through $R_{B2}$.

Limiting the gain of the resistor stabilizes the gain over a variety of operating parameters, so that your circuit will continue to work as the transistor heats up. Additionally, were you to manufacture the circuit, limiting the gain would make it less susceptible to manufacturing differences between individual parts.

In any case, if the output of the circuit has a resistance $R_O$, then the current gain from the input through the output can be calculated as

$$\text{gain} = \frac{R_{B2}R_C}{R_E R_O} \qquad (25.1)$$

To understand why this formula works, see Appendix D, Section D.5, "Output Gain Calculations in BJT Common Emitter Applications."[1] The formula just gives you a starting point, though you normally have to play around with resistor values a little to get it to work.[2] Also note that the formula only works when $R_O > R_C$.

When you think about your circuit, you will want to analyze it at two points—when the source current coming in at the input is at its highest and at its lowest (which in this case will be negative). If you have developed your circuit correctly, this should give a good swing in the voltage across $R_C$, but without ever clipping (the transistor turning off or going into saturation).

The best place to start is to recognize that your voltage divider must always provide enough current to keep the transistor on even when the source current swings negative. Therefore, the current coming in to the base through the voltage divider should be a little larger than the signal's current. This is known as the **quiescent current**.

In our case, we are going to develop our circuit to handle passive microphones, so the source signal current will only be on the order of about 10 microamps (0.01 mA). Therefore, we will set our quiescent current to be 0.1 mA. The means that $R_{B1}$ should be a little less than 50 kΩ. We will use a standard 47 kΩ resistor here. $R_{B2}$ can tolerate a wide range of values—basically anything that is at least a quarter the size of $R_{B1}$ (we can't let the voltage drop below the emitter voltage, or the transistor will stop conducting). We'll make it 20 kΩ here.

---

[1] I will warn you that the calculations are pretty ugly (which is why they are in the appendix). Also, to fully understand what is happening, you need to read the rest of this chapter through Chapter 26.

[2] The reason for this is that the formula itself was made by making a *lot* of assumptions and simplifications. Those don't always hold in the real world, so you have to make adjustments.

We want a value for $R_C$ that will swing the voltage about half as far as we can go (we have to save headroom for both the 0.6 V drop on the transistor and the actual output to the rest of the system). If we want a 25x gain, then, if our max base current will be 0.11 mA (quiescent current plus source current), that will put our max collector current at 2.75 mA (25 * 0.11). We want $R_C$ to be dropping about 1.5 V at this level (we need to save some headroom for a number of purposes, including staying above the voltage drop at $R_E$, the additional diode drop to stay above the base voltage, and some additional which will be used for the current going out of this stage of the amp). Therefore, the resistance for a 1.5 V voltage drop at 2.75 mA is $R = \dfrac{V}{I} = \dfrac{1}{0.00275} \approx 545\Omega$. Anything near that value should work fine, so we will go with a 510 Ω resistor.

Then, we mentioned earlier that the total gain will be given by $\dfrac{R_{B2}RC}{R_E R_O}$. So far, we have $\dfrac{20,000 \cdot 510}{R_E R_O}$. We can estimate the next stage of the amplifier as having a resistance of 2,000 Ω (this is the base resistor of the next stage of the amplifier—see Appendix D, Section D.5, "Output Gain Calculations in BJT Common Emitter Applications," for why this works as an estimate). Therefore, to get a 25x gain, we can do

$$\text{gain} = \frac{R_{B2}R_C}{R_E R_O}$$

$$25 = \frac{20,000 \cdot 510}{R_E 2,000}$$

$$R_E = \frac{20,000 \cdot 510}{2,000 \cdot 25}$$

$$R_E = 204$$

In testing, I found that a smaller resistor worked better for $R_E$, so I used a 47 Ω resistor. Again, the equations are greatly simplified and only give a starting point for experimentation.

# 25.4 Adding a Second Stage

A single amplification stage is not always enough. If your signal source is weak enough, sometimes you need more power just to hear it. This can be accomplished in a number of ways. The simplest, conceptually, is to add another output stage to your amplifier.

In order to do this, we need to design the next stage to take into account the output of our first stage. We will need to use a coupling capacitor to handle the change in voltage from the output of the first stage into our bias circuit for the second stage. Without the coupling capacitor, the voltage characteristics of the transistor would severely alter the way that our previous stage works. Therefore, the coupling capacitor helps us to isolate the different parts of the circuit.

Now, the current coming in to this stage will be significantly larger than the previous stage. Our previous stage had about 0.01 mA coming in. While not exact, with an actual 25x gain, the current coming in will probably be about 0.25 mA. Therefore, we have to plan this stage differently (i.e., using a different quiescent current).

Using the same procedure as we used for the previous stage, we can use 0.75 mA as the quiescent current and utilize a 5.1 kΩ resistor (to choose a standard value) for $R_{B1}$ and a 2 kΩ resistor for $R_{B2}$. Our largest swing forward will now be 1 mA, and therefore, the amplified current will be 25 * 1 = 25 mA. To get the 1.5 V drop, we will need a resistor for $R_C$ of $\dfrac{1.5}{0.0025} = 60\Omega$. We will approximate to a 100 Ω resistor.

The output resistance will be our headphones, which we can estimate at 16 Ω. Doing the calculation gives

$$\text{gain} = \frac{R_{B2}R_C}{R_E R_O}$$

$$25 = \frac{2,000 \cdot 100}{16 \cdot R_E}$$

$$R_E = \frac{2,000 \cdot 100}{25 \cdot 16}$$

$$R_E = 100\Omega$$

Again, I had to modify the $R_E$ to get better performance. This is unsurprising because the equation is only even moderately reliable when $R_O > R_C$. Lowering $R_E$ of this stage to 10 $\Omega$ seemed to work well.

The output of the second stage will again be coupled through a coupling capacitor to your headphone output and can be attenuated by another resistor (or a variable resistor for volume control) if needed.

Figure 25-5 shows the complete two-stage amplifier. With this circuit, you can use most microphones and most headphones to get enough output power to hear yourself in your headphones (in fact, if you don't have a microphone, headphones can actually work as a microphone in a pinch). Figure 25-6 shows the two-stage amplifier built into a breadboard.

All of the capacitors can be pretty much any standard capacity above around 100 nF. The ones that couple the DC bias signal, if they are polarized, should have their negative side toward the unbiased signal. The coupling capacitor between the two stages should ideally be non-polarized, though with these power levels it doesn't matter too much. If you do need to use a polarized capacitor here, it is best to have the negative side facing the second stage, since that should be right around 0.6 V, while the positive side should be swinging in the positive range.

One thing in this circuit we haven't discussed is the bleed-off resistors connected right next to the coupling capacitors for the input and output circuit. These are very large (1,000,000 $\Omega$) resistors. They are large so that they do not have any effect on the calculations in the circuit itself, but they do provide a place for the negative side of the capacitor to drain out when nothing is connected. Otherwise, any residual charge on the capacitor has no place to go and will remain even when the circuit is turned off and the devices are unplugged.

## 25.5  Using an Oscilloscope

Designing transistor amplifiers can be tricky because there are a lot of things that can go wrong. Although there is some leeway, using the wrong resistors can result in distortion or a loss of gain. Misconnecting a single component can render the entirety of the circuit inaudible.

Because of the variety of things that can go wrong when building audio circuits, it is best to use an oscilloscope. An oscilloscope can help you visually see what the voltages look like at each point in your circuit. Oscilloscopes can cost as little or as much as you want them to. There are pocket oscilloscopes that you can purchase for less than a nice dinner out, and there are bench oscilloscopes that you would need several months' salary to purchase. Any of those are helpful in analyzing your circuit, so you can see what is happening to your voltages at every point in the circuit.

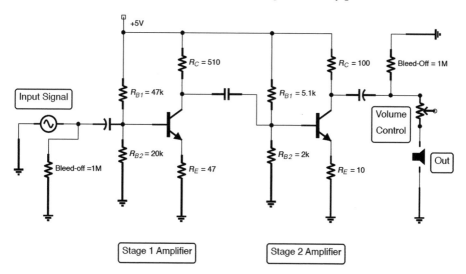

***Figure 25-5.*** *The Complete Two-Stage Amplifier Circuit*

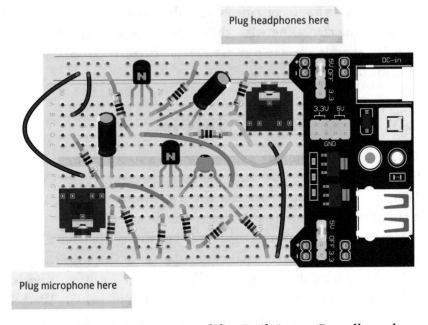

**Figure 25-6.** *The Two-Stage Amplifier Built into a Breadboard*

# Review

In this chapter, we learned the following:

1. Although transistors provide current amplification, current changes can be transformed into voltage changes using Ohm's law.

2. Using a resistor at the collector allows us to "read" a voltage change based on the changes in the currents going through the transistor.

3. Using a resistor in this way *inverts* the waveform—it will show low voltage when there is a lot of current and high voltage when there isn't much current.

4. Adding in an emitter resistor limits the amount of voltage gain in the circuit in order to compensate for variable/drifting transistor betas.

5. In order to amplify an audio signal, we have to add a DC bias to the signal so that the transistor stays in its operating range (positive voltage).

6. The simplest way to use a transistor to amplify a signal is to add a voltage divider to the base of the transistor, with a coupling capacitor feeding the signal into the voltage divider.

7. The neutral, "no signal" design point is known as the quiescent point of a circuit. The quiescent point is the state of the circuit when the AC signal coming in is neutral (0 V).

8. The AC signal is coupled into the voltage divider through a coupling capacitor in order to manage the difference between the pure AC signal and the DC biased signal.

9. The circuit should be analyzed both at the highest and lowest swings around the quiescent point from the input signal.

10. The collector resistor should be chosen in order to maximize voltage swing while preventing overdrive.

11. Weak AC signals often need multiple amplification stages to provide sufficient output power for driving outputs.

12. The output of one amplifier can be coupled through a capacitor into the input of a second amplifier.

13. If the signal sources and outputs are not permanently connected, adding a bleed-off resistor will enable the coupling capacitors to drain out after the jacks are disconnected.

14. There are numerous things that can go wrong in a transistor amplifier, including clipping the audio signal, having a bad quiescent current, or accidentally losing your gain through bad resistor choices, not to mention just simply building the circuit wrong.

15. Because of the number of things that can go wrong, it is easiest to diagnose problems in an amplifier using an oscilloscope, which allows you to visualize what is happening at each point in the circuit.

# Apply What You Have Learned

1. What is the purpose of the resistor in the collector of a transistor amplifier?

2. What is the purpose of the resistor in the emitter of a transistor amplifier?

3. Why is there a bias voltage on the base of the transistor? Why can't the signal just be connected in directly to the base?

4. Why is the signal coupled in through a capacitor?

5. Why does the single stage voltage amplifier discussed in this chapter invert its output?

6. If the output of the two-stage amplifier is coupled into a third stage, the signal current would swing 1.85 mA in either direction. Design a third amplification stage which can handle this amount of current.

# CHAPTER 26

# Examining Partial Circuits

We will end our discussion of amplification by discussing partial circuits. Oftentimes you will need to design a circuit which connects to another circuit, either powering it or receiving power from it. For instance, in the amplification circuits from Chapter 25, the outputs were connected to a speaker. They could also be connected to another amplifier or to a stomp box (a device to modulate the incoming signal in some way) or to a recording circuit.

## 26.1 The Need for a Model

In order to connect circuits together, we need to be able to describe, in general terms, the ways that circuits fit together. When dealing with transistors and other power amplification devices, we often need to come up with a simplified model for how the input to a circuit or the output from a circuit behaves. Early on (in Chapter 7), we learned how to take multiple resistors in series and parallel and combine them into an equivalent single resistor.

When dealing with a power amplification circuit, it is often necessary to look at various parts of the circuit by themselves and figure out how they *look* to other parts of the circuit. The way that a partial circuit looks to other parts of the circuit is called the circuit's **Thévenin equivalent** circuit.

© Jonathan Bartlett 2020
J. Bartlett, *Electronics for Beginners*, https://doi.org/10.1007/978-1-4842-5979-5_26

A Thévenin equivalent circuit takes a partial circuit and reduces it to

- A single voltage source (AC, DC, or DC-biased AC, expressed in RMS voltage)

- A single impedance (i.e., resistance) in series with the voltage source

Note that the single voltage source may be *different* than the voltage source that is actually connected. What you are doing is seeing what the circuit looks like to another circuit. For instance, a voltage divider circuit makes the output of the voltage divider *look like* it is coming from a lower voltage source.

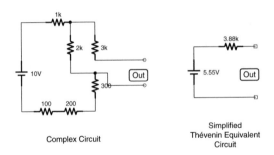

Complex Circuit

Simplified
Thévenin Equivalent
Circuit

***Figure 26-1.*** *A Complicated Circuit and Its Thévenin Equivalent Circuit*

Figure 26-1 shows a circuit and its Thévenin equivalent circuit. For purposes of thinking about and understanding the relationship between the circuit and things attached to the circuit, we can view the circuit as being the same as its Thévenin equivalent. Thus, having a Thévenin equivalent circuit greatly simplifies our modeling, calculating, and understanding of how circuits work together.

Any network of power sources and resistances can be converted into a Thévenin equivalent circuit. You can also get a Thévenin equivalent circuit for a circuit that includes capacitors and inductors, but the calculations become more difficult and the results are only valid for a specific frequency (each frequency will have a different Thévenin equivalent circuit). For simplicity, we will just focus on resistive circuits.

## 26.2  Calculating Thévenin Equivalent Values

To see how to calculate the voltage and resistance for a Thévenin equivalent circuit, this section will take a classic voltage divider circuit and analyze how it "looks" to other attached circuits. Figure 26-2 shows an example of a partial circuit. Like most partial circuits, this circuit has two output points—A and B. What we are wanting to know is this—if we attach another circuit up to A and B, is there a model that we can use to understand how the other circuit "sees" our circuit? The goal of making a Thévenin equivalent circuit is to understand what our circuit will look like to other attached circuits.

So, since our Thévenin equivalent circuit will have a voltage source and a single resistor, we need to calculate what the voltage and resistance of this circuit will be. To calculate the voltage, find out what the voltage of the circuit at the output is when there is *nothing connected*. That is, if we were to leave A and B disconnected and I were to connect my multimeter to A and B, what would the voltage be? This is your Thévenin voltage. Since this is a voltage divider, you can just use normal voltage divider calculations to find this out. In this case, we have a 12 V source, and the voltage divider divides it exactly in half (1 kΩ for each half). Therefore, the output voltage is 6 V. Therefore, our Thévenin equivalent circuit will have a 6 V source.

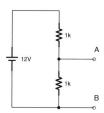

***Figure 26-2.*** *A Voltage Divider Partial Circuit*

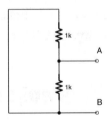

**Figure 26-3.**  *Calculating the Thévenin Resistance of the Circuit*

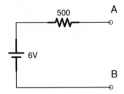

**Figure 26-4.**  *The Thévenin Equivalent of the Voltage Divider*

Now we need to find our Thévenin resistance. There are multiple tricks to do this, but the simplest one is to replace all voltage sources in your circuit with a wire (i.e., a short circuit) and simply compute the total resistance between A and B.[1]

Figure 26-3 shows what this looks like. Therefore, to calculate the Thévenin resistance of this circuit, simply calculate the total resistance from A to B. In this case, there are two parallel paths from A to B—one through the first resistor and one through the second. Therefore, we add up the resistors as parallel resistances. As a result, our Thévenin resistance will be

---

[1]We haven't talked about *current* sources much in this book. However, for completeness, I should note that if you have a current source, you should replace it with an open circuit (i.e., a gap in the wire) when calculating Thévenin resistance.

$$R_T = \cfrac{1}{\cfrac{1}{R_1} + \cfrac{1}{R_2}}$$

$$= \cfrac{1}{\cfrac{1}{1000} + \cfrac{1}{1000}}$$

$$= \cfrac{1}{0.001 + 0.001}$$

$$= \cfrac{1}{0.002}$$

$$= 500\,\Omega$$

Therefore, we would say that this partial circuit has a Thévenin voltage of 6 V and a Thévenin resistance of 500 Ω. Whenever we attach a circuit to this circuit, what that other circuit will "see" is a circuit like the one in Figure 26-4.

If you wanted to prove this to yourself, you can imagine a variety of different circuits attached to both our original circuit and to the Thévenin equivalent circuit. You will find that, in all cases, the amount of voltage and current the Thévenin equivalent circuit provides to the other circuit is the exact same as what the original circuit will provide.

That isn't to say that the circuits themselves are exactly equivalent. Our original voltage divider uses up a lot of current stepping down the voltage of the voltage source. Not only does that waste energy from our battery but it probably also causes a lot of heat. However, *any subcircuit that gets attached to A and B* will see both our original circuit and the Thévenin equivalent circuit as providing the same output.

# 26.3 Another Way of Calculating Thévenin Resistance

There is another way of calculating Thévenin resistance. In this method, we first calculate what the current would be if you shorted A to B directly with a wire. This is known as the short-circuit current, or $I_{SHORT}$. Then, after calculating this, you can divide the Thévenin voltage by $I_{SHORT}$ to obtain the Thévenin resistance.

When doing this, you have to remember that anything in parallel with our short will be essentially ignored—the current will always want to go through our short circuit.

Figure 26-5 shows what this looks like. What we want to do is to calculate the current going from A to B. Since A to B is a short circuit in parallel with our second resistor, we know that *all* of the current will prefer the short circuit. This means that the current going through A and B will simply be the current that is limited by the first resistor.

So, since we have a 12 V source and a 1 kΩ resistor, the short-circuit current will be

$$I_{SHORT} = \frac{V}{R}$$
$$= \frac{12}{1000}$$
$$= 0.012 \text{A}$$

Now, to determine the Thévenin resistance, we divide the Thévenin voltage by this number:

$$R_{Thevenin} = \frac{V_{Thevenin}}{I_{SHORT}}$$
$$= \frac{6}{0.012}$$
$$= 500\Omega$$

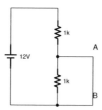

**Figure 26-5.** *Finding the Short Circuit Voltage*

As you can see, this is the same value that we got from the previous method.

# 26.4  Finding the Thévenin Equivalent of an AC Circuit with Reactive Elements

If a circuit has reactive elements (inductors and capacitors), we have to do a little more work to find the Thévenin equivalent circuit.

For DC circuits, this is relatively simple. Since capacitors block DCs and inductors are a short circuit for DCs, we can simply treat the capacitors as open circuits (i.e., unconnected) and treat the inductors as short circuits (simple wires). For AC circuits, you can get a feel for what this will be by assuming the opposite—that capacitors will be short circuits and inductors will be open circuits.

However, if you were to try to solve it explicitly, the problem is a little more difficult. The problem is that a full analysis of such circuits requires math involving complex numbers (i.e., numbers involving the imaginary unit $i$). While the technique is roughly equivalent to adding resistances in series and parallel as we have done before, it is much more difficult to do the math with complex numbers.

For the purposes of this book, the previous statements about DC and AC should suffice for a general understanding of how your circuit works.

# 26.5 Using Thévenin Equivalent Descriptions

Many circuits are described to their users using Thévenin equivalent descriptions. For instance, many circuits are described by their input or output impedance. This gives you a rough guide to imagine what will happen if you connect your own circuit to such circuits.

Imagine that you have a circuit that has a Thévenin equivalent output impedance of 500 Ω. If you connect an output circuit that only has 250 Ω of resistance, what do you think that will do to the signal? Well, since the output of the circuit is equivalent to going through a 500 Ω resistor (that's what Thévenin equivalence means), then if I connect a 250 Ω resistor, then I will have created a voltage divider in which two-thirds of the voltage will be dropped by the circuit I am connecting to and I will only get one-third of the output voltage.

On the other hand, if the impedance of my circuit is 50, 000 Ω, then the voltage drop coming out of the circuit in question is negligible compared to the voltage drop within my circuit. This means that my circuit will essentially receive the full Thévenin equivalent voltage.

We can also use this to calculate the amount of current that our circuit will draw. Let's say that a circuit yields a Thévenin equivalent output of 4 V with an 800 Ω impedance. If I connect a 3,000 Ω output circuit, how much current will flow? The total resistance will be 3,800 Ω, so the current will be $V/R = 4/3800 \approx 1.05$ mA.

The same is true for connecting an input circuit that you make to an output circuit someone else made. For instance, speakers and headphones are normally rated as an impedance—8 Ω, 16 Ω, and so on. They aren't, strictly speaking, resistors, but at normal audio frequencies, they behave essentially like one—they have a Thévenin equivalent impedance (their Thévenin equivalent voltage is zero).

**Example 26.29** If I have an output circuit which is a Thévenin equivalent to 3 V RMS and 200 Ω and I connect it to a set of 16 Ω headphones, what will the power of the headphones be in watts?

We can understand this circuit as simply being a voltage source followed by two resistors in series. The voltage source will be 3 V, and the resistances will be 200 Ω and 16 Ω, totaling 216 Ω. The current will therefore be $V/R = 3/216 \approx 0.0139$ A. The voltage drop in the headphones will be $I \cdot R = 0.0139 \cdot 16 \approx 0.222$ V. Therefore the power delivered to the headphones will be $V \cdot I = 0.222 \cdot 0.0139 \approx 0.00309$ W, or 3.09 mW.

# 26.6  Finding Thévenin Equivalent Circuits Experimentally

In addition to using circuit schematics to determine Thévenin equivalent circuits, it is also possible to determine them experimentally. This way, if you are unsure of the input or output characteristics of your device, you can measure it yourself. The problem with measuring it yourself is that it requires attaching a load to the circuit. Some circuits will fry if a wrongly sized load is attached. You have been warned.

The easiest way to determine Thévenin equivalency experimentally is rather unsafe, but it will help us understand better why the method works. Imagine a voltage divider where the bottom resistor has an extremely large resistance—say, 100 MΩ. In such a voltage divider, the bottom resistor will have almost the entirety of the voltage drop, right? In fact, if the bottom resistor was infinite, it would in fact have all of the voltage drop.

Because of this, we can determine the Thévenin equivalent voltage by measuring the output voltage when there is nothing connected, because no connection means that there is infinite resistance between the output and ground. Measuring this value will give us the Thévenin equivalent voltage.

To determine the Thévenin equivalent current, we can short-circuit the output. This is physical equivalent to the conceptual method we used in Section 26.3, "Another Way of Calculating Thévenin Resistance." When doing this, the *only* impedances to the current will be within the device itself. Therefore, using Ohm's law, the amount of current this draws will tell us how large of a resistance the output is yielding.

> **Example 26.30** If I measure the open-circuit (i.e., disconnected) voltage of the output of an unknown circuit as 8 V and the short-circuit current of the output as 10 mA, what is the Thévenin equivalent circuit?
>
> To find this out, we simply use Ohm's law. What resistance would cause an 8 V source have 10 mA of current?
>
> $$R = V / I$$
> $$= 8 / 0.010$$
> $$= 800$$

Therefore, our Thévenin equivalent circuit is 8 V with an impedance of 800 Ω.

The problem with this method is that you don't normally want to short-circuit your output. Additionally, some circuits require some sort of a load to work properly. In order to adjust to such scenarios, there is a set of equations that allow us to measure the voltage drop across a large and small resistance (instead of infinite and no resistance) and come up with a Thévenin equivalent circuit.

The equations are a little complex, but you can actually derive them directly from Ohm's law if you work at it (see Appendix D, Section D.6, "The Thévenin Formula," to see it derived). The first one calculates the Thévenin equivalent voltage ($V_T$) from the voltage with a high resistance ($V_H$), the high resistance value ($R_H$), the voltage with a low resistance ($V_L$), and the low resistance value ($R_L$):

$$V_T = \frac{\dfrac{V_H}{R_H}\left(R_H - R_L\right)}{1 - \dfrac{V_H R_L}{R_H V_L}} \qquad (26.1)$$

Then, we can calculate the Thévenin equivalent resistance:

$$R_T = \frac{V_T R_L}{V_L} - R_L \qquad (26.2)$$

For a fairly safe and basic starting point, you can use 1 MΩ for the high resistance value and 1 kΩ for the low resistance value.

**Example 26.31** I have a circuit that generates an output for which I need to know its Thévenin equivalent properties. I tested the circuit with a 200 Ω resistance for my low resistance and a 1000 Ω resistance for my high resistance. With the 200 Ω resistance, there was a 2 V drop across the resistance. With the 1000 Ω resistance, there was a 5 V drop across the resistance. What is the Thévenin equivalent circuit for this circuit?

First, we find the Thévenin equivalent voltage using Equation 26.1:

$$
\begin{aligned}
V_T &= \frac{\dfrac{V_H}{R_H}\left(R_H - R_L\right)}{1 - \dfrac{V_H R_L}{R_H V_L}} \\[2em]
&= \frac{\dfrac{5}{1000}\left(1000 - 200\right)}{1 - \dfrac{5 \cdot 200}{1000 \cdot 2}} \\[2em]
&= \frac{0.005 \cdot 800}{1 - \dfrac{1000}{2000}} \\[2em]
&= \frac{4}{0.5} \\[1em]
&= 8\text{V}
\end{aligned}
$$

Next we can find the Thévenin equivalent resistance using Equation 26.2:

$$
\begin{aligned}
R_T &= \frac{V_T R_L}{V_L} - R_L \\[1.5em]
&= \frac{8 \cdot 200}{2} - 200 \\[1em]
&= 800 - 200 \\
&= 600\Omega
\end{aligned}
$$

Therefore, our unknown circuit has a Thévenin equivalent voltage of 8 V and a Thévenin equivalent impedance of 600 Ω.

What makes this method valuable is that it allows a way to *experimentally* determine the Thévenin equivalent of a partial circuit that you don't have a schematic for or for which determining the Thévenin equivalent circuit might be difficult due to nonlinear components such as transistors.

# Review

In this chapter, we learned the following:

1.  In order to be able to connect circuits together without knowing all of the details of how they are implemented, we need a simplified model of how those circuits work with other circuits they are connected to.

2.  A Thévenin equivalent circuit is a combination of a single voltage source and a single series impedance which models the way that the given circuit will respond to other attached circuits.

3.  To calculate Thévenin equivalent voltage, calculate the voltage drop for an open circuit between the two terminals. This is the Thévenin equivalent voltage.

4.  To calculate Thévenin equivalent impedance, calculate the impedance from one terminal to another (or to ground if there is only one terminal), replacing any voltage sources with short circuits.

5.  Alternatively, to calculate Thévenin equivalent impedance, calculate the current flowing from one terminal to another if there was a short circuit between them. Then use Ohm's law to calculate the resistance.

6.  Thévenin equivalent circuits can be used to understand how the resistances of attached circuits will affect the signal coming out of or into a circuit.

7.  Thévenin equivalent circuits can also be found experimentally.

8.  Although not recommended, the Thévenin
    equivalent voltage and resistance can be found easily
    by simply measuring the voltage drop of an open
    circuit across the terminals and the current flowing
    through a short circuit between the terminals.

9.  A better option for experimentally measuring
    Thévenin equivalencies is by measuring the voltage
    with two different load resistances across the
    terminals. Then the Thévenin equivalencies can be
    found using Equations 26.1 and 26.2.

# Apply What You Have Learned

1.  Why would we want to know what a circuit's
    Thévenin equivalent circuit is?

2.  What are the two components of a Thévenin
    equivalent circuit?

3.  Think about the two-stage amplifier that you built
    in Chapter 25. How would you go about finding
    the Thévenin equivalent circuit as it is seen by the
    headphones?

4.  Suppose I have a circuit where the output terminals
    have a 2 V drop when it is an open circuit and have
    2 mA of current flowing through it when it is a short
    circuit. Draw the Thévenin equivalent circuit.

5.  If I have a Thévenin equivalent circuit of 4 V with an
    impedance of 400 $\Omega$, what will be the voltage drop
    of the load if I attach a 2000 $\Omega$ resistor across the
    output?

6.  If I have a Thévenin equivalent circuit of 3 V with an impedance of 100 Ω, what will be the voltage drop, the current, and the power of the load if I attach headphones rated at 32 Ω?

7.  Calculate and draw the Thévenin equivalent circuit of the following circuit:

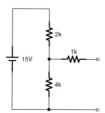

8.  Suppose I have a circuit where when I add a load of 350 Ω, I get a 7 V drop and when I add a load of 2000 Ω, I get an 8 V drop. Calculate and draw the Thévenin equivalent circuit.

**CHAPTER 27**

# Using Field Effect Transistors for Switching and Logic Applications

In Chapter 24, we discussed two kinds of transistors—bipolar junction transistors (BJTs) and field effect transistors (FETs). The previous chapters have focused primarily on BJTs because they are, in fact, great at various tasks that are commonly considered "amplification."

However, there are two amplification tasks for which BJTs are terribly suited—switching and logic circuits. Many people don't think of amplification when they think of logic circuits, but, indeed, they do require amplification. Think about the memory of a computer (which is a type of logic circuit). The memory of the computer has to continue to last after it has been written to. If there was no amplification, the signal would fade over time.[1] Therefore, in order to just "hold on" to the signal, amplification is required.

---

[1]Note that there are indeed some types of memory that can last significant amounts of time without amplification. I'm simplifying to help make the point.

© Jonathan Bartlett 2020
J. Bartlett, *Electronics for Beginners*, https://doi.org/10.1007/978-1-4842-5979-5_27

While this can be done with BJTs, since BJTs are *current* amplifiers, they tend to utilize a lot of current to get this done. Field effect transistors (FETs) operate instead on voltage and require very little current to operate. Therefore, they are very efficient for logic-type applications.

# 27.1  Operation of a FET

A FET has a very similar set of parts to a BJT. There are three parts—a **gate**, a **source**, and a **drain**.[2]

The basic operation of the FET is that a *voltage* at the gate controls the *current* conduction between the drain and the source. The gate controls the conduction between the drain and the source. Like BJTs, FETs have fully off, fully on, and partially on states. However, unlike BJTs, even when "fully on," FETs still offer a resistance between the drain and the source. This is why, for current-focused applications, BJTs are often used—in their fully on state, they don't limit the current from the collector to the emitter.

Unlike the BJT, the FET is operated by voltages rather than current. Because of this, the gate essentially consumes almost no current whatsoever (it can have a Thévenin equivalence of hundreds of megaohms of resistance). So, while BJTs consume current to perform their operation, FETs consume almost none.

FETs can be built to perform in one of two operating modes:

- A **depletion mode** FET is normally "on" (allowing current to flow between the drain and the source), but turns off when a sufficient voltage (compared to the source) is applied at the gate. The voltage works to "deplete" the transistor of its conducting ability.

---

[2]Some FETs also have a **substrate** (also called a **body**), but that is beyond the scope of this book.

- An **enhancement mode** FET is normally "off" (blocking current flow between the drain and the source), but turns on when a sufficient voltage (compared to the source) is applied at the gate. The voltage works to "enhance" the transistor's ability to conduct.

FETs are distinguished as **N-channel** or **P-channel** based on their orientation. In an N-channel FET, the current flows from the drain to the source (i.e., the drain acts like the collector, and the source acts like the emitter). In a P-channel FET, the current flows from the source to the drain (i.e., the source acts like the collector, and the drain acts like the emitter). For an enhancement mode FET, the gate activates the channel when the gate voltage (compared to the source) is sufficiently positive if it is an N-channel and sufficiently negative if it is a P-channel. For a depletion mode FET, the gate closes the channel when the gate voltage (compared to the source) is sufficiently negative if it is an N-channel and sufficiently positive if it is a P-channel.[3]

So, for instance, in a P-channel depletion mode FET, the source will be positive, the drain will be negative, and the channel will close as the gate voltage becomes more and more negative compared to the source.

Additionally, most FETs have a "threshold voltage" that the gate must achieve before it switches on.

In addition to the channel and the mode, FETs are made in a variety of different ways, which leads to numerous different types of FETs— MOSFETs, JFETs, QFETs, MNOSs, and others. Each of these has its own distinct operating characteristics (threshold voltage, channel resistance, etc.). We will focus on one particular FET to make life easier—the N-channel enhancement mode MOSFET. This is the most commonly used FET by hobbyists.

---

[3]I know this is a lot of information, but there are so many terms that you are likely to encounter that I want to be sure you are familiar with what they mean on a practical basis. As you will see in the following, we are only going to actually use one kind of FET here.

## 27.2 The N-Channel Enhancement Mode MOSFET

The most popular general FET is probably the N-channel enhancement mode MOSFET. Because it is N-channel, the drain operates as the collector, and the source operates as the emitter (if we think of it in terms of our BJT terminology). That is backward from the way we normally think of things, but that is the reality of the naming scheme. Because it is an enhancement mode device, the bridge between the drain and the source is closed, unless a positive voltage (compared to the source) is applied at the gate.

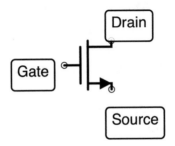

**Figure 27-1.** *The Schematic Symbol for an N-Channel MOSFET Transistor*

Figure 27-1 shows the schematic symbol for the N-channel MOSFET. Notice that the arrow is pointing out from the *source*. Again, that is because in this transistor, the source performs the same function as the emitter on a BJT.

## 27.3 Using a MOSFET

Figure 27-2 shows a schematic of a simplistic usage of a MOSFET. In this figure, the gate of the MOSFET is controlled by a switch. When the switch is on, the MOSFET conducts. However, the important thing to note is that the pathway into the gate of the MOSFET consumes basically no current whatsoever!

This is especially important when dealing with small microcontrollers. Some of them have extremely low tolerances for what currents they can deliver. By putting a MOSFET on the output pin, you can make the actual current output from the microcontroller effectively zero and simply have the current delivered through the MOSFET. Figure 27-3 shows this configuration. This is basically the same circuit as Figure 27-2 except that (a) a microcontroller is controlling the gate and (b) we added a pull-down resistor at the gate (note—Figure 27-2 also needs a pull-down resistor, but we left it off for simplicity). The pull-down resistor will make sure that even when the pin is not actively sending a signal, the gate is tied to a known voltage. This is especially important with MOSFETs since they do not consume very much current at all, so charge can stay on the circuit after disconnection.

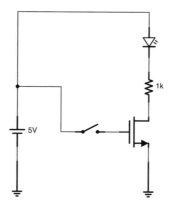

*Figure 27-2. A Simple MOSFET Circuit*

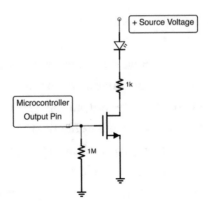

***Figure 27-3.*** *A Microcontroller Pin Controlling a MOSFET*

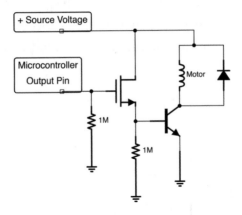

***Figure 27-4.*** *Combining a MOSFET with a BJT to Power a Motor*

One issue, however, is that, as we mentioned, MOSFETs always have resistance between the drain and source, limiting the amount of current that a MOSFET can source. If we wanted to power a motor, for instance, we would need to increase the current. We can do this by adding a BJT to the output of our MOSFET. Figure 27-4 shows this configuration. Notice that both transistors have a pull-down resistor attached. This prevents any accidental conduction of our devices.

In this configuration, when the gate to the MOSFET is pulled high, it will open up the connection from the drain to the source. Current will flow into the base of the BJT, which will allow current to flow from the collector to the emitter. The amount that it allows is based on the $\beta$ of the transistor. This current is used by the motor.

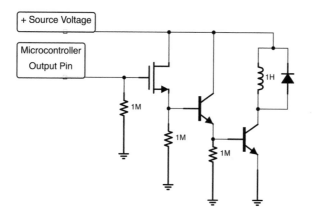

*Figure 27-5.* *A MOSFET with Two BJTs for Higher Current*

However, even this configuration may not provide enough current. The transistor can only amplify what it gets from the MOSFET, and the current output from the MOSFET is sometimes just not high enough for a single-stage amplification. Therefore, we can use the output from the first BJT as an input to the base of a second BJT to open up the power even more. Figure 27-5 shows this configuration. Note that each transistor has a pull-down resistor to make sure that it gets shut off when the pin goes low.

This configuration provides practically unlimited current through the collector of the transistor and doesn't utilize any current output from the microcontroller.

# 27.4 MOSFETs in Logic Circuits

MOSFETs are also great to use in logic circuits, again, because they use practically no current at all. While the pathway from the drain to the source can draw current, if the output coming from the source goes to *another* MOSFET, then it won't utilize any current either. As we mentioned earlier, we can think of the gate of a MOSFET as having a resistance on the order of a hundred megaohms. Therefore, Ohm's law will prevent any significant amount of current running into them.

In Chapter 12, we learned about integrated circuits that could perform logic functions such as AND, OR, and NOT. We can mimic these same logic functions with MOSFET transistors (we can also mimic them with BJTs, but we would waste a lot of current doing it).

Figures 27-6, 27-7, and 27-8 show how these gates could be wired using MOSFETs. Note that each transistor requires a pull-down resistor as well, which is not pictured for simplicity of understanding.

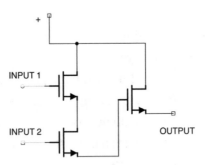

*Figure 27-6. An AND Gate Using MOSFETs*

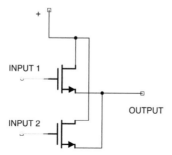

***Figure 27-7.*** *An OR Gate Using MOSFETs*

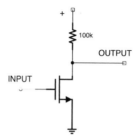

***Figure 27-8.*** *A NOT Gate Using MOSFETs*

# Review

In this chapter, we learned the following:

1.  Field effect transistors (FETs) are similar to BJTs, but they are controlled by voltage instead of current.

2.  The parts of the FET transistor are the gate, the source, and the drain, though whether the source or the drain is on the positive side depends on the type of transistor.

3. The N-channel depletion mode MOSFET is wired (somewhat confusingly) so that the drain is on the positive side and the source is on the negative side. Applying a positive voltage at the gate allows current to flow from the drain to the source.

4. Because FETs operate using voltage, the gate consumes almost no current, making it ideal for controlling devices from microcontrollers.

5. When a device is truly power-hungry, a FET can be used in combination with one or two BJTs to provide additional current output to the device.

6. FETs can also be used in combination with each other to produce logic circuits that utilize very little current.

# Apply What You Have Learned

1. Why is it especially important to include pull-down resistors with FET transistors?

2. Which types of FETs are normally conducting between the drain and the source? Which ones are normally not conducting?

3. Create a circuit that combines an AND gate and an OR gate using N-channel MOSFETs. It should turn on an LED if buttons 1 and 2 are pressed or if button 3 is pressed.

4. Why is a BJT needed to power an electric motor in addition to the MOSFET?

# CHAPTER 28

# Going Further

Congratulations! You have reached the end of this book! Hopefully, though, this is just the beginning of your electronics journey. From here, there are many directions you can go.

If you are mostly into digital electronics (programming and using microcontrollers), then this book probably has all of the electronics knowledge you need. From here, you should learn more about programming and more about the devices you want to use for your projects. Additionally, there are a ton of add-on devices that can be controlled with these sorts of microcontrollers. Learning about how to program and what devices are available would be your best next step. A good start to this would be Michael McRobert's book *Beginning Arduino*, Brian Evans's book *Beginning Arduino Programming*, or Bob Dukish's *Coding the Arduino*.

If you were more interested in the sound and amplification sections, the next steps would be to either learn how to do this with microcontrollers or learn to do it directly with capacitors, inductors, and other electronic components. For the microcontroller path, try out Mike Cook's *Arduino Music and Audio Projects* or Alexandros Drymonitis's *Digital Electronics for Musicians*. For direct work in electronics, check out Craig Anderton's classic, *Electronic Projects for Musicians*, or, if you can find a copy, Nicholas Boscorelli's *The Stomp Box Cookbook*. Ray Wilson's *Make: Analog Synthesizers* is also good.

© Jonathan Bartlett 2020
J. Bartlett, *Electronics for Beginners*, https://doi.org/10.1007/978-1-4842-5979-5_28

If you want to learn more about electric motors and devices that move, there are a lot of options as well. David Cook's *Robot Building for Beginners* is a great place to start, as well as the follow-up book *Intermediate Robot Building*. Jeff Cicolani also has a book, *Beginning Robotics with Raspberry Pi and Arduino*, that is worth looking into. The book *Arduino Robotics* has a lot of more advanced ideas as well, including a DIY Segway clone.

If you want to know more about the operation of the components themselves, the best in-depth guidebook (though very expensive!) is Paul Horowitz's *The Art of Electronics*. If electronics is going to be your profession, it's worth every penny. Otherwise, it is probably a little too advanced (and expensive) for the casual hobbyist.

If you enjoyed the math and wanted to know more, I suggest that you start by learning calculus, as much of the math of electronics is based in some way on calculus. The book I would suggest for that is my own *Calculus from the Ground Up*.

Anyway, I wish you well on your electronics journey. You are well prepared to begin!

# APPENDIX A

# Glossary

**AC** See *alternating current.*

**AC mains** This is the type of current that is supplied to your house by the public utility companies. This is usually 120 volts AC and cycles back and forth 50–60 times per second.

**AC signal** This is the type of current usually picked up by a microphone or antenna. It has very low current and usually must be amplified before processing.

**alternating current** Current where the flow of current continually changes direction. This can also refer to a continual stream of fluctuations of voltage.

**amp** A shorthand way of saying ampere. See *ampere.*

**ampere** An ampere is a measurement of the movement of charge. It is equivalent to 1 coulomb of charge per second moving past a given point in a circuit.

**amplification** Taking a low-power signal and converting it to a high-power signal. This is usually done by using the low-power signal to control a high-power source and manipulate it to mimic the low-power signal.

**AND function** A logic function which yields a true value when all of its inputs are true.

**AND gate** A logic gate which implements the AND function.

**anode** An anode is the "positive side" of a polarized device. Note that, in batteries, the anode is actually the negative terminal (because the positive charge *enters* here).

© Jonathan Bartlett 2020
J. Bartlett, *Electronics for Beginners*, https://doi.org/10.1007/978-1-4842-5979-5

**Arduino** A popular environment for programming microcontrollers, including a standard set of development boards for a variety of microcontrollers.

**Arduino IDE** A software program used to write and upload programs for Arduino-based microcontrollers.

**atomic number** The number of protons that a given element has.

**auto-ranging multimeter** A multimeter which does not require that you know the likely value of the measured value ahead of time.

**baud** A way of expressing rates of communication. Means "bits per second."

**beta** The amount of gain that a BJT can generate.

**bit** Binary digit. A true or false (or 1 or 0) value.

**BJT** Bipolar junction transistor. In this type of transistor, current at the base of the transistor controls the conduction between the collector and the emitter.

**boost converter** See *DC-DC power converter.*

**breadboard** A device which makes it easier to attach components together. See also *solderless breadboard.*

**breakdown voltage** The voltage drop that occurs when a diode is blocking current, but the voltage goes beyond the capacity of the diode itself and "breaks down" the blockade. This is problematic in normal diodes, but an expected part of operation of Zener diodes.

**bridge** A space in the middle of a breadboard separating terminal strips.

**brushed electric motor** A motor that operates by changing its interior magnetic configuration based on wires that are rotating in the shaft.

**brushless electric motor** A motor that operates by changing its exterior magnetic configuration based on generating an alternating current inside the motor. Brushless motors are less prone to fail because of fewer parts that wear down.

**capacitance** Capacitance is the ability to hold an electric charge.

**capacitive reactance** The reactance that comes from capacitor-like components.

**carrier frequency** A frequency on which another signal is laid.

**cathode** A cathode is the "negative side" of a polarized device. Note that, in batteries, the cathode is actually the positive terminal (because the positive charge *leaves* here).

**charge** Charge is a fundamental quantity in physics. A particle can be positively charged (like a proton), negatively charged (like an electron), or neutrally charged (like a neutron). Charge is measured in coulombs.

**chip** See *integrated circuit.*

**circuit diagram** The drawing of a circuit using special symbols to show how the components are connected without worrying about how the circuit will be physically laid out on the breadboard.

**circuit pattern** A circuit pattern is a common way of building (and understanding) certain types of circuits or subcircuits.

**closed circuit** A circuit is closed if there is a complete pathway from the positive to the negative.

**CMOS** CMOS is a technology for building integrated circuits (especially MOSFETs) and stands for "Complementary Metal Oxide Semiconductor." It is also a standard for true/false voltage levels used by logic chips made using CMOS technology.

**coil** See *inductor.*

**comment** In computer programming, a comment is a line of code that the computer ignores and is meant to communicate information to the person reading the code.

**common point** See *ground.*

**common emitter** A transistor circuit pattern where the emitter is tied to a known, fixed voltage.

**connection point** A place on a breadboard where a wire or component can be attached.

**conserved quantity** A quantity is conserved if, in the normal course of action, it cannot be created or destroyed. Energy is a conserved quantity—it cannot be created or destroyed but only transferred.

**conventional current flow** Conventional current flow traces the flow of positive charge in a circuit from a positive source (often a battery) to either ground or a negative terminal.

**coulomb** A coulomb is a quantity of electric charge. One coulomb is roughly equivalent to the charge of 6.242Œ10¹8 protons. The same number of electrons produces a charge of −1 coulomb. Coulombs are represented by the symbol C.

**coupling capacitor** A coupling capacitor is a capacitor that links to circuits, usually at different DC offsets. The coupling capacitor transmits changes in voltage (i.e., AC) while blocking the DC offset voltages from influencing each other.

**datasheet** The documentation provided by a component or an integrated circuit which provides technical details about the component's operation.

**debugging** The process of finding errors in electronic circuits or computer code.

**DC-DC power converter** A device which converts voltage levels (like a transformer) but for DC circuits.

**DC bias voltage** See *DC offset.*

**DC** See *direct current.*

**DC motor** A device that converts DC electrical power into mechanical power.

**DC offset** If an alternating current is centered around a voltage other than zero, the center voltage is the DC offset.

**depletion mode** A FET which uses depletion mode means that the FET normally conducts between the drain and source, but will be inhibited by sufficient gate-to-source voltage (sufficiently positive for a P-channel or sufficiently negative for an N-channel).

**development board** A development board is a prebuilt circuit board that makes trying out certain chips and components (and building example projects with them) much easier.

**digital logic** A convention where voltages (usually a positive voltage and zero voltage) are used to represent "true" and "false" values (or "1" and "0").

**diode** An electric component that only allows current to flow in one direction.

**DIP** See *dual in-line package.*

**direct current** Current where the flow of current maintains the same direction. It can also be viewed as steady voltage from a positive terminal to a negative terminal (i.e., voltage which does not continually vary/change directions).

**dissipation** Dissipation refers to the ability to get rid of something. Heat dissipation deals with the removal of extra heat generated in circuits.

**drain (transistor)** One side of the main current pathway of a FET. This is the positive side in an N-channel FET and the negative side in a P-channel FET.

**dual in-line package** A type of package for integrated circuits which has two parallel sets of pins which fits nicely across the bridge of a breadboard.

**electric field** This is the force of attraction of opposite charges which are separated but near to each other.

**electromagnet** A magnet that is created through an inductor. Electromagnets allow electronics to manipulate the larger physical world.

**electron current flow** Electron current flow traces the flow of negative charges from a negative source or ground to its destination (often a positive terminal on a battery).

**electron** A negatively charged particle that is usually on the outside of an atom.

**energy** The ability to do work, usually measured in joules.

**enhancement mode** A FET which uses enhancement mode means that the FET normally does not conduct between the drain and source, but sufficient gate-to-source voltage will allow conduction (sufficiently positive if it is an N-channel and sufficiently negative if it is a P-channel).

**equivalent resistance** If multiple resistors are connected in series or in parallel, their operation can be mimicked by a single resistor. This resistor is said to have equivalent resistance of the resistor circuit that it replaces. See also *Thévenin equivalent circuit*.

**farad** The basic unit of capacitance named after Michael Faraday.

**feedback** When the output of a process feeds back into the input of a process.

**FET** Field effect transistor. This is a type of transistor where the gate controls the conduction between the drain and the source.

**filtering capacitor** A capacitor used to remove signals of a certain range of frequencies from the signal.

**flash memory** A type of memory in integrated circuits that is retained even after the power to the device is removed.

**flux** See *magnetic flux*.

**flyback diode** See *snubber diode*.

**forward voltage drop** The amount of voltage that a diode utilizes when the current flows forward.

**frequency** How often a cycle of an oscillator completes a full cycle, measured in hertz (cycles per second).

**function** In computer programming, a function is a block of code that accomplishes a task and may return a value to the code that invoked the function.

**gain** The amount of amplification that a component provides to a signal.

**gate (logic circuit)** See *logic gate*.

**gate (transistor)** In a FET, the gate is the input that controls the pathway between the drain and the source using voltage levels. Gates generally utilize a negligible amount of current.

**ground** The chosen point on a circuit by which to measure other voltages. On DC battery circuits, this is usually simply the negative terminal of the battery.

**H-Bridge** A device which makes it easier to control a two-way motor drive.

**headers** Places on a circuit board where additional circuits or wires can be attached.

**heat** Undirected energy. In electronics, heat is usually due to inefficiency in circuits. All circuits are inefficient to some degree, and that inefficiency is released as heat into the environment.

**heatsink** A heatsink is an object, usually large and metallic, which attaches to a part of a circuit to dissipate heat into the environment and away from the circuit itself.

**henry** The unit of measure for inductance.

**hertz** A unit of measurement of frequency/oscillation. Abbreviated Hz. Hertz refers to the number of cycles per second.

**IC** See *integrated circuit.*

**in-system programmer** A device that connects your computer to a microcontroller which will transmit a new program to the microcontroller.

**inductance** The amount of resistance an inductor offers to changes in current. Measured in Henries.

**inductive kick** When current is suddenly blocked to an inductor, the magnetic field suddenly collapses and generates a sudden large voltage at the cathode.

**inductive reactance** The reactance that comes from inductor-like components.

**inductor** A component, usually made of coiled wire, that stores energy in a magnetic field. Inductors resist changes in current.

**impedance** The amount of resistance a circuit offers to alternating current which combines resistance and reactance. Impedance is usually based on a specific frequency.

**inefficiency** In energy terms, inefficiency is the amount of energy that is wasted in performing a process. All processes are inefficient to some degree.

**integrated circuit** A miniaturized circuit that is built on a silicon chip.

**International System of Units** See *SI Units.*

**inverted input or output** An input or output is inverted if you send it (or receive from it) the opposite of what you might normally expect.

**ISP** See *in-system programmer.*

**joule** A standard unit of work or energy. It is defined as the amount of work performed when a 1-kilogram object is moved 1 meter. It can also be defined as the work performed when moving a coulomb of charge through 1 volt of electric potential difference.

**junction** The point where two or more wires or components are connected together.

**Kirchhoff's current law** At any junction, the total amount of current going into a junction is exactly the same as the total amount of current going out of that junction.

**Kirchhoff's voltage law** Given any two specific points on a circuit (at a particular point in time), no matter what path is traveled to get from one point to the other, the difference in voltage between the two points is the same. This can also be stated equivalently as saying that any complete, closed path around a circuit has a total voltage drop of zero.

**latch** A simple type of memory that stores a single bit using logic gates.

**lead** A metallic connection point of a component.

**leg** See *lead.*

**logic function** A function that takes in one or more logic (true/false) values as input and produces one or more (usually one) logic values as output.

**logic gate** A circuit which implements a logic function. This is different from a transistor gate. Confusingly logic gates are built from transistors which can have a gate.

**loop** In computer programming, a loop is a group of commands that is repeated multiple times.

**magnetic flux** The energy stored in an electric field.

**mechanical fit** The ability of two objects to be joined just by pushing them together.

**memory** The capacity of a circuit to hold on to previous values. Often used in computer programming to store values.

**microchip** See *integrated circuit*.

**microcontroller** An integrated circuit which operates as a standalone computer. Usually used for controlling small electronic devices.

**milliamp** A short way of saying milliampere. See *milliampere*.

**milliampere** One thousandth of an ampere. See *ampere*.

**MOSFET** A specific (and common) type of FET transistor.

**multimeter** A device used to measure a variety of electrical quantities in circuits and devices, usually including voltage, current, and resistance.

**N-channel** A type of FET. Refers to the physical construction of the FET.

**NAND function** A logic function which yields a false value only when all of its inputs are true. A combination of the AND and NOT functions.

**NAND gate** A logic gate which implements the NAND function.

**NPN** A type of BJT.

**neutron** An uncharged particle in the nucleus of an atom.

**no load RPM** The speed at which the shaft of a motor rotates with nothing attached to the shaft at its rated voltage.

**no load current** The amount of current that a motor utilizes with nothing attached to the shaft at its rated voltage.

**non-polarized component** A circuit component (such as a resistor) where it does not matter which end is used as the anode or cathode.

**NOR function** A logic function which yields false if any of its inputs (or combination of inputs) are true. A combination of the OR and NOT functions.

**NOR gate** A logic gate which implements the NOR function.

**NOT function** A logic function which takes one input and yields its opposite.

**NOT gate** A logic gate which implements the NOT function.

**nucleus** The nucleus is the part of the atom where protons and neutrons reside.

**ohm** The unit of measurement of resistance.

**open circuit** An open circuit is a condition where there is no electrical pathway for the current to flow. See also *closed circuit, short circuit.*

**open collector** A type of output from a circuit where the "positive" state is actually disconnected, while the "zero" state is an actual ground voltage. This is often used to allow the user of the circuit to supply their own voltage through a pull-up resistor.

**OR function** A logic function which yields a true value when any of its inputs are true.

**OR gate** A logic gate which implements the OR function.

**oscillation** Oscillate means going back and forth. In electronics, oscillation usually means periodic back-and-forth fluctuations in current or voltage.

**oscillator** An oscillator is a circuit that switches back and forth between two or more states (e.g., positive voltage to zero voltage) in a regular fashion.

**oscilloscope** A device used to probe circuits and visualize the behavior of circuits over time.

**P-channel** A type of FET. Refers to the physical construction of the FET.

**package** The way that an integrated circuit is encased, including the physical casing, the pinout, and the type of pins.

**parallel circuit** A circuit is a parallel circuit if one or more components are arranged into multiple branches.

**period** The length of a full cycle of an oscillating circuit. Usually measured in seconds.

**pad** See *pin.*

**pin** On an integrated circuit, this is one of the legs protruding from the chip that you can connect to your circuit. Can also refer to the leg/lead of other types of components.

**pinout** The pinout refers to the meaning/purpose assigned to each pin of a particular integrated circuit.

**PNP** A type of BJT.

**polarized component** A circuit component (such as a diode) which has an explicit anode and cathode (i.e., the sides of the component are not interchangeable).

**power** The continual supply of energy, usually measured in watts. In DC circuits, power is calculated as the voltage (in volts) multiplied by the current (in amperes).

**power buses** See *power rails*.

**power rails** The part of a breadboard (usually indicated by red and blue lines) which is usually used for power connections.

**power transistor** A transistor made to handle large amounts of voltage and current.

**programming environment** A set of tools which makes programming for certain devices, or in certain ways, easier.

**protection diode** A diode that protects a circuit, usually either from putting in a battery backward or, in the case of a snubber diode, from inductive kick.

**proton** A positively charged particle in the nucleus of an atom.

**pull-up resistor** A resistor connected to a positive voltage which gives a default positive voltage if no other voltage is connected on the line.

**pull-down resistor** A resistor connected to a positive voltage which gives a default zero voltage if no other voltage is connected on the line.

**pulse-width modulation** Sending a signal using a fixed pulse frequency, but where the percentage of time the signal is high vs. low varies. This is a way of outputting voltage levels on devices that don't support outputting at different voltage levels.

**PWM** See *pulse-width modulation*.

**quiescent current** In a transistor amplifier, the quiescent current is the amount of current that is flowing into the base of the transistor when no signal is applied.

**RC circuit** A resistor in series with a capacitor, usually used for timing.

**reactance** This is a part of impedance which is similar to resistance but operates by preventing flow rather than dissipating energy. Reactance is usually based on the frequency of the signal.

**resistance** Resistance measures how much a component resists the flow of electricity. Resistance is measured in ohms ($\Omega$).

**resonant frequency** The resonant frequency of a circuit is the frequency of the circuit where the inductive and capacitative reactances cancel each other out.

**RMS** A way of computing averages that focuses on magnitudes.

**RPM** Revolutions per minute. How often the shaft of a motor rotates in a minute.

**RS-232** A protocol for serial communication describing voltage levels, timing, and other important signaling features for sending and receiving bits using two wires.

**saturation mode** This occurs in a transistor when it is fully on and cannot amplify the signal further. In saturation mode, the transistor acts more like a switch that is on rather than as an amplifier.

**schematic** See *circuit diagram.*

**serial interface** A type of input/output mechanism that sends data a single bit at a time, oftentimes using the RS-232 protocol.

**series circuit** A series circuit is a circuit or part of a circuit where all of the components are connected one after another.

**servo motor** A motor that, instead of spinning, creates an angle.

**set screw** A screw whose purpose is to apply pressure to another part to join it together.

**shaft** The rotating part of a motor.

**short circuit** A short circuit is what happens when the current pathway has no resistance from the positive to the negative.

**SI Units** The international standard for physical units of measure.

**sink** When a component or circuit receives incoming current.

**snubber diode** A diode that is wired backward across the terminals of an inductor to protect the circuit against inductive kick.

**solder (noun)** A substance which can be heated up to attach wires, components, and other metallic objects together.

**solder (verb)** The activity of attaching things together using solder.

**solderless breadboard** A device consisting of a number of connected terminals where components can be inserted and removed at will, which allows for the construction of circuits in a nonpermanent way.

**source (general)** When a component or circuit provides current output.

**source (transistor)** One side of the main current pathway of a FET. This is the negative side in an N-channel FET and the positive side in a P-channel FET.

**square wave** An oscillating signal where the signal spends almost all of its time either in the high or low state and almost no time in between.

**SR latch** A simple type of memory which can store a single bit.

**stall condition** In an electric motor, this is the condition where the motor is not turning while it is exhibiting its maximum torque.

**stall current** The amount of current that the motor uses in a stall condition.

**stator** The fixed outside container of a motor.

**terminal** See *lead*. Can also refer to a female receiver for a lead.

**terminal strip** On a breadboard, a terminal strip is a row of connection points which are connected together within the breadboard, so that putting in multiple components or wires on a terminal strip connects them together.

**Thévenin equivalent circuit** A generalization of how one circuit "sees" another circuit, as if it solely consisted of a power source and an impedance/resistance.

**TO-220 package** A way of packaging an integrated circuit, usually for transistors, voltage regulators, or other power-oriented devices. It consists of three terminals and a heatsink.

**torque** Rotational power. In a motor, this is the amount of rotational power that the motor applies to the shaft.

**transformer** A pair of inductors which utilize the magnetic field in one coil to generate a current in the other inductor. Usually used to convert voltage levels in different circuits and to isolate parts of a circuit. Transformers only operate on AC circuits. For DC circuits, see *DC-DC power converter*.

**transistor** A circuit component used for switching, logic, and amplification. Generally, a transistor operates by having one terminal control the flow of current between two others. See also *FET* and *BJT*.

**TTL** An acronym for transistor-to-transistor Logic. This is an old standard for logic chips for signaling true and false values, usually operating at 5 V.

**unit of measurement** A standard marker used for quantification, such as grams (weight), seconds (time), or meters (length).

**unit prefix** A unit prefix is a modifier that can be added to a word to indicate that it should be multiplied by some amount. For instance, a kilometer means a thousand meters. A millimeter means a thousandth of a meter.

**variable** In computer programming, a variable is a storage location where a value is held that can change.

**variable resistor** A resistor whose value changes.

**voltage** A voltage is the "power" of an electric charge. Formally, it is the ratio of potential energy of a charge to the magnitude of a charge. It can also be described as the change in magnetic flux over time.

**voltage divider** A voltage divider occurs when there are two components (usually resistors) connected together with a terminal coming out from between them meant to have a voltage between that of the two components.

**voltage drop** The voltage difference between two points on a circuit. This usually refers to the amount of voltage consumed within a specific component on a circuit.

**watt** A unit of power. A watt is the delivery of one joule per second.

**work** Work occurs when force causes a displacement (change of position). Work is often measured in joules.

**XOR function** A logic function which yields a true value when any one (and only one) of its inputs is true.

**XOR gate** A logic gate which implements the XOR function.

**Zener diode** A diode which is meant to be wired in such a way as to take advantage of its breakdown voltage.

# Electronics Symbols

| Symbol | Component | Description |
|---|---|---|
| (battery symbol) | Battery | A battery is represented by a long line and a short line stacked on top of each other. Sometimes, there are two sets of long and short lines. The long line is the positive terminal, and the short line is the negative terminal (which is usually used as the ground). |
| (resistor symbol) | Resistor | A resistor is represented by a sharp, wavy line with wires coming out of each side. |
| (potentiometer symbol) | Potentiometer | A potentiometer is represented by a resistor with an arrow in the middle. This indicates that the positioning of the dial will affect how the voltage is divided. |

*(continued)*

| Symbol | Component | Description |
|--------|-----------|-------------|
| | Diode | A diode is represented by an arrow with a line across it, indicating that current can flow from positive to negative in the direction of the arrow, but it is blocked going the other way. |
| | LED | An LED symbol looks similar to a diode (since it is a diode), but it also has two short lines coming out of it, representing the fact that it emits light. |
| | Zener diode | A Zener diode is represented like a normal diode, but with angled lines coming out of the blocking bar, representing the fact that the "blocking" action is not its only use. |
| | Button | A button is represented by a line that could connect two wires. This represents the fact that if the button is pushed down, it will connect the two parts of the circuit. |
| | Switch | A switch is like a button, but it is anchored on one side. This represents the fact that the position of the switch is semipermanent. Unlike a button, which pushes and then releases, the switch will stay where you put it. |
| | Capacitor (unpolarized) | A capacitor is represented by two parallel lines separated by a space, representing the fact that a capacitor is built from two plates that are not physically touching. |

*(continued)*

| Symbol | Component | Description |
|---|---|---|
| ⊣)⊢ | Capacitor (polarized) | A polarized capacitor is similar to an unpolarized capacitor, except that the negative side of the capacitor has a curve applied to it. |
| ⟋ⲙⲙⲙ⟍ | Inductor | An inductor is represented by a curling line to represent the fact that the wires in an inductor are coiled. This symbol is often used to represent not just basic inductors, but also applications of inductors such as motors and electromagnets. |
| (BJT NPN symbol) | BJT NPN | The BJT NPN transistor is a three-terminal device with a line going in from the collector and a line going out to the emitter, with an arrow pointing toward the emitter. The line coming to the solid flat line is the base, which controls the flow. You can remember that this is an NPN transistor because the arrow "Never Points iN." |
| (MOSFET symbol) | N-channel enhancement mode MOSFET transistor | The N-channel enhancement mode MOSFET transistor has a similar symbol to that of the BJT, but the gate doesn't actually touch the line connecting the drain to the source. This is because the gate of a FET does not actually participate in current flow, but only controls the gate itself with voltage. |

# Integrated Circuit Naming Conventions

The naming conventions for ICs can be bewildering at first. In truth, there is no official standard for chip names, but there are some conventions that are often followed. When a chip is invented, the company that invented it assigns it a part number. However, the courts have ruled that part numbers cannot be copyrighted. Therefore, if another manufacturer makes a similar or identical chip with the same pinout, they will often use the same part number.

## C.1 Logic Chip Basic Conventions

Logic chips are often broken up into two families based on the voltage levels that they expect and produce. **TTL** (which stands for transistor-to-transistor logic) is an old standard for logic chips which usually operates at 5 V. TTL chips consider a signal to be "false" when it is below 0.8 V and "true" when it is above 2.2 V and can break if they receive voltages significantly higher than 5 V. Between 0.8 V and 2.2 V is a region where the resulting value is unpredictable. TTL originally referred to *how* the logic chips were constructed, but now it usually refers to the expected input/output levels of the chip.

© Jonathan Bartlett 2020
J. Bartlett, *Electronics for Beginners*, https://doi.org/10.1007/978-1-4842-5979-5

439

**CMOS** is a newer technology, and with it came a newer standard for how logic levels are interpreted. CMOS chips support a much wider supply voltage range than TTL, but their logic levels are a little different. For CMOS, false is from 0 V to one-third of the supply voltage (whatever it is—CMOS can usually operate from 3 V to 15 V), and true is from two-thirds of the supply voltage to the full supply voltage.

Chips are often made in a series—a whole set of chips which all perform complementary functions. The most common series of logic chips is the 7400 series originally designed by Texas Instruments. The 7400 series started as a set of TTL chips. Some common chips in this series are the 7400 itself (a quad–NAND gate), the 7408 (a quad–AND gate), and the 7432 (a quad–NOR gate).

Chips names will often have a prefix that relates to either their manufacturer or the company that originally designed them. As some examples, National Semiconductor chips are usually prefixed with LM; Texas Instruments chips have a whole slew of prefixes, including SN and TI; Motorola chips usually have an MC prefix; and Signetics chips usually have an NE prefix. There are many others, but this is just to give you an example. The 7400 series usually has part numbers starting with SN74 because TI built them. So a SN7408 is an AND gate based on designs by TI.

Now, the series is 7400. The last two digits refer to the function and pinout of the chips. That is, in the 7400 series, "08" will refer to quad–AND gates which all have the same pin configuration. However, sometimes they will insert letters in between "74" and "08." This usually refers to some modification to the electrical characteristics of the chip. For instance, a low-power version of the 7400 series has a "74LS" prefix. So the "SN74LS08" chip is a version of the 7408 (i.e., has the same pinout and function) that was originally designed by TI (the SN prefix) but is built for lower-power consumption (LS).

Then, part numbers often have suffixes as well. Suffixes often refer to some external characteristics of the chip. For instance, in Chapter 11, we mentioned different chip packages, such as DIP and SMD. These different packages will have different suffixes. For the 7400 series, the DIP package is usually suffixed with "P," so an SN74LS08P is the DIP version of the SN74LS08, and the NS74LS08NSR is an SMD version. You may also have suffixes which are based on temperature, hardiness, and even occasionally electrical output characteristics.

Sometimes, if a different manufacturer builds the same chip, they may change the manufacturer code and use different suffixes. For instance, Texas Instruments sells a SN74HC08P, which is a DIP 7408 which uses CMOS levels up to 6 V (that's what the HC is for). Essentially the same chip is available from Fairchild, which calls it the MM74HC08N. The MM prefix is one that Fairchild uses, and it is the same 74HC08 chip, and, for Fairchild, they use an "N" suffix to designate a DIP chip.

As I mentioned, these are only conventions, not standards, so they don't always apply. However, they can be helpful, so that you know that if someone specifies a 7432 chip and you see part numbers that say SN74LS32P, you might be able to determine that this at least has some relationship to the chip you are looking for.

# More Math Than You Wanted to Know

This appendix is a catalog of equations in electronics and where they came from for those who are curious. This book is meant more for an introductory approach, but nonetheless many people are curious. This chapter isn't for the faint of heart, and it may involve lots of math you haven't taken. That's why it is stuck in an appendix.

However, if you are curious, these are the mathematical answers to your questions.

## D.1 Basic Formulas

### D.1.1 Charge and Current Quantities

- 1 coulomb = 6.241509 * $10^{18}$ electrons (how many electrons in a coulomb)
- $I = \dfrac{dc}{dt}$ (current is the derivative of charge with respect to time)
- $1A = 1\dfrac{C}{s}$ ($A$ = ampere; $C$ = coulomb; $s$ = second)
- $3.6C = 1mAh$ ($C$ = coulomb; $mAh$ is milliamp-hour, a common unit for batteries)

J. Bartlett, *Electronics for Beginners*, https://doi.org/10.1007/978-1-4842-5979-5

## D.1.2  Volt Quantities

Volts are basically measures of energy per unit of charge. Volts are also known as electromotive force (EMF), or $\in$. Volts can be expressed in a number of ways:

- $V = \dfrac{J}{C}$ ($J$ = joules; $C$ = coulombs)

- $V = \dfrac{\text{potential energy}}{\text{charge}}$

- $V = \dfrac{N \cdot m}{C}$ ($N$ = newtons; $m$ = meters; $C$ = coulombs)

- $V = \dfrac{kg \cdot m^2}{A \cdot s^3}$ ($kg$ = kilograms; $m$ = meters; $A$ = amperes; $s$ = seconds)

- $V = \dfrac{d\phi}{dt}$ (Faraday's law of induction—voltage is the derivative of the flux of the magnetic field with respect to time)

## D.1.3  Resistance and Conductance Quantities

Resistance is in ohms. The inverse of resistance is conductance (the ability of current to flow through a wire) and is measured in siemens (S). The siemens unit is also called a mho (ohm spelled backward) and is sometimes marked by an upside-down omega ($\mho$):

- $G = \dfrac{1}{R}$ ($G$ = conductance in siemens, $R$ = resistance)

- $G = \dfrac{I}{V}$ ($G$ = conductance; $I$ is current; $V$ is voltage)

- $R = \dfrac{V}{I}$ (Ohm's law)

Individual materials have a resistivity $(\rho)$.

$$R = \rho \cdot \frac{\text{length}}{\text{cross-sectional area}} \qquad \text{(D.1)}$$

In other words, from beginning to end, resistance decreases with cross-sectional area and increases with length.

## D.1.4 Ohm's Law

$V$ is voltage (in volts), $I$ is current (in amperes), and $R$ is resistance (in ohms):

$$V = I \cdot R \qquad \text{(D.2)}$$

## D.1.5 Power

$P$ is in watts. The following hold true for DC circuits. For AC circuits, they hold true if the resistance is actually an impedance:

- $P = V \cdot A$
- $P = I^2 R$
- $P = \dfrac{V^2}{R}$

## D.1.6 Capacitance

Capacitance is the ability to store charge.

The fundamental equation for a capacitor is

$$Q = V \cdot C \qquad \text{(D.3)}$$

$Q$ is the amount of charge stored, $V$ is the voltage across the terminals, and $C$ is the capacitance in farads.

The derivative of this equation with respect to time is

$$\frac{dQ}{dt} = \frac{dV}{dt} \cdot C \tag{D.4}$$

Because current is the derivative of charge, we can then say

$$I = C\frac{dV}{dT} \tag{D.5}$$

The capacitance of capacitors is given by the equation

$$C = \epsilon_r \, \epsilon_0 \, \frac{A}{d} \tag{D.6}$$

Here $C$ is capacitance, $\epsilon_r$ is the dielectric constant of whatever separates the capacitor's plates, $\epsilon_0$ is the dielectric constant of free space, $A$ is the area of the plates in square meters, and $d$ is the distance between the plates in meters.

## D.1.7 Inductance

The fundamental equation for an inductor is

$$\phi = L \cdot I \tag{D.7}$$

Here, $\phi$ is the flux of the magnetic field in Webers, $L$ is inductance in Henries, and $I$ is current in amperes. The derivative gives you voltage:

$$\frac{d\phi}{dt} = L\frac{dI}{dt} \tag{D.8}$$

$$V = L\frac{dI}{dt} \tag{D.9}$$

In other words, the voltage produced is proportional to the change in current.

The inductance of a coil of wire can be calculated by

$$L = \frac{\mu \cdot N^2 \cdot A}{l} \tag{D.10}$$

Where $N$ is the number of turns of wire, $A$ is the area of the coil, $l$ is the length of the coil, and $\mu$ depends on the core being used.

# D.2 Semiconductors

Components made from silicon are known as semiconductors and have very useful nonlinear properties.

## D.2.1 Diodes

Diodes do not have a fixed voltage drop as we assume in this book. It is an exponential function, but is steep enough to act like a fixed 0.6 V voltage drop for most purposes. The actual equation is

$$I = I_S\left(e^{\frac{V}{\eta V_T}} - 1\right) \tag{D.11}$$

$I_S$ is the saturation current (depends on the construction of the diode), $V$ is the voltage, $\eta$ is either 1 for germanium or 2 for silicon, and $V_T$ is known as the thermal voltage (the amount of voltage created just by particles moving around at a given temperature, usually about 0.026 V at room temperature).

## D.2.2 NPN BJT

While we discussed general rules about BJTs, the technical model used to model them is known as the Ebers-Moll model. This model is much more complex to use, which is why we don't discuss it much in the chapter.

There are also several different Ebers-Moll models, depending on the level of detail required. The basic Ebers-Moll model for a conducting but unsaturated transistor is as follows:

$$I_E = I_S \left( e^{\frac{V_B E}{V_T}} - 1 \right) \tag{D.12}$$

In this $I_E$ is the emitter current (you can also use it for the collector current, since they are approximately equal). $I_S$ is the saturation current of the base-emitter diode, and $V_T$ is the thermal voltage, just like for diodes.

# D.3 DC Motor Calculations

The voltage drop across a motor ($V_m$) is defined by the following equation:

$$V_m = V_b + R_m I_m$$

where $V_b$ is the back EMF of the motor, $R_m$ is the internal resistance of the motor's wiring, and $I_m$ is the current flowing through the motor—so, basically, just Ohm's law plus the back EMF generated by the spinning of the motor.

So how much back EMF is created? We can determine that like this:

$$V_b = K_e \omega$$

In this equation, $K_e$ varies by the motor and is usually given in volts per RPM or volts per radians per second. $\omega$ is merely the rotational speed in the units given.

Likewise, the torque generated can be determined from this equation:

$$T = K_T I_m$$

In this equation, $K_T$ is the torque constant for the motor (be careful of the units), and $I_m$ is the current going through the motor. Knowing the peak (stall) current, you can find the maximum torque available for the motor.

Interestingly, you can see that increasing the torque will actually affect, to some degree, the RPM of the motor. The full equation for the voltage across the motor is

$$V_m = K_e \omega + R_m I_m$$

The torque will affect $I_m$. That, in effect, will increase the voltage drop given by $R_m I_m$. Given a fixed voltage source, this will leave less voltage available for the $K_e \omega$ part of the equation. Since $K_e$ is a constant, that means that $\omega$ will be reduced to some extent.

# D.4 555 Timer Oscillator Frequency Equation

In Chapter 18, we learned to make oscillators using the 555 timer chip. In the actual chapter, I wanted you to focus on actually learning what was happening with the 555 timer rather than using a formula. However, there is a nice, simple formula that allows you to relate the resistor/capacitor network of the 555 timer to the final output frequency.

The formula is as follows:

$$f = \frac{1.44}{C\left(R_1 + 2R_2\right)} \qquad \text{(D.13)}$$

In this equation, $f$ is the frequency, $R_1$ is the resistor coming from the supply voltage, $R_2$ is the resistor next to the capacitor, and $C$ is the timer capacitor.

To understand where this equation comes from, remember that frequency is just $\dfrac{1}{\text{period}}$. We can use time constant formulas to find the period and then just flip it to find the frequency.

If you recall, the period is just the total time it takes to complete a charge/discharge cycle. The 555 charges through *both* $R_1$ and $R_2$, but only discharges through $R_2$. Additionally, since it is just bouncing back and forth between $\dfrac{1}{3}$ and $\dfrac{2}{3}$ full, it only uses 0.693 time constant.

Therefore, we can have two formulas, one for the time charging and one for the time discharging:

$$T_{\text{CHARGE}} = 0.693C\left(R_1 + R_2\right)$$
$$T_{\text{DISCHARGE}} = 0.693R_2$$

The total period is just these two time periods added together. Therefore, you get

$$
\begin{aligned}
T_{\text{PERIOD}} &= 0.693C\left(R_1 + R_2\right) + 0.693CR_2 \\
&= 0.693C\left(\left(R_1 + R_2\right) + R_2\right) \qquad \text{Factoring out } 0.693C \\
&= 0.693C\left(R_1 + 2R_2\right) \qquad\qquad \text{Regrouping}
\end{aligned}
$$

Since $f = \dfrac{1}{T_{\text{PERIOD}}}$, we can flip the preceding equation and get

$$
\begin{aligned}
f &= \frac{1}{0.693C\left(R_1 + 2R_2\right)} \\
&= \frac{1}{0.693}\frac{1}{C\left(R_1 + 2R_2\right)} \qquad \text{Regrouping} \\
&\approx 1.44\frac{1}{C\left(R_1 + 2R_2\right)} \\
&= \frac{1.44}{C\left(R_1 + 2R_2\right)}
\end{aligned}
$$

At the end of the day, this is exactly what you did when you solved those problems; you just did it by hand instead of using a nice little formula. All a formula does is encapsulate the things that you normally do anyway, but simplifies it down to a set of predefined steps.

I have a love/hate relationship with formulas. Formulas are nice because they are easy to use. However, when you use them, it makes it easy to forget the basic facts behind them. The basic facts are more important than the formula, because you can rearrange the basic facts and develop all sorts of formulas depending on your needs. In fact, if you know the basic facts and you know how to make formulas, if you ever forget a formula, it is easy to determine one from the basic facts. Therefore, while memorizing formulas is important, knowing *why* formulas work is just as important, as it allows you to think more deeply and broadly and adapt your knowledge to new situations.

# D.5 Output Gain Calculations in BJT Common Emitter Applications

In Chapter 25, we showed how to put together a multistage amplifier for sound coming in from a microphone.

However, we handwaved away a lot of the calculations needed for it. That's because they are, well, difficult.

Anyway, if you don't like handwaving, then this section is for you.

In Chapter 25, we said that, on a common emitter amplifier, the gain on the output current compared to the incoming current was determined by $\dfrac{R_{B2}R_C}{R_E R_O}$, where $R_{B2}$ is the bottom resistor from the voltage divider that the signal is fed into, $R_C$ is the collector resistor, $R_E$ is the emitter resistor, and $R_O$ is the output resistance (see Figure 25-4 for the diagram).

Recognize that any incoming current into the circuit from the input (as opposed to the quiescent current coming from the voltage source through $R_{B1}$) will have two alternative paths to take—through $R_E$ or through $R_{B2}$. The relative amounts that do this are going to be based on the amount of voltage that $R_E$ utilizes.

What we want to do is to analyze the gain between our *incoming* current (let's call that $I_{IN}$) and the current at the collector ($I_C$). That is our real gain from the incoming current.

The problem is knowing how much the actual amount of the incoming current ($I_{IN}$) will be going through $R_{B2}$ or $R_E$. It will depend on the voltage in $R_E$. More voltage in $R_E$ will mean that the current is likely to go down $R_{B2}$ instead. This already tells us that the size of $R_E$ will limit the amount of gain, as increased beta in the transistor will also increase the voltage of $R_E$ which will also limit the amount of incoming current, which will have an equivalent effect of reducing gain.

Now, our circuit will primarily be working at a quiescent currentc, $Q$. We have already noted that this current will be the dominant signal. That means that the voltage between the base and the ground will be a combination of the diode voltage drop, the current in $R_E$ from $Q$, and the current in $R_E$ from the transistor's beta ($\beta Q$). Therefore, the total voltage drop from the base to the ground will be $V_{BG} = QR_E + \beta QR_E + 0.6$.

We can treat this as a "virtual resistance." The current coming in at $I_{in}$ will be small comparatively, so we can reverse Ohm's law to see what this looks like as a resistance to the incoming current. Because $R = \dfrac{V}{I}$, we can say that the resistance here to new current is

$$R_{BG} = \frac{QR_E + \beta QR_E + 0.6}{Q} = R_E + \beta R_E + \frac{0.6}{Q} \approx R_E + \beta R_E \qquad \text{(D.14)}$$

We dropped the $\dfrac{0.6}{Q}$ term because it would give us a very small comparative resistance, and we are trying to simplify our lives.

So now, when we have new current coming in at $I_{IN}$, it has two branches it can follow, each with its own resistance. Some of it will be wasted through $R_{B2}$, and some of it will be amplified through $R_{BG}$. The amount going through $R_BG$ we will call $I_U$ (for *usable* incoming current). The amount going through $R_{B2}$ will just be $I_{IN} - I_U$.

In parallel resistances, the relative amount of current going through each resistor can be calculated as

$$\frac{I_1}{I_2} = \frac{R_2}{R_1} \tag{D.15}$$

You can see this from Ohm's law. Since $I_1 = \frac{V_1}{R_1}$ and $I_2 = \frac{V_2}{R_2}$, the ratio of the currents becomes $\frac{I_1}{I_2} = \frac{\frac{V_1}{R_1}}{\frac{V_2}{R_2}}$. Since $V_1 = V_2$ (the resistors are parallel and so have the same voltage drop), then this reduces to Equation D.15.

So, for this, $I_{IN}$ will be divided between $R_{B2}$ and $R_{BG}$. Therefore, we can say

$$\frac{I_U}{I_{IN} - I_U} = \frac{R_{B2}}{R_{BG}} \tag{D.16}$$

$$I_U = I_{IN} \frac{R_{B2}}{R_{BG}} - I_U \frac{R_{B2}}{R_{BG}} \tag{D.17}$$

$$I_U + I_U \frac{R_{B2}}{R_{BG}} = I_{IN} \frac{R_{B2}}{R_{BG}} \tag{D.18}$$

$$I_U = \frac{I_{IN} R_{B2}}{R_{BG} \left( 1 + \frac{R_{B2}}{R_{BG}} \right)} \tag{D.19}$$

$$I_U = \frac{I_{IN} R_{B2}}{R_{BG} + R_{B2}} \tag{D.20}$$

The amount of current through the collector that comes through the usable current from the signal (and not from the quiescent current, $Q$) we can denote as $I_{CQ}$. Therefore

$$I_{CQ} = \beta I_U \tag{D.21}$$

So the total amplification of our signal will be the ratio of the amplified output $I_{CQ}$ to the incoming current $I_{IN}$:

$$\frac{I_{CQ}}{I_{IN}} = \frac{\beta I_U}{I_{IN}} \tag{D.22}$$

$$= \frac{\beta \left( \dfrac{I_{IN} R_{B2}}{R_{BG} + R_{B2}} \right)}{I_{IN}} \tag{D.23}$$

$$= \frac{\beta}{I_{IN}} \frac{I_{IN} R_{B2}}{R_{BG} + R_{B2}} \tag{D.24}$$

$$= \frac{\beta R_{B2}}{R_{BG} + R_{B2}} \tag{D.25}$$

$$\approx \frac{\beta R_{B2}}{R_E + \beta R_E + R_{B2}} \tag{D.26}$$

As you can see, this attenuates the action of $\beta$ since it is in both the numerator and the denominator.

To see the extremes, if the $\beta$ is low (i.e., single digits) and $R_E$ is small compared to $R_{B2}$, this reduces to

$$\frac{I_{CQ}}{I_{IN}} \approx \beta \frac{R_{B2}}{R_{B2}} = \beta \tag{D.27}$$

As $\beta$ increases, the dominating terms become

$$\frac{I_{CQ}}{I_{IN}} \approx \frac{\beta R_{B2}}{\beta R_E} = \frac{R_{B2}}{R_E} \tag{D.28}$$

We will call this particular gain $\gamma$ (a lowercase Greek "g"). So therefore

$$\gamma = \frac{R_{B2}}{R_E} \tag{D.29}$$

Now, the actual output current (that goes through the capacitor to the next stage or to the speaker) is actually going to be determined largely by the resistance of the next stage!

What we have determined so far is the amount of current that goes through $I_C$ from $I_{IN}$. The total amount of current in $I_C$ is going to be $\beta(Q + I_U)$. However, $Q$ is going to be essentially stable and therefore is not going to change the voltage on $R_C$, and capacitors only see voltage *changes*. Therefore, the only part of that which will be transmitted through the capacitor is the voltage change on $R_C$ due to $I_U$, which will be $\beta I_U$ or, in terms of our actual input signal, $\gamma I_{IN}$.

Next, we have to figure out how much current we will actually be transmitting out of our amplification stage. This is the current that goes out through the coupling capacitor. Now, since the coupling capacitor is *only* transmitting changes, the only current that goes through that branch of the circuit is changing current. Therefore, the quiescent current does not travel through the capacitor.

So what we have to do is figure out how to estimate the amount of current coming into the capacitor. We have already designated $I_{IN}$ as our input current, $I_U$ as the usable current that is amplified at the base, and $I_C$ as the current coming in to the collector.

Current coming out of $R_C$ has two choices of where to go. It can either go out to the next part of the circuit through the capacitor, or it can go through the transistor. This will depend on the resistance of each route.

We need to start by calculating the quiescent resistance of the route that goes through the transistor and $R_E$. If $V$ is our positive voltage, then, when the current goes through $R_C$, it will have dropped. Then it will drop again in the rest of the circuit.

The amount that the voltage drops going through $R_C$ is $I_T R_C$ (because the total voltage goes through $R_C$). We can replace $I_T$ with $I_O + I_C$, which means the voltage drop will be $(I_O + I_C)R_C$. The rest of the voltage drop we will call the "transistor path" voltage. It is simply

$$V_{\text{TPATH}} = V - \left( \left( I_O + I_C \right) R_C \right) \tag{D.30}$$

Ohm's law says that $R = \dfrac{V}{I}$, so the resistance on this path will be

$$R_{\text{TPATH}} = \frac{V - \left( \left( I_O + I_C \right) R_C \right)}{I_C} \tag{D.31}$$

Since $I_C = \beta Q$, then

$$R_{\text{TPATH}} = \frac{V - \left( \left( I_O + \beta Q \right) R_C \right)}{\beta Q} \tag{D.32}$$

The resistance of the other path will essentially be the Thévenin resistance of the output circuit (whatever lies beyond the capacitor). We will talk about what it should be shortly, but for now let's just call it $R_O$.

So that gives us two resistance values: $R_O$ and $R_{TPATH}$. When we have a change in current (i.e., from $I_{IN}$), it will draw extra current, which will go down both paths. The amount that goes down each path will depend on the resistance of each path.

Because the current changes are small compared to the quiescent current, we can ignore the impact that these changes have on the resistances themselves (i.e., how the change in current affects $R_{TPATH}$). We will use $I_T$ to represent the total *additional* current that comes across $R_C$ due to the currents coming in at $I_{IN}$. $I_O$ will be the amount that actually goes on out of the circuit.

As mentioned earlier, given two parallel resistances, $R_1$ and $R_2$, $\dfrac{I_1}{I_2} = \dfrac{R_2}{R_1}$. Therefore, we can say that the relative amount of current between the amount of current that goes out $I_O$ and the amount of current that goes through the transistor ($\gamma I_{IN}$) is

$$\frac{I_O}{\gamma I_{IN}} = \frac{\dfrac{V - \left(\left(I_O + \beta Q\right)R_C\right)}{\beta Q}}{R_O} = \frac{V - \left(\left(I_O + \beta Q\right)R_C\right)}{\beta Q R_O} \tag{D.33}$$

We can then solve for $I_O$:

$$I_O \beta Q R_O = \left(V - \left(\left(I_O + \beta Q\right)R_C\right)\right)\gamma I_{IN} \tag{D.34}$$

$$I_O \beta Q R_O = V\gamma I_{IN} - \gamma I_{IN} R_C I_O - \gamma I_{IN} \beta Q R_C \tag{D.35}$$

$$I_O \beta Q R_O + \gamma I_{IN} R_C I_O = V\gamma I_{IN} - \gamma I_{IN} \beta Q R_C \tag{D.36}$$

$$I_O \left(\beta Q R_O + \gamma I_{IN} R_C\right) = I_{IN}\gamma \left(V - \beta Q R_C\right) \tag{D.37}$$

$$I_O = \frac{I_{\text{IN}}\gamma\left(V - \beta QR_C\right)}{\beta QR_O + \gamma I_{\text{IN}} R_C} \tag{D.38}$$

Therefore, the complete gain (we will denote with a capital gamma, $\Gamma$) will be the ratio of $I_{IN}$ (the actual input signal) to $I_O$ (the actual output to the next stage). By using the preceding equivalency for $I_O$, we can determine

$$\Gamma = \frac{I_O}{I_{\text{IN}}} = \frac{\dfrac{I_{\text{IN}}\gamma\left(V - \beta QR_C\right)}{\beta QR_O + \gamma I_{\text{IN}} R_C}}{I_{\text{IN}}} \tag{D.39}$$

$$= \frac{I_{\text{IN}}\gamma\left(V - \beta QR_C\right)}{\left(\beta QR_O + \gamma I_{\text{IN}} R_C\right)I_{IN}} \tag{D.40}$$

$$= \frac{\gamma\left(V - \beta QR_C\right)}{\beta QR_O + \gamma I_{\text{IN}} R_C} \tag{D.41}$$

Because we are using relatively low voltages, $V$ is going to be essentially irrelevant and can be removed. Because $I_{\text{IN}}$ is small and $R_C$ is likely small compared to $R_O$, we can remove the term $\gamma I_{\text{IN}} R_C$. Therefore, that leaves

$$\Gamma = \frac{I_O}{I_{\text{IN}}} \approx \frac{-\gamma \beta QR_C}{\beta QR_O} \tag{D.42}$$

$$\approx -\gamma \frac{R_C}{R_O} \tag{D.43}$$

Since $\gamma = \dfrac{R_{B2}}{R_E}$, we can also write this as

$$\Gamma = \frac{I_O}{I_{IN}} \approx -\gamma \frac{R_C}{R_O} = -\frac{R_{B2}R_C}{R_E R_O} \tag{D.44}$$

Also note that this assumes that $R_O > R_C$ and $R_C > R_E$.

This is the total current gain from the input to the output. Notice that this value is negative. As we mentioned earlier, this kind of amplifier *inverts* the signal. Therefore, the gain is negative.

As you probably noticed, there were a lot of steps and a lot of simplifications. There were a lot of things where we handwaved away "insignificant" values and the sort. That's the way that electronics often works—you have to figure out which pieces really matter.

Now, thankfully, not everyone has to write these equations out because someone came in before them and deduced them. Personally, I think it's fun, but I recognize that isn't everyone's experience. Most electronics projects utilize more basic and straightforward applications of Ohm's law. But, occasionally, you have to pull out your whiteboard and go to town.

Of course, one thing I left out was how to determine $R_O$, the resistance of the circuit that follows.

If the output goes to another amplification stage, you may have to do more math to find the resistance of the next stage. The hard way is to look at the calculations earlier in this section for calculating $R_{BG}$ and $R_{B2}$ and calculate them for the next stage and treat them as parallel resistors. However, an easy way is to simply use $R_{B2}$ to stand in for $R_O$. It's not exactly correct, but then that isn't what we are aiming for. We're just looking for the ballpark.

If the output goes to your headphones, then all you need to do is plug in the resistance of your headphones. Most headphones are less than $50\Omega$, with $16\Omega$ being a fairly typical value.

# D.6 The Thévenin Formula

In Chapter 26, we used two formulas which allowed us to calculate the Thévenin equivalent circuit for circuits experimentally. Equations 26.1 and 26.2 seem strange and complicated, but they are actually directly deducible from Ohm's law and the concept of an equivalent circuit.

The Thévenin Theorem states that any combinations of voltage sources and resistances can be replaced by a single voltage source and a single resistance. We will call this our Thévenin voltage source ($V_T$) and our Thévenin impedance ($R_T$). If we hook up a load (i.e., a fixed resistance) across the output terminals of this circuit, we will know the resistance that was added (because *we* added it), and we can measure the voltage drop across the resistor easily enough with a multimeter or oscilloscope.

We will need to measure this using two different loads because we have two unknowns—$V_T$ and $R_T$. Using two different loads will give us two different equations using Ohm's law that will allow us to solve for two variables. We will call our lower-resistance load $R_L$, and the voltage drop across the $R_L$ resistor will be $V_L$. Likewise, our higher-resistance load we will call $R_H$, and the voltage drop across it will be $V_H$. The current running through each of these loads ($I_L$ and $I_H$) can be given by

$$V_L = I_L \cdot R_L$$
$$V_H = I_H \cdot R_H$$

That is just simply Ohm's law. We can also use Ohm's law to develop equations for the whole circuit, including the Thévenin equivalent voltage and impedance. Remember, because of the current rules, whatever current is flowing through our resistor must also be flowing in our Thévenin equivalent impedance. Therefore, the Thévenin equivalent voltage will be the current multiplied by the two impedances together. Therefore, this yields the following equations:

$$V_T = I_L\left(R_L + R_T\right)$$
$$V_T = I_H\left(R_H + R_T\right)$$

Both of these equations solve for $V_T$, given an unknown of $R_T$. We can also rearrange either of these to solve for $R_T$. Let's rearrange the first one to do that:

$$V_T = I_L\left(R_L + R_T\right) \quad \text{Original equation}$$

$$\frac{V_T}{I_L} = R_L + R_T \quad \text{Divide both sides}$$

$$\frac{V_T}{I_L} - R_L = R_T \quad \text{Subtract } R_L$$

$$R_T = \frac{V_T}{I_L} - R_L \quad \text{Solved for } R_T$$

This is the same as Equation 26.2. However, it requires $V_T$ to work. Now that we have an equation for $R_T$, we can substitute that back in and get an equation for $V_T$ without using $R_T$. Using basic algebra manipulations, we can do the following:

$$V_T = I_H\left(R_T + R_H\right) \quad \text{Original equation}$$
$$V_T = I_H R_T + I_H R_H \quad \text{Distributive rule}$$
$$V_T = I_H\left(\frac{V_T}{I_L} - R_L\right) + I_H R_H \quad \text{Substituting for } R_T$$

$$V_T = I_H \frac{V_T}{I_L} - I_H R_L + I_H R_H \quad \text{Distributing}$$

$$V_T - I_H \frac{V_T}{I_L} = -I_H R_L + I_H R_H \quad \text{Get the } V_T\text{s together}$$

$$V_T \left( 1 - \frac{I_H}{I_L} \right) = I_H \left( R_H - R_L \right) \quad \text{Factor both sides}$$

$$\frac{V_T}{I_L} = R_L + R_T \quad \text{Divide both sides}$$

$$V_T = \frac{\dfrac{V_H}{R_H} \left( R_H - R_L \right)}{1 - \dfrac{V_H R_L}{R_H V_L}} \quad \text{Replace currents with Ohm's law equivalents} \left( \frac{V}{R} \right)$$

As you can see, this is Equation 26.1.

# D.7  Electronics and Calculus

Calculus is a favorite subject of mine, and many parts of electronics make a lot of sense in the light of calculus.

# D.7.1  Current and Voltage

First of all, recognize that electronics includes both static and dynamic quantities. Charge, for instance, is a static quantity. Current, though, is the *movement* of charge and thus is a dynamic quantity. Current entering or leaving a point can be written as a differential:

$$I = \frac{dQ}{dt} \tag{D.45}$$

Like current, voltage is a dynamic quantity, which is the change in the magnetic flux ($\phi$):

$$V = \frac{d\phi}{dt} \tag{D.46}$$

## D.7.2 Capacitors and Inductors

The static equation governing a capacitor is

$$Q = V \cdot C \tag{D.47}$$

where $Q$ is the charge, $V$ is the voltage, and $C$ is the capacitance. Taking the derivative of both sides, this can be converted into a dynamic equation:

$$\frac{dQ}{dt} = C\frac{dV}{dt} \tag{D.48}$$

Since $\dfrac{dQ}{dt} = I$, we can rewrite this as

$$I = C\frac{dV}{dt}. \tag{D.49}$$

What this means is that the current is proportional to the *change* in voltage.

The static equation governing an inductor is similar:

$$\phi = L \cdot I \tag{D.50}$$

Taking the derivative of both sides yields

$$\frac{d\phi}{dt} = L \cdot \frac{dI}{dt} \tag{D.51}$$

Since $V = \dfrac{d\phi}{dt}$, this can be rewritten as

$$V = L \cdot \frac{dI}{dt}. \qquad \text{(D.52)}$$

In other words, on inductors, the voltage is proportional to the change in current.

# D.7.3 Time Constants

If an ideal capacitor were connected to an ideal voltage source, then the capacitor would charge instantaneously. However, as described in Chapter 17, when charged through a resistor, it takes a certain amount of time to do the charging. The RC time constant combined with Figure 17-1 gives a simple way of figuring out these timings.

A more complete way of understanding this is with the following equation:

$$V_C = V_S \left( 1 - e^{\frac{-t}{RC}} \right) \qquad \text{(D.53)}$$

Here, $V_C$ is the voltage across the capacitor, $V_S$ is the voltage source, $t$ is the time from the start of charging (in seconds), and $R$ and $C$ are the resistance and capacitance. $e$ is Euler's constant. To find the amount of time, we can solve for $t$:

$$t = -RC \ln\left( 1 - \frac{V_C}{V_S} \right) \qquad \text{(D.54)}$$

Here, $\dfrac{V_C}{V_S}$ is the voltage percentage (expressed as a decimal). Therefore, the number of time constants is given by $-\ln\left( 1 - \dfrac{V_C}{V_S} \right)$.

465

So how was Equation D.53 even determined? Since the voltage across the capacitor depends on the charge in the capacitor, then $V_C = \dfrac{Q}{C}$. Since the amount of current flowing through the resistor can be determined by the voltage and the voltage will be based on the difference between the source and the capacitor, then $I = \dfrac{V_S - V_C}{R}$. From the capacitor side, $I = C\dfrac{dV}{dt}$. Since the current had to come from somewhere, it had to come from the resistor. So that means these currents are equal. Therefore, $\dfrac{V_S - V_C}{R} = C\dfrac{dV_C}{dt}$.

We can solve this as a differential equation, by separating the variables. This gives $\dfrac{1}{R}dt = \dfrac{dV_C}{V_S - V_C}$. Since battery voltages are constant, $V_S$ is a constant, so this integrates to $\dfrac{t}{R} + D = -C\ln(V_S - V_C)$, where $D$ is the constant of integration.[1] Rearranging, this becomes $\dfrac{-t}{RC} + D = \ln(V_S - V_C)$. Exponentiating both sides gives $De^{\frac{-t}{RC}} = V_S - V_C$. At time $t = 0$, $D = VS - VC$. Since we are assuming that the starting capacitor voltage is zero, this means at that time, $D = V_S$. Now this becomes $V_S e^{\frac{-t}{RC}} = V_S - V_C$. Rearranging to solve for $V_C$ yields $V_C = V_S - V_S e^{\frac{-t}{RC}}$. This can be simplified to yield Equation D.53.

---

[1] $D$ undergoes lots of changes, and I'm not going to justify them all, but they are based on the fact that $D$ is an unknown constant, and any manipulation of other constants will still yield an unknown constant.

# APPENDIX E

# Simplified Datasheets for Common Devices

Datasheets are what electronics manufacturers use to communicate the specifications of their components to the engineers who will use them in projects and products. However, datasheets tend to be horrendously complex. Typical datasheets run about 10–30 pages, and most of that is completely useless for someone just trying to get a circuit to work. Sometimes the first pages of the datasheet are all of the different packages the chip is available in, and the pages detailing what the component *actually does* are almost in the very back. I've even seen many sheets that never speak of what a device is for or why you would want to use it.

So, to simplify your life, I have created some simplified datasheets. All of these focus on the typical component styles used in solderless breadboards. These datasheets are also oriented toward *generic* parts. Each manufacturer has their own parts with their own specs and their own benefits and drawbacks. Some manufacturers may have higher or lower current specifications, faster or slower switching times, or other variations. These datasheets should be used as a starting point, but not as a final authority.

Use these datasheets to find the component you want and find its general characteristics, what each of the pins are for, and what they should be hooked up to. However, the manufacturer's datasheet should be consulted for final specifications.

© Jonathan Bartlett 2020
J. Bartlett, *Electronics for Beginners*, https://doi.org/10.1007/978-1-4842-5979-5

# E.1  Batteries

## E.1.1  Overview

A battery is a voltage source, meaning that it provides a fixed voltage over a wide range of currents.

Batteries have two terminals—positive and negative (or ground). The rated voltage for the battery is the typical voltage between these two terminals. However, a battery's actual voltage will vary quite a bit over the battery's lifetime.

Batteries also exhibit a small amount of *internal resistance* (also known as *equivalent series resistance*) which limits the amount of current they can provide.

## E.1.2  Variations

| Battery Type | Typical Voltage | Voltage Range | Typical Capacity |
| --- | --- | --- | --- |
| AAA | 1.5 | 1.1–1.5 | 540 mAh |
| AA | 1.5 | 1.1–1.5 | 1100 mAh |
| C | 1.5 | 1.1–1.5 | 3800 mAh |
| D | 1.5 | 1.1–1.5 | 8000 mAh |
| E(9 V) | 9 | 7.2–9.6 | 1200 mAh |
| Coin cell (all sizes) | 3 | 2–3.6 | 30–620 mAh |

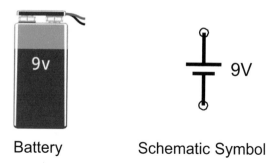

Battery            Schematic Symbol

## E.1.3 Notes

Putting batteries together in parallel increases their available current but does not alter their voltage. Putting batteries together in series adds their voltages but does not change the available current.

Coin cell batteries are designated CRxxxx, where the first two digits of xxxx are the diameter in millimeters and the remaining digits tell the height in tenths of millimeters.

# E.2 Resistors

## E.2.1 Overview

Resistors are devices that resist the flow of current from one terminal to the other. The resistance of a resistor is measured in ohms.

The power (in watts) dissipated by a resistor is measured by the current flowing through it multiplied by the voltage drop across it. Resistors are rated for their maximum safe amount of power dissipation.

Resistors are often used to provide a safe limit to the amount of current flowing in a circuit or to provide a voltage drop for an input to another circuit.

# E.2.2 Finding a Resistor Value

The colored bands on a resistor tell you how much resistance it has. However, these are very tiny, and sometimes it is easier just to measure it with a multimeter.

To interpret the colored bands, you first need to orient your resistor so that the last band is on the right (it is usually slightly thicker and set off from the others). This band is the *tolerance* band (use the tolerance column on the right).

The next band to the left is the *multiplier*. Use the multiplier column to read this value. The other bands are used as digits of a number which are then multiplied by the multiplier.

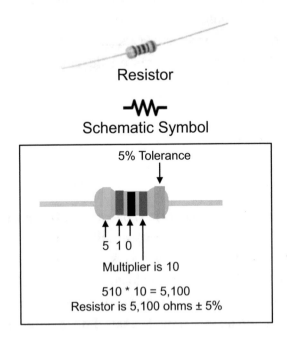

Resistor

Schematic Symbol

5% Tolerance

5  1  0

Multiplier is 10

510 * 10 = 5,100
Resistor is 5,100 ohms ± 5%

| Color | Digit | Multiplier | Tolerance |
|-------|-------|------------|-----------|
| Black | 0 | 1 | |
| Brown | 1 | 10 | ± 1% |
| Red | 2 | 100 | ± 2% |
| Orange | 3 | 1,000 | |
| Yellow | 4 | 10,000 | |
| Green | 5 | 100,000 | ± 0.5% |
| Blue | 6 | 1,000,000 | ± 0.25% |
| Violet | 7 | 10,000,000 | ± 0.1% |
| Grey | 8 | 100,000,000 | ± 0.05% |
| White | 9 | 1,000,000,000 | |
| Gold | | 0.1 | ± 5% |
| Silver | | 0.01 | ± 10% |

# E.3  Diodes

## E.3.1  Overview

A diode is a device that only permits current to flow in one direction and blocks current in the other direction.

All diodes exhibit a *forward voltage drop*, which is the amount of voltage they consume when current is flowing. This is typically 0.6 V, though it varies a little based on current flow.

Diodes also have a *reverse breakdown voltage* which is the amount of voltage they can handle in the blocking direction before they start conducting anyway.

# E.3.2 Variations

- An LED is a light-emitting diode. LEDs vary in their forward voltage drop based on their color (red=1.8; blue=3.3).

- A Zener diode is a diode that is built for a specific (usually lower than usual) reverse breakdown voltage. The reverse breakdown voltage of a Zener is more fixed/reliable than its forward voltage drop.

- A Schottky diode has a lower forward voltage drop (0.15–0.45V) and is able to turn on and off faster than ordinary diodes and accordingly also dissipates less heat.

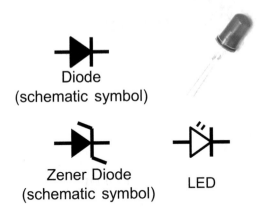

Diode
(schematic symbol)

Zener Diode
(schematic symbol)

LED

# E.3.3 Forward Voltage Drop

Diodes are often considered to not have a resistance, but instead to have a simple voltage drop. That is, you apply the voltage drop and ignore resistance. That works for the math, but the reality is a bit different. Essentially, a diode is a variable resistor, where the resistance varies in order to keep the voltage drop essentially fixed. Therefore, diodes dissipate power just like other components, with the voltage drop multiplied by the current flowing through them.

## E.3.4 Usages

- Prevent batteries from being inserted backward in a circuit

- Provide a fixed voltage drop between two points on a circuit, either through the forward voltage drop (regular diode) or the reverse breakdown voltage (Zener diode)

- Convert AC to DC by only allowing the positive flows through the circuit

# E.4 Capacitors
## E.4.1 Overview

A capacitor is a device that stores energy using a charged electric field. The size of the capacitor is proportional to the amount of charge that it can store. This size is measured in farads.

Changes in the voltage of one side of the capacitor will be transmitted through to the other side, but a steady-state DC voltage will not after the capacitor initially charges up.

This means that capacitors are ideal for sending AC signals through different DC bias levels, as merely the changes in voltage (the AC component) will be transmitted through the capacitor, while the bias voltages themselves will be blocked. A simplified description says that capacitors allow AC and block DC.

## E.4.2 Variations

- Capacitors can be made of a variety of materials, which affect several of their properties.

- Capacitors can be non-polar (it doesn't matter which side is which) or polar (one side should always be more positive than the other).

- Ceramic disk capacitors are the classic example of non-polar capacitors, and electrolytic capacitors are the classic example of polar capacitors.

- Capacitors also vary in the amount of voltage that can be used with them.

Common Capacitor Types
(tantalum, electrolytic, ceramic disk)

$$\dashv\vdash$$

Schematic Symbol (nonpolar)

$$\dashv\hspace{-0.3em}\rightarrow\vdash$$

Schematic Symbol (polar)
(straight line is the positive side)

# E.4.3 Finding Capacitance Values

Larger capacitors simply have their capacitance values printed on them. Smaller capacitors just have a set of digits printed on them, such as "104," sometimes with a letter after them. These are a little harder to interpret.

On these capacitors, the first digits should be read as is, and the last digit is the number of additional zeroes that should be tacked onto the end. This value is then interpreted as picofarads.

So the value "104" means we take "10" and then add "4" zeroes, giving us "100000." This is the capacitance in picofarads. This is the same as 100 nanofarads. If there is any code starting with a letter, this is a tolerance marking.

# E.5 Inductors

## E.5.1 Overview

An inductor is a device that stores energy in its magnetic field. The size of the inductor (in Henries) is proportional to the size of the magnetic flux it can create for a given level of current.

Inductors prevent changes in current by varying their electric field. Reducing the current through an inductor causes a partial collapse of the field, creating a voltage on the other side, which feeds current.

A simplified way of understanding inductors is to think of them as allowing DC but blocking AC.

Inductors are generally constructed by winding wire around an iron core material.

# E.5.2 Uses

- Inductors serve as the main gateway between electrical and mechanical actions through the magnetic field.

- Inductors are used to open and close valves and switches magnetically.

- Inductors are used to drive electric motors.

- Inductors are used to limit certain frequencies in circuits.

- Inductors are used in speakers, where changes in magnetism cause the speakers to move.

- Inductors can be used as transformers to convert power from one voltage/current combination to another of equal power.

Various styles of inductors

Schematic Symbol

# E.5.3 Inductive Kick

Inductors use current to maintain their magnetic fields. When the current decreases suddenly, the magnetic field is converted into a large voltage, creating what is known as an inductive kick.

This kick can be damaging to electronic components. To mitigate this, a diode can be placed backward across the inductor so that, under normal circumstances, it does not conduct, but when an inductor produces a voltage spike, it re-routes the current back through the inductor where it can dissipate slowly in a loop rather than building up and damaging other components with a large voltage spike.

## E.5.4  Inductor Color Codes

Simple inductors (i.e., those in packaged casings) are marked identically to resistors, except that the resulting value is in *micro*henries rather than just Henries.

# E.6  NPN BJTs
## E.6.1  Overview

Transistors come in a variety of configurations. BJTs (bipolar junction transistors) are *current-amplifying* devices.

In an NPN (negative-positive-negative) transistor, small changes to the current at the base result in large changes in current coming into the collector.

In a transistor, the voltage at the emitter is one diode drop (0.6 V) below the base, and if it is not, the transistor does not conduct. The transistor's beta is the multiplier between the base current and the collector current. The collector's voltage must be above the base voltage, or the transistor is saturated (acts as a short circuit from collector to emitter).

If these conditions are met, the transistor acts as a variable resistor which keeps the collector current as an amplification of the base current.

## E.6.2 Variations

- A PNP transistor is the opposite of an NPN—the current applied at the base *reduces* the flow of current into the collector.

- A FET (field effect transistor) operates using voltages rather than current. This allows for negligible current usage on the inputs, but also reduced gain and more complicated support considerations.

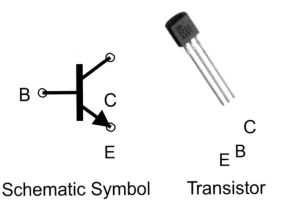

Schematic Symbol        Transistor

## E.6.3 Pin Configuration

- Base (B): This is the terminal that contains the current to be amplified.

- Collector (C): This is the terminal where the amplified current will flow into.

- Emitter (E): This is the terminal where the currents from both the base and the collector will flow out of, at a voltage level of one diode drop (0.6 V) less than the base.

## E.6.4 Design Considerations

Transistor designs are based on which terminals the signal itself passes through (the third terminal is referred to as the "common" terminal).

In common collector configurations (also called emitter followers), the signal passes from base to emitter with an increased current but no increased voltage.

In common emitter configurations, the signal passes from the base to the collector, with the increase in current converted to a voltage through a collector on the resistor.

# E.7  YwRobot Power Module
## E.7.1  Overview

This device allows you to supply power to your breadboard projects from a variety of sources through its barrel jack. The module down-steps the voltage to 5 V or 3.3 V (selectable with jumpers).

The power module comes with an on/off switch and a set of header pins that can be used to wire power to other places.

The module is made to fit on a standard breadboard, where the output pins align directly onto the power rails of the breadboard.

Be sure to align the positive and negative markings on the module with their matching power rails!

Note that this part is not technically part of any schematic and simply acts as a voltage source within a schematic.

# E.7.2 Variations

- On some boards, the USB jack can be used as a power input, and on some it is a power output only.

- The popularity of this module has prompted a number of manufacturers to build similar devices with a variety of shapes and input/output methods.

Align these with the +/- power
rails on your breadboard

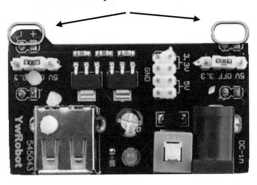

# E.7.3 Pin Configuration

The power module connects directly to your breadboard. Each side can be independently selected for 3.3 V or 5 V power via jumpers.

In the middle is a set of male headers for 3.3 V, 5 V, and ground.

# E.7.4 Limitations

- Minimum input voltage: 6.5 V (DC)

- Maximum input voltage: 12 V (DC)

- Output voltage: 3.3/5 V (selectable)

- Maximum output current: 700 mA

- Barrel jack plug size: 5.5 mm × 2.1 mm

# E.8  555 Timer

## E.8.1  Overview

The 555 timer is a collection of components that can be configured to provide timings and oscillations.

It uses two voltage levels—one-third supply voltage and two-thirds supply voltage. Internally, it consists of

- Two comparators (one for each voltage level)

- A flip-flop (single-bit storage) to know what state it is in and to switch states at the appropriate time

- An output driver

- A reset input

The timer relies on external circuitry (such as an RC time circuit) to supply timings.

The timer effectively has two states. In the "charging" state, the **Discharge** pin is disconnected, and the **Threshold** pin is waiting for a high (2/3) voltage. In the "discharging" state, the **Discharge** pin is connected to ground, and the **Trigger** pin is waiting for a low (1/3) voltage. The typical usage is to provide an oscillating circuit.

## E.8.2 Variations

- Can be implemented using CMOS/FETs or BJTs. FET implementation consumes less power, but can source less output.

- Many variations in maximum oscillation frequency.

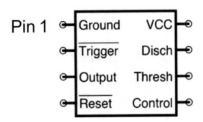

## E.8.3 Pin Configuration

- **Trigger** and **Threshold** detect going below 1/3 and above 2/3 voltage, respectively.

- **Discharge** provides a ground that is only attached when the chip is in the discharging state.

- **Output** supplies a high voltage when the chip is in the charging state and a low voltage when it is in the discharging state.

- **Reset** should be normally tied to a positive supply—it resets the circuit when it goes low.

- **Control** is normally connected to ground with a capacitor (10 μF recommended).

## E.8.4  Specifications

- Supply Voltage: Usually 2–15 V

- Output Current: 100–200 mA

## E.8.5  Implementation Example

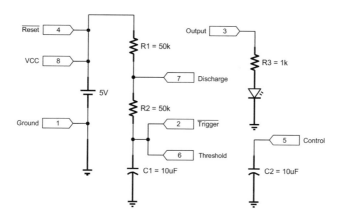

# E.9  LM393 and LM339 Voltage Comparator

## E.9.1  Overview

The LM393 is a dual voltage comparator. Each channel has two inputs—designated IN+ and IN-. When the voltage at IN+ is greater than the voltage at IN-, the output (OUT) is positive (actually, it is disconnected; see more later). Otherwise, the output is connected to ground.

The output is called an "open collector" output, which means that the "positive" state has no output current and is essentially disconnected. However, in the negative state, the output is connected to ground. This means that to use the output, you need to provide your own positive voltage through a pull-up resistor (this allows you to set your own output voltage).

The LM339 is identical except that it has four channels instead of two. Note that the schematic symbol for this is the same as that of an op-amp, largely because they perform similar (though not identical) functions.

## E.9.2 Variations

Various chips differ in the amount of current they can sink, how fast they respond to changes in input voltage, how smooth the transition is from one state to the other, and the minimum amount of difference required to trigger.

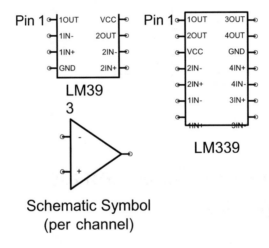

Schematic Symbol
(per channel)

## E.9.3 Specifications

- Supply Voltage: 2–36 V

- Input Voltage: -0–1.5 V less than supply voltage

- Maximum Sink Current: 20 mA (when output is grounded)

- Input Impedance: High (inputs use very negligible amounts of current)

- Quiescent Chip Current: 1 mA

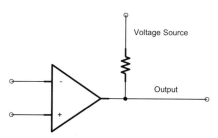

## Usage of the Comparator with a pull-up resistor

# E.10  CD4081 and 7408 Quad-AND Gate

## E.10.1  Overview

The quad-AND gate is a set of four AND logic gates on a single chip. The output (Y) will be high only if *both* inputs (A and B) are high.

The required voltages for low and high on input and the guaranteed voltages for low and high on output are listed in the specifications section.

For the output to be high, both A and B must be high. Otherwise, the output (Y) will be low.

The 7408 and the CD4081 are the TTL and CMOS versions of the chip, respectively.

## E.10.2  Variations

- 74HC08: Pin compatible with the 7408; voltage and current characteristics of the CD4081

- 74HCT08: Pin compatible and voltage-level compatible with 7408; similar current usage as the CD4081

- 74LS08: Fast-switching version of the 7408

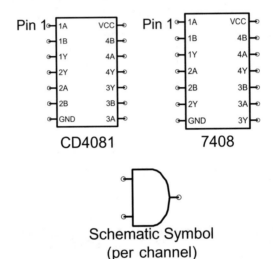

CD4081

7408

Schematic Symbol
(per channel)

# E.10.3 Specifications (CD4081)

- Supply Voltage: 3–15 V

- Input (High) Voltage: > 2/3 supply

- Output (High) Voltage: Supply – 0.05

- Input (Low) Voltage: < 1/3 supply

- Output (Low) Voltage: 0–0.5 V

- Maximum Output Current: ~5 mA

## E.10.4  Specifications (7408)

- Supply Voltage: 5 V

- Input (High) Voltage: > 2 V

- Output (High) Voltage: > 2.7 V

- Input (Low) Voltage: < 0.8 V

- Output (Low) Voltage: < 0.4 V

- Maximum Output Current: 100 mA

# E.11  CD4071 and 7432 Quad-OR Gate

## E.11.1  Overview

The quad-OR gate is a set of four OR logic gates on a single chip. The output (Y) will be high if *either or both* inputs (A and B) are high.

The required voltages for low and high on input and the guaranteed voltages for low and high on output are listed in the specifications section.

For the output to be high, either A or B (or both) must be high. Otherwise, the output (Y) will be low.

The 7432 and the CD4071 are the TTL and CMOS versions of the chip, respectively.

## E.11.2  Variations

- 74HC32: Pin compatible with the 7432; voltage and current characteristics of the CD4071

- 74HCT32: Pin compatible and voltage-level compatible with 7432; similar current usage as the CD4071

- 74LS32: Fast-switching version of the 7432

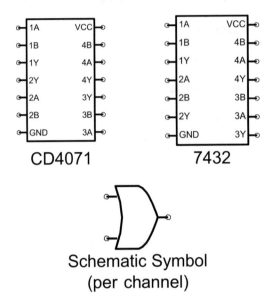

Schematic Symbol
(per channel)

# E.11.3 Specifications (CD4071)

- Supply Voltage: 3–15 V

- Input (High) Voltage: > 2/3 supply

- Output (High) Voltage: Supply – 0.05

- Input (Low) Voltage: < 1/3 supply

- Output (Low) Voltage: 0–0.5 V

- Maximum Output Current: ~5 mA

# E.11.4 Specifications (7432)

- Supply Voltage: 5 V

- Input (High) Voltage: > 2 V

- Output (High) Voltage: > 2.7 V

- Input (Low) Voltage: < 0.8 V

- Output (Low) Voltage: < 0.4 V

- Maximum Output Current: 100 mA

# E.12  CD4001 and 7402 Quad-NOR Gate

## E.12.1  Overview

The quad-NOR gate is a set of four NOR logic gates on a single chip. The output (Y) will be high if *both* inputs (A and B) are high or if *both* inputs are low.

The required voltages for low and high on input and the guaranteed voltages for low and high on output are listed in the specifications section.

For the output to be high, either both A and B must be high or neither must be high. Otherwise, the output (Y) will be low.

The 7402 and the CD4001 are the TTL and CMOS versions of the chip, respectively.

## E.12.2  Variations

- 74HC02: Pin compatible with the 7402; voltage and current characteristics of the CD4001

- 74HCT02: Pin compatible and voltage-level compatible with 7402; similar current usage as the CD4001

- 74LS02: Fast-switching version of the 7402

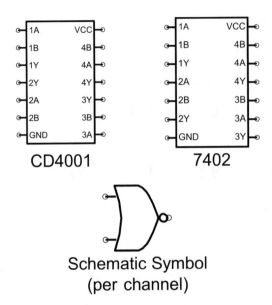

Schematic Symbol
(per channel)

# E.12.3  Specifications (CD4001)

- Supply Voltage: 3–15 V

- Input (High) Voltage: > 2/3 supply

- Output (High) Voltage: Supply – 0.05

- Input (Low) Voltage: < 1/3 supply

- Output (Low) Voltage: 0–0.5 V

- Maximum Output Current: ~5 mA

# E.12.4  Specifications (7402)

- Supply Voltage: 5 V

- Input (High) Voltage: > 2 V

- Output (High) Voltage: > 2.7 V

- Input (Low) Voltage: < 0.8 V

- Output (Low) Voltage: < 0.4 V

- Maximum Output Current: 100 mA

# E.13  CD4011 and 7400 Quad-NAND Gate

## E.13.1  Overview

The quad-NAND gate is a set of four NAND logic gates on a single chip. The output (Y) will be low unless *both* inputs (A and B) are high.

The required voltages for low and high on input and the guaranteed voltages for low and high on output are listed in the specifications section.

For the output to be high, A and B can be anything as long as they are not both high. Otherwise, the output (Y) will be low.

The 7400 and the CD4011 are the TTL and CMOS versions of the chip, respectively.

## E.13.2  Variations

- 74HC00: Pin compatible with the 7400; voltage and current characteristics of the CD4011

- 74HCT00: Pin compatible and voltage-level compatible with 7400; similar current usage as the CD4011

- 74LS00: Fast-switching version of the 7400

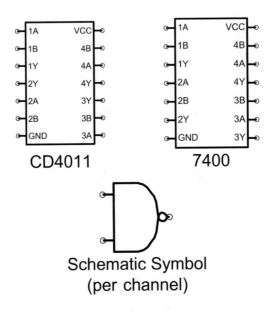

Schematic Symbol
(per channel)

# E.13.3  Specifications (CD4011)

- Supply Voltage: 3–15 V

- Input (High) Voltage: > 2/3 supply

- Output (High) Voltage: Supply – 0.05

- Input (Low) Voltage: < 1/3 supply

- Output (Low) Voltage: 0–0.5 V

- Maximum Output Current: ~5 mA

# E.13.4  Specifications (7400)

- Supply Voltage: 5 V

- Input (High) Voltage: > 2 V

- Output (High) Voltage: > 2.7 V

- Input (Low) Voltage: < 0.8 V

- Output (Low) Voltage: < 0.4 V

- Maximum Output Current: 100 mA

# E.14  CD4070 and 7486 Quad-XOR Gate

## E.14.1  Overview

The quad-XOR (exclusive OR) gate is a set of four XOR logic gates on a single chip. The output (Y) will be high if either input (A or B) *but not both* is high.

The required voltages for low and high on input and the guaranteed voltages for low and high on output are listed in the specifications section.

For the output to be high, either A or B must be high but not both of them. Otherwise, the output (Y) will be low.

The 7486 and the CD4070 are the TTL and CMOS versions of the chip, respectively.

## E.14.2  Variations

- 74HC86: Pin compatible with the 7486; voltage and current characteristics of the CD4070

- 74HCT86: Pin compatible and voltage-level compatible with 7486; similar current usage as the CD4070

- 74LS86: Fast-switching version of the 7486

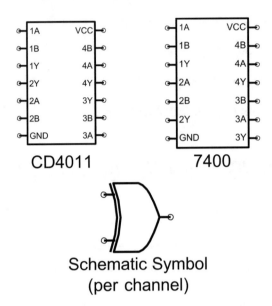

CD4011        7400

Schematic Symbol
(per channel)

# E.14.3  Specifications (CD4070)

- Supply Voltage: 3–15 V

- Input (High) Voltage: > 2/3 supply

- Output (High) Voltage: Supply – 0.05

- Input (Low) Voltage: < 1/3 supply

- Output (Low) Voltage: 0–0.5 V

- Maximum Output Current: ~5 mA

# E.14.4  Specifications (7486)

- Supply Voltage: 5 V

- Input (High) Voltage: > 2 V

- Output (High) Voltage: > 2.7 V

- Input (Low) Voltage: < 0.8 V

- Output (Low) Voltage: < 0.4 V

- Maximum Output Current: 100 mA

# E.15  LM78xx Voltage Regulator

## E.15.1  Overview

The LM78xx voltage regulator is actually a series of chips to provide a consistent voltage output from a variety of voltage inputs. Each chip is named with the number of volts it supplies in its output. For instance, the LM7805 outputs a constant 5 V, and the LM7812 outputs a constant 12 V.

These chips are linear voltage regulators, which means that they regulate voltage by dissipating excess power as heat. If significant heat develops, the LM78xx can have a heatsink attached to the back plate, which also serves as a second ground.

The LM78xx requires an input voltage at least 2.5 V above the regulated voltage. This is known as the "drop-out" voltage of the chip.

## E.15.2  Variations

- The 78xxSR is a line of switching regulators, meaning that they do not dissipate significant power when regulating (they operate by turning the power on and off quickly rather than dissipating excess power). They waste significantly less current but do have a significant cost.

- The TL750Mxx chips are similar to the LM78xx chips, but have a very low "drop-out" voltage (~0.6 V).

- The LM79xx chips are similar to the LM78xx chips, but act as *negative* voltage supplies (-5 V, etc.).

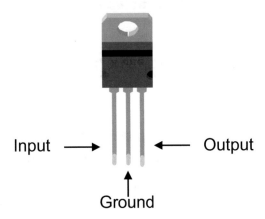

Input $\longrightarrow$        $\longleftarrow$ Output

Ground

## E.15.3  Specifications

- Maximum Input Voltage: 35 V

- Maximum Output Current: 1 A

- Built-in overcurrent protection

- Protection against short circuits

- Overheating protection (shuts off when overheating)

# E.15.4 Usage Notes

- The specifications require two capacitors for operation—a 330 nF capacitor on the input and a 100 nF capacitor on the output (see below).

- These capacitors are generally not required for very simple projects—you can simply hook the input directly to your positive power source, the ground to your ground, and the output to your project.

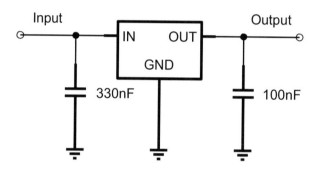

# Index

## A

Abbreviation, 14, 15
Adjustable resistors, 298
Amplification, 455
Amplification
  definition, 355
  gain of an amplifier, 356
  microcontroller, 355
  NPN transistors, 371, 372
  parable, 356
  parts, 358, 360
  transistors, 357
Analog Inputs
  current value, 226
  darkness sensor, 224, 225
  debugging, 226
  photoresistor, 224
  pin number, 223
  serial interface, 225
  values, 223
Analog output
  Arduino, 229
  darkness sensor, 227
  dimmer, 227–229
  pin numbers, 227
  PWM, 226
  variable, 228

  voltages, 227
  while command, 228
  while loop, 228
analogRead() function, 223, 229
analogWrite() function, 227, 230
AND Gate, 183, 193
Arduino environment, 205
  programming, 207
Arduino IDE, 207, 208
Arduino Programming/Bob
  Dukish's Coding, 417
Arduino Uno, 206
  breadboard, 213, 214
  LEDs, 216
  modifications, 219
  rewiring, 219
  wiring inputs/outputs, 214, 215
ATmega328/P, 203, 355
Auto-ranging multimeter, 73

## B

Bipolar junction transistors (BJTs),
  357, 370, 407
Boost converters, 153
Breakdown voltage, 106, 122
Brushed electric motor, 343
Buttons/switches, 4

# C

Printed in the United States
By Bookmasters